Unilever Foodsolutions
2200 Cabot Drive
Lisle, IL 60532

Tel: 800-323-6490
unileverfoodsolutions.us

Unilever Foodsolutions is proud to be a part of *Cooking with America's Team*. This outstanding collection of recipes showcases the creativity, talent and diversity of the 2004 ACF Culinary Teams USA.

As Grand Platinum-level sponsors of the American Culinary Federation, we believe this book once again demonstrates the Unilever Foodsolutions commitment to chefmanship. In the same way these talented chefs are committed to raising culinary standards, so are we at Unilever Foodsolutions. Our team of chefs - unmatched in the industry - has a real passion for food, which we share with our customers. By striving to provide the foodservice industry with the highest quality products, we help operators consistently attain the "gold standard" in their dishes.

The **KNORR**® name is known worldwide for its wide range of culinary-inspired products. From time-saving bases and sauces to fully prepared soups, **KNORR**® products deliver ease of usage with delicious flavor every time.

HELLMANN'S® is the first name in mayonnaise. Chefs have trusted and used **HELLMANN'S**® products for years to prepare delicious salads and sandwiches. Now **HELLMANN'S**® also provides versatile, chef-developed salad dressings and a full line of convenient condiments for every culinary need.

Your Unilever Foodsolutions representative can show you how all our products help you save time and labor while pleasing your patrons. Now, we invite you to join us in *Cooking with America's Team*. Bon appetit!

Steve Jilleba, CMC, CCE, AAC
Unilever Foodsolutions Corporate Executive Chef

Cooking with America's Championship Team

Sizzling recipes from Chef Edward G. Leonard, CMC and the American Championship Culinary Team

First published in the United States of America in 2005 by:

Feeding Frenzy, Inc. • 400 E. 5th North Street, Suite C • Summerville, SC 29483 • 1-888-311-8442 phn.

Publisher: Feeding Frenzy, Inc.
Author: Chef Edward G. Leonard, CMC
Art Direction/Design/Layout: Graham Walters, Rhino Design Group
Photography: John Ormond, Vaughn St. Imaging
Contributing Photographer: Ron Manville
Copy Editor: Roger Cook
Line Editor: Susan Cook/Kevin Cook
Recipe Editor: Alex Trassman

Copyright © 2005 Feeding Frenzy, Inc.

All right reserved, including the right of reproduction in whole or part in any form without written permission from the publisher, except brief quotes in connection with reviews written specifically for inclusion in a magazine or newspaper.

Notice: Although every precaution has been taken to ensure the accuracy of published materials, Feeding Frenzy, Inc., *Cooking with America's Championship Team: Sizzling Recipes from Chef Edward G. Leonard, CMC and the American Championship Culinary Team* and the American Culinary Federation cannot be held responsible for opinions expressed and facts supplied by its contributors. All recipes are true and correct to the best of our knowledge and are offered with no guarantee on the part of the author or Feeding Frenzy, Inc.

ISBN# 0-9728697-5-1

Printed & Bound in China
Four Colour Imports, Ltd..

Cooking with America's Championship Team

Sizzling recipes from Chef Edward G. Leonard, CMC and the American Championship Culinary Team

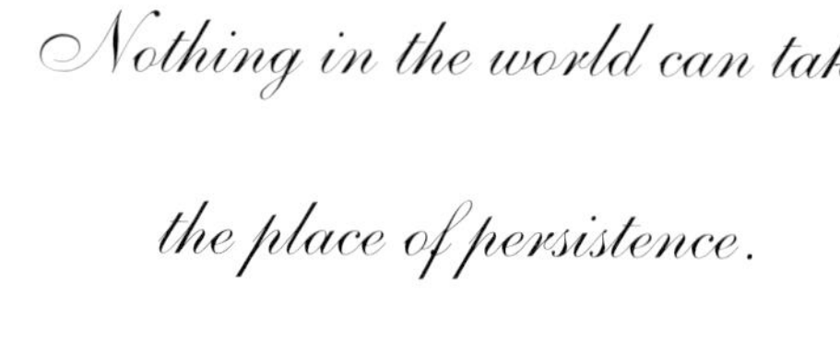

Nothing in the world can take

the place of persistence.

Talent will not;

nothing is more common than

unsuccessful men with talent.

Genius will not;

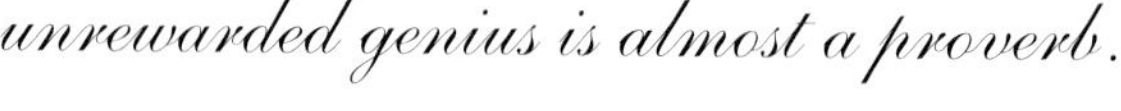

unrewarded genius is almost a proverb.

Education will not;

the world is full of educated derelicts.

Persistence and determination

alone are omnipotent.

—John Quincy Adams

Congratulations ten times — bravo, bravo to Chef Leonard and ACF Culinary Team USA 2004! As a French-American chef, I cannot be more pleased with the incredible success the U.S. team has achieved. It is further proof of how much American cuisine has developed and advanced in the last four decades, earning a privileged place in the global culinary community.

Reading and studying the recipes from this book is a pleasure. It sets the basis of a real, classic American cuisine originated from the international melting pot and adapted to today's cooking philosophy, which is lighter, fresher and healthier.

It is a pleasure to note how clearly and simply the recipes are written, so that they can be easily executed by professionals as well as amateur chefs. I also like the chefs' tips for each recipe. I am convinced that this book will set the standard of American cooking for current and future chefs of America, and will certainly be of great interest internationally. It already has a privileged place in my library.

—Andre Soltner

Former chef/owner of New York's legendary Lutèce, current dean of classic studies at the French Culinary Institute (New York), délegué général of the Master Chefs of France, and co-author of *The Lutèce Cookbook* (Alfred A. Knopf, 1995).

A chef's life is usually comprised of long hours in the kitchen, with very little time for family and friends. However it is times like these, when one gets to represent one's country, that the sacrifice and effort are truly gratifying. The American Culinary Federation is all heart and guts--and incredibly talented. Their trials described within are heart pounding. The recipes they have compiled are the culmination of their craft, their persistence and their belief in each other.

It is with great pride and honor that I introduce you to their incredible journey and their award-winning cuisine.

Thomas Keller
The French Laundry

We salute the members of the ACF Culinary Team Foundation and the ACF members who fully embraced our ambitious goal of elevating the image of the American chef. They provided the financial means, the organizational strength, the support needed and the professional know-how that made it all work. The major corporations that stepped to the forefront as sponsors of the 2004 U.S. culinary team have, through their support, invested in the culinary future of America.

The leadership of Unilever Foodsolutions made the objectives at hand possible, because that leadership was followed by support from many other sponsors. Individual supporters also answered the call: Chefs and ACF chapters rallied to encourage their team and its endeavors. We thank each and every one of them.

Early on, the team held numerous practice sessions that required excellent facilities, cooperation and availability of the finest ingredients. Westchester Country Club, as team headquarters, provided the perfect environment for the chefs and even provided rooms for them to stay over comfortably during three- to four-day practice sessions.

Our team advisors and coaches, along with the ACF Culinary Competition Committee, provided invaluable advice, as they encouraged us to forge ahead and seek new dimensions in food displays regardless of the risks engendered by innovation.

While working in Weimar, we were fortunate to have the wonderful cooperation of Chef Christian Damm at the Dorint Hotel and host Chef Olaf Dienel at the hospital, who provided the facilities, food, a great space and a lot of hot coffee. The services of L. Edwin Brown and Garret Sanborn were invaluable as the team searched for the impossible ingredient, equipment, the perfect vegetable. Brad Barnes, a Certified Master Chef, since 1999 developed, put together, broke down, packed, shipped and unpacked our tables, our china and equipment. The dedication and persistence of Ron Manville, the team's photographer, allowed us to publicize our success and record it for posterity.

Special recognition goes to the many Americans who came to support the teams; the directors on ACF's board, who traveled to Erfurt to show their support for such a global endeavor; and members of the American regional team, student team, military team and our first-ever pastry team who represented themselves so well for the members of the American Culinary Federation and the cuisine of the USA.

Our thanks go to the national team sous chef, James Decker, CEC, who was there for us and never let us down, along with the many apprentices who worked day and night to make it happen.

Major contributions were made by men and woman behind the scenes: team members' employers, managers and culinary staffs. Thanks to such support, team members were able to concentrate on their assignments and spend the time needed for success.

Our success in 2004 was also based on the hard work and efforts of past American teams that paved the way for the international recognition of the American chef.

Finally, my heartfelt and extreme gratitude to the five members of ACF Culinary Team USA 2004's national team: Joachim Buchner, Patricia Nash, Richard Rosendale, Daniel Scannell, and Russell Scott. You did what you set out to do, and everyone won as a result.

As contributors of this book with outstanding recipes, ACF Culinary Team USA 2004 members designate all proceeds of the books purchased by Team USA toward support of the 2008 team and its goal of education in the field of cookery.

Chef Edward G. Leonard, CMC at Westchester Country Club

The world's oldest, largest and most prestigious cooking competition is the International Kochkunst Ausstellung (IKA), or International Culinary Exhibition, held every four years in Germany since 1896 with the exception of the years of conflict marking World War II. The United States, represented by the American Culinary Federation, Inc., has competed quadrennially since 1956.

In 2004, the official culinary teams of 38 nations competed for bronze, silver and gold medals and the highest honors: a place among the top three nations, determined over the course of four days at the Erfurt Messe in what used to be East Germany. The event, which for decades has been better known worldwide as the "Culinary Olympics," brought tens of thousands of professional cooks and enthusiastic spectators to this part of the world.

The "Culinary Olympics" has always been hosted by Germany's leading chefs' organization, the Verband der Köche Deutchlands, or German Cooks Association. The IKA tests the mettle of the world's greatest culinary talent in two classifications: cold buffet (food that is prepared hot or cold, but preserved to perfection and presented cold) and hot food (restaurant style) cooking. The latter category is, by far, the more prestigious of the two because it accurately reflects a real-life kitchen and dining environment.

Each day of the four days, eight countries' national teams displayed their cold-buffet program. Meanwhile, eight other national teams cooked their three-course menus under the watchful eyes of international judges, then served 110 portions of each course to avid diners at the Restaurant of Nations, that accommodated nearly 900 people daily.

On October 21, 2004—the final day of the "Culinary Olympics," devoted solely to recognizing how teams and nations fared—judges conferred the title of World Champion on the top-three-ranking nations: Sweden, Switzerland and the United States, respectively. The Swedish team deserves much credit for defending its first-place win in 2000.

The United States was judged third-best in cooking worldwide! For a land known globally more for its fast food than its fine cuisine, this was a significant achievement. It said to all nations that the United States is able to stand up to the best cooking from all corners of the planet, and even lead the world.

But the judges of the 2004 IKA were not finished with America. Championships were awarded in the four categories of the two classifications: A, B and C in the cold-buffet program and R in the hot kitchen. The most coveted of all the category titles—R for restaurant-style cooking—went to the United States of America for being the best team of chefs in the hot kitchen!

Within these pages is the story of the American team and its road to the World Championship in the hot kitchen and its placement among the top three nations. The story of the five teams making up ACF Culinary Team USA 2004—national, regional, youth, pastry and military—is told through personal reflection and anecdote and demonstrated through winning formulas for the dishes that earned the United States the prestigious cooking title.

It is the story of a group of chefs dedicated to their craft with a passion that drove them to be the best. This story is owned by all professional cooks in America, because it is their story, too, embodied in the men and women who cooked internationally on their behalf in the largest and most prestigious culinary event in the world.

I hope you enjoy our book, not only the story of the teams, but the recipes that are easy to make and so full of flavor. The recipes from Culinary Team USA members are simplistic, elegant, and can be prepared and enjoyed by the home cook as well as the professional in his or her kitchen setting. It is our way of sharing with you what we love most: good food.

Have a flavorful day, every day.

– Chef Edward G. Leonard, CMC

The most coveted of all the category titles—R for restaurant-style cooking—went to the United States of America for being the best team of chefs in the hot kitchen!

Left: Honey-cream and pistachio cake with rhubarb soup, a category C cold entry from Patricia Nash.

Right: Black-kale-wrapped smoked tofu with baby corn-husk cracker: one of four vegetarian platters by Daniel Scannell, CMC.

Left: A cold platter of hors d'oeuvres by Russell Scott, CMC: poached king crab-leg terrine; green asparagus/goat-cheese triangle; marinated green asparagus spears; mango/cucumber salad with green asparagus mousse; shrimp/white asparagus roulade; roasted corn and sweet pepper en geleé with a crab cracker; and herbed mustard sauce and crab-roe vinaigrette.

Right: Stuffed lobster tail with lemon/dill mayonnaise: one of five cold-display finger foods by Richard Rosendale, CC.

Left: Smoked Alaska salmon terrine with dilled baby cucumber, pickled celery salad roe and rye cracker: the starter course of a three-course cold-display entry by Daniel Scannell, CMC.

Right: Warm Alaska sole terrine and braised salsify, roasted salmon fillet with pancetta/chive hollandaise, baby artichokes and tomato fondue: a cold-display appetizer from Joachim Buchner, CMC.

Left: Plantain-wrapped Florida group with red-pepper infusion, candied-yam swirl, yellow-squash boat, black-eyed peas, hominy and charred-corn salsa: a cold-display main dish from Daniel Scannell, CMC.

Right: Vanilla-bean mousse, apple jelly, almond cake and chocolate "obsession," with a praline crunched topped with a spiced sugar button: a cold-display banquet dessert by Patricia Nash.

America's Pursuit of Gold

By Edward G. Leonard, CMC

Members of ACF Culinary Team USA 2004 take their place on the roster of distinguished American chefs who have competed every four years since 1956 in the International Kochkunst Ausstellung (IKA) in Germany.

In my final memo to the 2004 team before we departed the States for Germany, I shared thoughts with them that can really apply to any endeavor a person undertakes.

The Quest for Excellence

Excellence can be yours if you:

- See the invisible, feel the intangible, strive for the impossible.
- Meet challenges with an eager attitude and a curious mind. Set your expectations a notch higher than others.
- Strive to exceed your expectations.
- Regard adversity as a building block rather than a stumbling block.
- Offer respect as readily as you expect it.
- Listen to your inner voice, not the voices of skeptics.
- Know that the real danger in life is doing nothing.
- Use the intensity of your disappointments to fuel your endeavor.
- Live by the decisions you make and move on without regret.
- Rise every time you fall.
- Use your imagination to explore the possibilities.

The teams' objectives were as follows:

1. For the national team to win the overall World Championship and/or the hot-food championship at the 2004 "Culinary Olympics,"
2. For all teams to finish within the top three in their respective divisions (youth, pastry, military, etc.),
3. To make a difference in the world of cuisine,
4. To showcase the cuisine of our country in a contemporary style with a solid classical foundation,
5. To become better at our craft and be the best we can be, and
6. To learn and educate by sharing knowledge and absorbing all that is new.

It is an extraordinary journey for a team that started out in 2001 with a mission and goal to represent the cuisine of the United States.

America has competed in the "Culinary Olympics" for nearly a half-century. The United States sent its first team to Frankfurt in 1956 to compete against nations that did not recognize America for its cuisine. Over the years that followed, especially beginning with the strong performance of the 1976 team, the cuisine of America became well represented and has shown other nations the fine caliber of cooks and chefs in the U.S.A.

The character of these talented teams has changed from predominantly older, European-born-and-trained chefs, to the first team, in 1988, to feature an overwhelming majority of young, American-born-and-trained chefs. This tradition has grown and continued with the 1992, 1996, 2000 and 2004 teams.

The American teams now have prestige and rank among the top world competitors from all over the globe.

The perception of a team once considered easy to beat has also changed to that of a world-champion team that was ranked third in the world (tied with Canada) just prior to the 2004 competition in Germany.

The character of these talented teams has changed from predominantly older, European-born-and-trained chefs, to the first team, in 1988, to feature an overwhelming majority of young, American-born-and-trained chefs.

The ACF Team meets to review before the events commence.

Prior to the "Culinary Olympics" team members discuss how to improve upon the crab trio.

1956 American Culinary Federation National USA Culinary Team

Fred Wohlkopf (manager)
Paul Laesecke (captain)
Paul Debes
Paul Leuppe
Otto Spielbichler

1960 American Culinary Federation National USA Culinary Team

Paul Laesecke (manager)
Charles Finance (captain)
Tony Ackermann
Charles Daniel
Edmond Kasper

1964 American Culinary Federation National USA Culinary Team

John Monbaron (manager)
Willy Rossel (captain)
Richard Mack
Otto Spielbichler
Hubert Schmieder
Fred Borman
Willi Rahmig
Casey Sinkeldam

Culinary Team USA's success in 2004 is the success of all teams that have shared in making American cookery world class and something that all cooks, chefs and food enthusiasts can be proud of.

American cuisine was a concept that the world did not acknowledge when the United States first competed at the IKA in 1956. Then, Europeans believed Americans were culinarians of a lesser order. Seeing America as the land of fast food, hamburgers and hot dogs, Europeans believed that the United States consisted of cooks at best, not world-class chefs.

Even as recently as a generation ago, the American team realized what the rest of the world still had to learn: True culinary art is preparing real food for real people, not arcane displays for other chefs.

Early U.S. teams focused their menus on favorite foods from home, such as steak, stuffed baked potatoes and succotash. U.S. menus sold out within minutes at the public restaurant—the Restaurant of Nations—in Frankfurt with fair-goers preferring simpler, straightforward, flavorful food over other nations' more esoteric offerings.

It was the 1976 U.S. team that brought America its first recognition as a world culinary leader. That year, the team developed its philosophy about the relationship between chefs and food in the United States. The philosophy was based on America's tradition of wholesome, nutritious and simple eye-appealing preparations as the foundations of cookery.

That philosophy has matured and been honed to a sharp, competitive edge. As it collected more medals in the 1980s, the American team began establishing its identity as a country whose national cuisine is based firmly on a deep understanding of our native foods. By 1988 the global attitude toward American cuisine had changed dramatically. Both the American team and the world's idea of fine cuisine had undergone an evolution. Today, American chefs are considered formidable competition, their dishes among the avant-garde of the world.

In the 1990s, the teams' philosophy evolved further to demonstrate the melting pot that is America, with flavors of multiple cultures making up a distinctly American cuisine. U.S. diners began to crave flavor, and welcomed the melting pot of our country that delivered the flavors of Italy, Asia, Spain, Mexico and more.

The 2000 and 2004 teams developed dishes and menus that competed in Germany not only to bring home medals, but also to add new dimensions to menus in foodservice operations across the United States and to show a balance of the traditions of the past with the new concepts and flavors of today.

Competing Today

All types of professional culinary competitions are on the rise today. From the Food Network's "Iron Chef" to Sutter Home Winery's Build a Better Burger, from regional seafood cook-offs to the Pillsbury Bake-off, not to mention the vast array of ACF competitions held coast-to-coast annually, people are cooking and presenting their creations for judging, to become better at what they do. There are forums, conferences, culinary tours and more venues where chefs, cooks and those from all countries who love food can exchange ideas and be inspired by the ideas of others. Culinary competitions are also the research and development laboratories for world-class chefs, encouraging innovation and experimentation. Most important, competitions such as the International Kochkunst Ausstellung, or "Culinary Olympics," allow chefs to test themselves against their peers at professional and personal levels. The competition challenges every chef, no matter how successful, to strive for the next level of excellence.

Competitions today at the international level are at an all-time high in both attendance and the high level of craftsmanship.

The Road to the 2004 "Culinary Olympics"

Putting together a world-class team of chefs to represent the United States in international culinary competitions is a process that begins two to three years prior to the IKA.

Only chefs who are members of the American Culinary Federation and United States citizens are eligible for the team. Chefs seeking a place on the U.S. culinary team must first compete and excel in one of the several regional tryouts held around the country.

Chef Edward G. Leonard, CMC, who captained the 2000 U.S. team and was given overwhelming support by the ACF Foundation to lead the 2004 team, changed the tryout system for 2004 from simply displaying cold platters of food and pastry to an edible cold-food and pastry display.

The new system showed the judges much more about the chefs trying out—how they work, their character, and their ability to plan and prepare. Also, having the displays judged on taste singled out the chefs with the greatest talent to present great-tasting food in an awesome fashion.

Among the scores of contestants, only 24 winners of these regional cold-food and pastry competitions were invited to compete in the hot-food competition held in Chicago during the 2001 National Restaurant Association's Restaurant, Hotel-Motel Show. The Chicago competition was the final tryout for the U.S. culinary team, and the event at which the team members were selected.

In Chicago, four chefs and two pastry chefs competed each of four days in glass-enclosed kitchens designed to approximate the working environments of international competitions. The final tryout in Chicago was specifically structured and designed to test the professional skills and creativity of pastry chefs, who in past years had shown great talent in cold display and centerpiece work, but now needed to indicate proficiency in a key element, namely, flavor.

Each chef contestant was assigned to a kitchen and given a mystery box of randomly selected food materials. Contestants were directed to prepare a three-course menu using at least some quantity of all items in the basket. Each was challenged to produce a meal that would reflect his or her style of cuisine while demonstrating the skill to use given ingredients in a simple, but elegant, manner. The contestants were judged on six criteria: presentation, creativity, workmanship, composition, sanitation and the most important element, taste.

Once the tryouts were over, the official American Culinary Federation judging committee selected the team from among the highest-ranking finalists. Culinary skills and combined scores alone were not enough to guarantee a place on the team, however. Each contestant was also judged on the neatness of his or her workplace, ability to function under pressure and ability to make last-minute, qualitative decisions. Other important factors were the chef's ability to be a team player, professional and personal references, and one-on-one interviews. Also, evaluating how the chef worked with an assigned apprentice was heavily taken into consideration.

Even a chef with great talent could be passed over if ego and selfishness were part of his or her demeanor, as being a true team player with a willingness to put the team first can spell the difference between success and failure at the IKA and other international competitions.

Practice makes perfect, as Chef Scannell, CMC prepares dishes for service in one of the many practice sessions.

Team cooperation plays a vital role as Chef's Leonard, Nash and Rosendale discuss improvements on the teams dessert.

1968 American Culinary Federation National USA Culinary Team
Jack Sullivan (manager)
Richard Mack (captain)
Ferdinand Metz, CMC
Gerhard Schmidt
Casey Sinkeldam

1972 American Culinary Federation National USA Culinary Team
Jack Sullivan (manager)
Bernard Urban (captain)
Milos Cihelka, CMC
Franz Eckert
Gerhard Grimeissen

1976 American Culinary Federation National USA Culinary Team
Richard Bosnjak (manager)
Ferdinand Metz, CMC (captain)
Bruno Ellmer, CMC
Gerhard Grimeissen
Gerhard Schmid
Fritz Sonnenschmidt, CMC
Helmut Loibi, CMPC (pastry)

Intensity grows as Chefs Buchner and Leonard discuss last minute changes to a dish just prior to the event.

Those chosen as team members by the ACF committee were then assigned to the national or regional team according to the highest overall scores and the judge's assessment on strengths, weaknesses and the balance of putting together a team. For example, a winning combination might be a chef who is extremely good in cold-food-display work and not bad in the hot kitchen, teamed up with a chef who is excellent in the hot kitchen and okay in the cold. Some regional-team members were considered alternates for national-team members, qualified to take the place of a chef on the national team should the need arise.

The official ACF Culinary Team USA 2004, selected as a result of tryouts in 2001, consisted of 11 chefs and two sous chefs. The new team made its announcement in May of that year to the culinary world and the ACF ranks.

The team's first official duty was to attend a meeting at the team manager's place of employment, Westchester Country Club in Rye, N.Y. The meeting's objectives were for team members to learn about the others' careers and places of employment, as well as personal lives. The meeting also carried out the goals, purpose and game plans for the team from that point on, and presented a schedule of practice times and competition dates.

"Making the team is not the end. It's just the beginning in a long road ahead," said team chef Dan Scannell, CMC, who was also a member of the 2000 team. Becoming a team is a process that takes two-plus years of practice, meetings, appearances, traveling together, working side by side and spending perhaps more time with each other than with their families and friends.

Early in practice, the team developed and expressed the philosophy that would guide it and become the foundation of future practices and other competitions outside of the IKA. The philosophy concerning other competitions leading up to the 2004 IKA was to consider them as intense practice sessions that would teach by trial and error. The mission, therefore, was not necessarily to win such events prior to the IKA, but rather, to expose the team to preparing, packing, traveling and practicing under circumstances of pressure that would reflect the big show in Erfurt, Germany.

The team would compete in Luxembourg the November following the tryout, which left the chefs only five months to prepare. The United States performed well, winning a silver in the hot kitchen and taking a gold in the cold program, finishing 6th overall.

In May 2003, nearly 18 months before the 2004 IKA, the U.S. culinary team gave a dramatic demonstration of how it was coming together by winning for the first time ever the American Culinary Classic that is held every four years at the National Restaurant Association's Restaurant, Hotel-Motel Show in Chicago. The American Culinary Classic is the only World Association of Cooks Societies-sanctioned international competition in the Western Hemisphere. The U.S. team displayed its readiness for the challenge by executing a cold display that won three gold medals and took first place among 11 international teams. The team went into the hot kitchen with a menu and game plan designed to correct the mistakes in Luxembourg. It succeeded with a gold medal and first place in the hot kitchen.

With the two category wins, the U.S. team took first place overall, winning the Classic cup. It was the first time a U.S. team had won the Classic since the competition's launch in 1983. Germany placed second, with Scotland finishing third.

Finally, The 2004 IKA

Practice for ACF Culinary Team USA 2004 did not stop when chefs boarded the plane for Germany, but continued day and night until the final day of competition.

The International Kochkunst Ausstellung (IKA), or International Culinary Exhibition, in Erfurt, Germany, in October 2004 attracted 38 international teams (with a waiting list) and scores of individual and regional-team chefs. The world's largest and oldest culinary competition would also be the largest ever in the competition's history. What a long way the competition had come from its roots of local cooking and food competition held on the Frankfurt fairground in 1896!

This competition attracts the world's most masterful chefs, who compete in a series of categories for gold, silver and bronze medals and the highest honors: the titles of World Champion in the cold displays, the most-important hot kitchen, and overall. Serious participation requires extensive preparation, an unbendable commitment, and support and encouragement of many organizations, families, friends and individuals alike, all of whom deserve our thanks and recognition.

Four competition categories include Category A, which mandates a cold platter, finger foods hot and cold, and six appetizers; Category B, which is hot food displayed cold and includes a three-course meal, a vegetarian platter for four and five main plates; and Category C, which includes complex pastry centerpieces, petit fours, a dessert plate displayed for six but able to be scaled for 200, and a pastry platter of the hardest level.

The most-challenging and highly coveted category is Category R, the hot kitchen. Only the official national teams of each country are eligible to compete in the hot-food competition. (Regional and city teams, as well as individuals, may compete in the cold-food categories.) Only national teams compete directly against one another for the top rankings in the world. Each national team consists of a team manager and/or captain along with five other chefs that include a pastry chef.

In Category R, each national team has five hours to prepare a three-course meal of 110 portions. The team cooks under the watchful eyes of kitchen judges along with a panel of tasting judges. The judges pull four plates from the 110 portions at a time of their choosing during service. As a result, no team knows which of the 110 portions will go to the jury. So all must be perfect.

The judge's panel is selected from the represented nations and senior German chefs drawn from the German Cooks Association. The judges themselves must have been chefs at the top of their profession and be past "Culinary Olympians" on national teams.

Teams competing in both cold and hot classifications compete against a point system that earns them total points for bronze, silver and gold medals. Those points are then totaled to produce the final standings.

The body of teams under the USA banner consisted of the national team, student team, regional team, pastry team and military team. In 2000, the U.S. national team won first place in Category B along with three gold medals and a silver for the hot kitchen, finishing seventh overall. Would it fare better in 2004?

On opening day at the IKA, one of the most stirring traditions is the Parade of Nations. Each national team is led onto the stage with the flag of its respective country, and the opening ceremony begins. One can feel the energy, the excitement and the culinary friendships, old and new. One can see the hard work of the German Cooks Association to execute a global event that is truly first class.

As the games begin, Chefs Leonard and Handke look for perfection and anticipate gold.

Ingredients arrive and Chef Rosendale begins preparations for one of the many dishes for which he is responsible.

The U.S. national team worked in the town of Weimar, about 25 minutes from the Erfurt Messe, or fair hall, where the competition took place. In the kitchens of the hospital at Weimar, the team prepared for the event for which they had trained the previous 30 months.

Still ironing out details, Chefs Leonard, Buchner, Rosendale, Scannell and Scott made plans for the first order of business: the cold-buffet program on Monday. The team went shopping, checked all equipment lists and food supplies and waited patiently for packages from the States to arrive in Germany. The cold program was a large program, and the team felt it had the goods to prevail as the leaders of this program. Since 1999, after the team won the cold-buffet championship in Basel, Switzerland, the United States had been a global leader and innovator in the cold-buffet program.

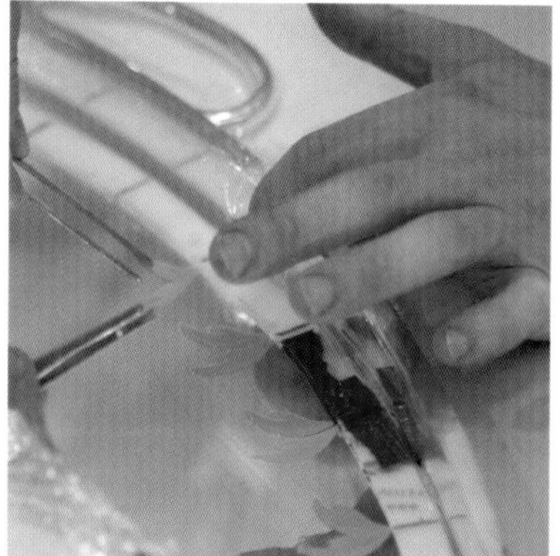

As the cold food plating begins, attention to detail and adept hands are a prerequisite.

Chef Nash assembles the display that won team USA a gold medal in category C (desserts) in cold food.

For the 2004 cold-buffet program, the U.S. team had a custom-designed centerpiece created by designers in New York with the Lucite Corporation.

Patricia Nash, the national team's pastry chef, worked on her portion of the cold-buffet display at the Victor's Residenz hotel in Erfurt with team pastry coach Thomas Vaccaro. Her work would consist of a theme centered on fashion, with techniques of chocolate, sugar and gum paste complemented by great-looking and flavorful pastries.

The team worked almost 30 straight hours with no sleep and met at the hall to set up its display.

On October 18, the second day of the IKA and the first time that the U.S. national team would compete, a finished cold-buffet table was presented with all the hard work and effort of Team USA against a strong showing that day from Canada, Germany, Sweden, Norway and many others. A group of official judges, score sheets in hand, scrutinized the show platters and plates on the U.S. national team's table.

In 2000, the U.S. table took three gold medals in the cold-buffet program, and a world championship in Category B—hot food presented cold. The pressure was on in 2004.

On the last hours of the second day, the U.S. team stood near the scoreboards, awaiting the results. In cold-food competition the day before, not one team had won three gold medals straight. When results of the second day were posted, the U.S. team's score was not quite what it expected: two silver and one gold. The gold, at least, was in Category C (pastry), and was the second-highest gold-medal score among all national teams that week. Sweden and Canada received straight gold medals for the three categories of the cold-buffet program. Perhaps the confidence of the other teams grew when one chef commented that the culinary super power from the United States had stumbled.

There is an old saying that it is never over until the fat lady sings, and she had some singing left to do.

The pressure on Team USA to excel in hot food at the highest level, and even to have a chance of finishing among the top three or five nations overall, was now growing.

Months after I became manager of the U.S. team in early 1999, the team's win in Basel, Switzerland, for the cold-buffet program launched a winning streak of straight gold medals in the buffet program from there on—15 in all, culminating with two cold championships and a championship in Category B at the 2000 IKA.

Although two silver and a gold in 2004 was a respectable showing, it was not what the U.S. team was accustomed to scoring in the cold-buffet program. My job, however, as leader, was to believe in his team and be proud of its performance. The biggest challenge was still two days ahead.

Indeed, a U.S. team had not won a gold medal in the hot kitchen since 1988. Achieving anything less than a gold medal in hot food would shatter the U.S. objective of placing among the top three or five nations overall. Less than a gold, in fact, and it would be difficult even to defend the team's seventh-place showing in 2000.

The U.S. chefs gathered at dinner to celebrate the silvers and gold earned in cold buffet. Afterward, they got some much needed rest.

I called for a private talk with the team the next morning. I told the chefs that the true character of the team would now be tested, that the showing of great character is not when one has everything going for himself or herself, when all is right and one is leading the pack. Rather, it is when things do not go as planned and one is backed into a corner that great character emerges. How you respond, how you come out of that corner is the true mark of your character, I said. I finished by saying how we cook, how we lift our heads when we walk into the kitchen with a confidence that says we can cook a meal that will rock the world, will be our legacy and the measure of whether the chefs representing the USA and ACF will have any character.

The USA Competes in the Hot Kitchen

The evening before Team USA would compete in hot food, team members left Wiemar for Erfurt to walk through their assigned kitchen, check out the equipment and discuss the game plan for the following morning. Competition regulations were reviewed and preparation procedures rehearsed.

In hot-food competition, judges evaluate not only taste and appearance of dishes, but kitchen judges also review all items brought into the kitchen to determine if they are prepared from basic products. There can be no shortcuts, and kitchen judges ensure that a team's prep is carried out to the letter of the official guidelines.

International culinary competitions in general, and the IKA in particular, are the research and development showcases of the food industry. New food products, techniques and presentations appear here first. The excitement of the hot kitchens is infectious, with a buzz and intensity like no other competition in the world. Many feel that the IKA separates the chefs from the cooks.

It was the success of the 1980, 1984 and 1988 teams, which won gold medals at each IKA in the hot kitchen, that showed Europe that the USA could indeed cook, winning the respect of all. The star chefs and TV food channels came long after. If not for the success of those teams, then perhaps the boom of food in America would not have happened.

The cuisine of today offers a variety of components, flavors, histories, stunning presentations and textures, giving the professional chef's art, whether savory or pastry, a more defined place. To produce food today at the highest level for 110 people in the time allowed and under the watchful eyes of judges is no easy feat.

The Restaurant of Nations at the IKA is a public restaurant, set up daily in front of the hot-food kitchens to serve the menus of the national teams competing that day. The public can purchase tickets to eat the menu of their choice. Each day's menu is printed in several languages, and following the theory that one picture is worth a thousand words, each team's actual menu is prepared and preserved in lighted display cases so all guests may see the meals being produced that day. As well, the judges may review the show plates to ensure the finished products come out of the kitchens as expected.

1980 American Culinary Federation National USA Culinary Team

Ferdinand Metz, CMC (manager)
Klaus Friedenreich, CMC (captain)
Gerhard Grimeissen
Klaus Loos
Richard Schneider, CMC
Gunther Heiland, CMPC (pastry)

1984 American Culinary Federation National USA Culinary Team

Ferdinand Metz, CMC (manager)
Richard Schneider, CMC (captain)
Marcus Bosiger
Daniel Hugelier, CMC
L. Timothy Ryan, CMC
Helmut Loivl, CMPC (pastry)

1988 American Culinary Federation National USA Culinary Team

Ferdinand Metz, CMC (manager)
Richard Bosnjak (advisor)
L. Timothy Ryan, CMC (captain)
Mark Erickson, CMC
Hartmut Handke, CMC
Daniel Hugelier, CMC
Christopher Northmore, CMPC (pastry)

2000 American Culinary Federation National USA Culinary Team

Edward G Leonard, CMC
Charles Carroll, CEC
Daniel Scannell, CMC
Alfonse Contrisciani, CMC
Derrin Moore, CMC
Darrin Aoyama, CEPC (pastry)

2004 American Culinary Federation National USA Culinary Team

Edward G. Leonard, CMC (manager and captain)
Joachim Buchner, CMC
Daniel Scannell, CMC
Richard Rosendale, CC
Russell Scott, CMC
Patricia Nash (pastry)
Harmut Handke, CMC (advisor)
Ferdinand Metz, CMC (advisor)
Victor Gielisse, CMC (team coach)
Thomas Vaccaro, CEPC (pastry coach)
James Decker, CEC (sous chef)

The ACF team prepares hot food service at the 2004 IKA while admirers wait in anticipation.

The U.S. hot-food menu sold out the first day of the competition, days before the team was scheduled to compete. The Restaurant of Nations would serve 890 meals each day to a full house of visitors from all nations, who would sit down to eat together and sample the fare from the competing countries.

On Wednesday, October 20, the U.S. national team started setting up in the display hot-food kitchen at 6:00 a.m. Team members were scrutinized by judges at every stage of bringing in the food and equipment, setting up, preparation and service.

Each national team prepared 110 portions of its three-course menu for sale, which consisted of a starter, main plate and pastry course. At some point during the service window, plates were taken for tasting and evaluation in a private room.

On the day that Team USA competed in hot food, only two of the 24 gold medals awarded thus far were in hot food. The judging was fair, but tough the past few days. Even the cold-buffet program at the start of the last day of the IKA still showed only two teams receiving three straight gold medals: Sweden and Canada.

Both countries also competed in hot food with the United States on the last day. A gold in the hot kitchen for either of them would ensure a shot at the overall title and some category championships.

With only the medals being shown on the daily scoreboard, and not the scores themselves, no one knew how the standings would measure up at the end. A gold medal might be a low gold, for instance; a silver might be a high silver. So the chance to place high overall was always there, and the excitement kept on building.

Team USA Hot-Food Philosophy

The team's philosophy and hot-food presentation was designed to the most important criteria: flavor, texture and taste, reflecting the food of America. The impression that Team USA wanted to make was one that would impress and show the judges that the team had solid fundamentals, a menu that harmonized and showed good seasonal flavor profiles, and tasted great.

The first impression—visual—gives the judges and diners a desire to taste the food because its appearance is attractive and appealing and makes you hungry.

The second impression comes from a pleasing aroma that reinforces the visual appeal and excites the taste buds.

The third and fourth impressions combine savory and sensory. The experience of taste is reinforced by the different textures, methods of preparation, harmony of flavors, and the correct balance of seasoning and complex combinations. The senses of sight, taste, aroma and mouthfeel are crucial to the entire dining experience, particularly when that experience is judged at the international level.

The U.S.A.'s hot-food menu at the 2004 IKA exhibited food that could be characterized as innovative, yet basic and honest, with a true reflection of the American bounty. It was a combination of traditional and comfortable flavors, and unique with an up-to-date presentation coupled with a solid classical foundation. All the correct elements were there to capture the judges' attention. Not only did the three courses conform to the team's philosophy, they also worked well with one another, creating a unified and compatible menu.

The trilogy of American crab featured a tasty and creamy she-crab bisque that was served in a roasted sugar pumpkin to reflect the season and the heritage of autumn in America. The crab terrine had a light, but pungent, mustard/butter sauce that truly complemented the terrine while letting it stand on its own. The fried crab finger over a spinach salad was the finish that balanced the richness of the plate with the perfect blend of tartness.

The main plate itself represented a unique balance of food that exhibited a very rich Pennsylvania Dutch influence. Much of the dish would have to be cooked at the last minute.

Preparing the venison-shoulder braise and then filling a dumpling was time consuming, but made the dish a signature item. The dumplings were the domain of Chef Buchner, who was affectionately known as "the dumpling man."

Flavors were enhanced by the tartness and sweetness of seared and caramelized apple rings along with braised cabbage served with very comforting, down-to-earth accompaniments of sautéed chanterelles, green beans and a potato/parsnip purée with a signature savory tuile that pulled all elements of the plate together.

The main protein of roasted venison loin featured all the necessary contrasts in sensory perception, yet maintained harmony. The flavors and textures were varied, with a unique mix of compatible ingredients. Most important, those ingredients enhanced the venison, while the surprise of the braised meat in the dumpling was a big winner.

The autumn dessert was dramatic in its presentation. While the vanilla cream wrapped around a baked-pumpkin brulée center, layers of cake, apple jelly and diced apple made this a truly unique and very seasonal pastry item. The team was able to use the best flavor memories of the fall while the pastry was finished with a cranberry sauce, cookie garnish and an awesome roasted-apple sorbet that left the diner wanting more.

The three-course meal exemplified one of the most-difficult things to achieve in professional cooking: simplicity and elegance. The proof is in the eating. Simple yet elegant food with a touch of innovation, pleasing presentation and the right combination of textures, colors and aromas is always a winner. Team USA's philosophy of focusing on flavors first, letting the rest follow, was true to course with this winning menu.

Among the eight national teams competing on the last day of the IKA, Team USA not only finished within the time window, but was first in finishing service. Each of the 110 dishes of each course was consistent, hot and flavorful.

Team USA cleaned up, proud of its work, but not knowing the result. Chefs hoped the judges would appreciate their effort and the three-course meal they worked so hard to prepare.

On the way back to the hotel we found out by cell phone that we had indeed scored a gold medal for our efforts—a first since 1988. The only other gold that day went to Sweden, resulting in a total of four gold medals in hot food among 32 teams. The USA was in the running, and the moment of character had been shown. It was a night to celebrate before the final awards and closing ceremony on Thursday.

American Excellence in Cold-Buffet Competition

At the IKA, hot-food competition, which most resembles the real-life world of a successful restaurant, is where the ultimate glory and honor for any nation lie. Nonetheless, the U.S. national team's success with cold food, combined with its gold-medal World Championship in hot food, is what earned this country its placement of third in cooking excellence among all nations after Sweden and Switzerland, respectively.

Chef Scott lends a hand when he can, helping Chef Buchner with his specialty, venison dumplings.

In the weeds? Chef's Buchner, Scott and Scannell begin to plate while hungry patrons eagerly await.

Culinary Team USA national made its first official appearance at the 21st IKA on October 18 in the cold-display category, and the buzz about the exquisite entry radiated throughout the Erfurt convention center known as the messe. From the striking table design itself—black tiers and spires sweeping inward from the perimeter of the table and reaching skyward, resembling the splash a stone makes when dropped in a calm pool of water—to the dessert theme of a seamstress' studio, smartly conveyed through such icons as scissors, thread and dress patterns, and even an overflowing confectionery sewing box as a centerpiece, the United States showed the world that we rule in cold-buffet work as well as hot food.

Indeed, the United States' national team won a gold medal in category C (patisserie), and a silver medal each in categories A and B, which denote food that is prepared hot but displayed cold, preserved for viewing and judging. Representative cold platters included one display of five hors d'oeuvres serving six people and consisting of rack of salmon, watercress mousse and tomato/citrus coulis; braised bacon-wrapped chicken tenderloin; steamed shrimp dumplings and lemon broth; smoked poussin stuffed with Smithfield ham and black-trumpet mushrooms; and savoy cabbage filled with sage sausage, with horseradish sauce. Another five courses, serving four, featured Hatch (New Mexico) chile rellenos filled with spinach and goat cheese and served with polenta fries; "tamales" in bric pastry, with millet- and corn-stuffed red onion; black-kale-wrapped smoked tofu with baby corn and a husk cracker; savory tofu/butternut-squash cajeta custard consisting of white beans, fried artichokes and mustard greens; and three salsas featuring ancho remoulade, piquillo-pepper sauce and pico de gallo.

Brad Barnes (l.) and national-team pastry coach Thomas Vacarro assemble dishes on the cold-buffet display.

The hot food served cold display which will win team USA a silver medal in both A and B categories.

Was the team disappointed that it didn't earn gold in categories A and B, which present hot food in a cold format for visual judging? Absolutely. Should it be? Absolutely not, says Leonard. Many countries earned diplomas or bronze medals for their cold-display work, and the two silver medals plus the gold in patisserie won by the United States was a very respectable showing. However, since 1999, Culinary Team USA has become accustomed to sweeping cold-food categories in international competition.

"The idea was to bring everything full circle," says Leonard of Culinary Team USA national's cold-buffet entries at the most-recent IKA. "The whole table worked together. No matter where you looked, you saw food, you saw everything in harmony. The categories weren't necessarily separated, so the whole flow of that table and design was a continuous circular motion."

Leonard admits that in 2004 the team approached cold food differently than at the last IKA in 2000, and that in doing so the team took a gamble. "In 2000 I was very firm against fusion cuisine in our food," Leonard says. "Yet we're a melting pot, and cuisine fusion is featured at some of the most popular places people eat." So Culinary Team USA decided to feature some of the fusion elements that mark contemporary American cuisine through several cold entries, one of which was a main plate of plantain-wrapped Florida grouper with red-pepper infusion created by team member Scannell.

"Everything was done excellently," says Leonard "Our hot-food-displayed-cold represented food that you would want to eat. There was less garde manger than in 2000, and more practicality. That's the balance: demonstrating expertise and still having some practicality behind it. Since 1999 we've dominated the cold sector. In general for the Americans team, our whole presentation was really big and bold. I'm proud of the results, which were high enough that, with our hot medal, put us third place in the world."

Other ACF Teams Impress the World, Too

Karin Ahlborg, a Swedish journalist, relayed how the Swedish youth team accidentally took the fish for its competition that was meant for the Swedish national team in the hot-food kitchen the next morning. Panic ensued. After calling all over Germany, the team found a supply of what it needed in Switzerland late in the night. Ultimately, Sweden was named overall winner of the IKA.

Images of solidarity and pride among cooks in the face of the highest stakes abounded at the 21st International Culinary Exhibition (IKA) in Erfurt, Germany, in October. The Icelanders all shaved their heads in a show of brotherhood. Spectators cheered the spirit of the upstart team from the Bahamas when it placed 29th among 32 teams in hot food. The Hungarian team stood out, looking resplendent in red chef's coats and black aprons. Cooks from Asian nations jumped up and down, pleased with themselves over any accomplishment, however large or small, at the greatest cooking arena in the world. One of the two Germans who accepted the gold medal for that nation's championship in the pastry competition, grabbed the microphone to propose marriage to his teammate in front of a thousand or more onlookers. As if people weren't already whipped up as they sat on the edges of their seats awaiting the results of scoring on the last day of the IKA, the declaration of love between two chefs winning the gold for their country was nearly too much to bear.

Of course, when the world learned that the United States was the global champion in hot-food, or restaurant-style, cooking among 32 nations, the roar was enough to lift the roof off the Erfurt messe.

However, the national team of six Americans who performed so well, winning for the United States third place overall among 38 countries, wasn't the only team that competed under the U.S. stars and stripes in Germany. Four other teams also did our nation proud. If one trait was shared by all U.S. teams in Erfurt, it was the desire to make an impression, to titillate by innovation or invention while remaining solidly rooted in the basics. In that regard, all U.S. teams—national, regional, pastry, youth and military—scored highest.

From the Army, Two Golds and Something New

America's participation in this year's IKA got off to a winning start thanks to the Fort Lee, Virginia-based U.S. Army team, which, along with the U.S. pastry team, competed in cold-buffet display on October 17, the first day of the "Culinary Olympics." Culinary Team USA's military team won a gold medal for its U.S. Cavalry-themed table that had as its centerpiece a three-tiered cake in rolled fondant crowned by a sugar stallion.

Showpieces included cocoa paintings of U.S. Cavalry generals through history, a salt-dough log cabin, a covered wagon in marzipan with goods and supplies in miniature, a marzipan horse saddle, pastillage medals affixed to a confectionery box, and a blown-sugar Cavalry hat with playing cards and spurs. At the awards ceremony following judging, Master Sgt. Mark Warren, CEC, the team's captain, accepted a whopping 11 silver and four gold medals on behalf of team members for the U.S. Army's showpiece and centerpiece work.

But the gold that counts most is the one the U.S. Army team received for the cold table as a whole. One of its three-course entries started with creamy chicken-liver mousse, crisp polenta cake with poached apple and mushrooms in a Madeira reduction, and sweet-and-sour currant sauce. The entrée was a boiled dinner of corned beef with a tomato/horseradish dumpling,

2004 ACF Culinary Team USA Military

Master Sgt. Mark Warren (captain),
Fort Bragg, North Carolina

Chief Warrant Officer Robert Sparks,
support,
Stuttgart, Germany

Master Sgt. Steve Magnin,
larder chef,
Carlisle Barracks, Pennsylvania

Sgt. 1st Class David Turcotte,
advisor,
Washington, D.C.

Sgt. 1st Class Rene Marquis,
expeditor,
Fort Shafter, Hawaii

Sgt. 1st Class Mark Morgan,
pastry chef,
Fort Benning, Georgia

Staff Sgt. Joshua Rine,
larder chef
Heidelberg, Germany

Staff Sgt. Jesus Camacho,
sugar centerpiece,
Fort Drum, New York

Sgt. Adam Lang,
marzipan centerpiece,
Fort Bragg, North Carolina

Sgt. Karen Glanzer,
cocoa painting,
Fort Shafter, Hawaii

2004 ACF Culinary Team USA Military (continued)

Sgt. Scott Graves, support, Heidelberg, Germany

Sgt. Carlene Robidoux, marzipan centerpiece, Fort Bragg, North Carolina

Spc. Luisa Concepcion, sugar centerpiece, Schofield Barracks, Hawaii

Spc. Florine Nevins, marzipan centerpiece, Schofield Barracks, Hawaii

Spc. Todd Bohak, larder chef, Fort Bragg, North Carolina

Spc. Billy Daugette, support, Fort Benning, Georgia

Pfc. Mathew Flemister, salt dough, Fort Wainwright, Alaska

Pfc. Joseph Oberly, support, Heidelberg, Germany

Pfc. John Page, support, Washington, D.C.

Chief Warrant Officer David Longstaff (Manager), Fort Lee, Virginia

US Military team wins gold.

root vegetables and a cabbage galette. Dessert was a chocolate/orange-cream gâteau slice with blood-orange and cumquat sauces, garnished with a chocolate decoration simulating wood grain.

The U.S. military team also did America proud on Tuesday by earning its second gold medal, this one in hot food. If competing for medals in the most prestigious culinary competition in the world wasn't pressure enough, military teams at the IKA were forced to cook outside the messe in tented kitchens that centered around the use of a Karcher unit—a German field kitchen equivalent to the MKT, or Mobile Kitchen Trailer, that the U.S. Army uses around the world. Further, three-course meals were required to cost out at no more than three euros total—the equivalent of about four U.S. dollars. Each military team had to prepare 75 portions each of two three-course meals that were preselected by judges ("They choose the hardest menus of all," according to Sgt. 1st Class Rene Marquis, CEC, CCE) from among the team's seven entries in category B of the cold-buffet division.

Four years ago, America's Army won the military division of the IKA. Not satisfied with merely trying to repeat its success from 2000, however, this year the Army added an innovation not seen before at this event: a stainless-steel insert to fit into the hot-water well of the Karcher to create a bain-marie for holding and serving food. According to Marquis, whereas other military teams served from the ovens and stoves stationed under the tent, the United States' new-fashioned bain-marie created moist heat for holding food and an efficiency of service that drew attention of the hosts of the IKA. Marquis said the Army plans to purchase a Karcher and bring it to Fort Lee long before the 2008 IKA so that that year's team won't have to wait until it gets to Germany to practice on one. Naturally, the Fort Lee Karcher will contain the inserts. So might all Karcher units at the 2008 IKA.

What does military cooking at the IKA say to the world? And why was it part of the "Culinary Olympics," where national teams consisting primarily of chefs of commercial kitchens vie for a singular IKA championship that the world's armed forces can't enjoy? Said Chief Warrant Officer David Longstaff, CEC, manager of the U.S. Army team, "What our being here demonstrates is that even though we're military chefs, we can produce the same cuisine as our civilian counterparts. Even though we're soldiers—and that's always our first mission—it's good to be able to show the world how well we cook food." Added Longstaff, even the U.S. Army is often surprised by the caliber and talent of its own enlisted men and women who cook. The medals, he said, prove what Army cooks can do on the world competition stage, but the real glory in competing comes from sharing. "Over half of our team has been deployed in theaters across the world, and have come together to do this competition," Longstaff said. "They'll deploy again shortly. There are foodservice people in the Army who will never achieve a place on this team, because it's such a small group. Because our team is based all over the world, team members can take these skills out to the soldiers and teach them the highest cooking standards."

Among 11 teams representing their nations' armed forces, the United States placed second overall (after Germany), and is already looking ahead to 2008.

Pastry: Pushing the Envelope

The United States also made a first showing at the launch of the IKA in the national pastry competition's cold-presentation category, in which it offered a chocolate showpiece, two gâteaux, a sugar showpiece, six unique plated desserts and a display of six pieces of eight different friandises including a showpiece. With the U.S. space program as its theme, the U.S. pastry team earned a silver medal—not a bad showing for a first-time involvement, according to pastry judge John Hui, CEPC, 2004 Pastry Chef of the Year from ACF's Western Region.

Team USA's national pastry team earned a gold medal in hot-food presentation on October 19, augmenting its silver in cold-buffet display two days earlier. Before he knew how well he and Roy Pell had fared in hot food, Darrin Aoyama, CEPC, captain of the two-person team, said that medals weren't the reason the United States was represented in pastry at the IKA.

"Medals are what we want to win, of course, but the issue is that we want to put something new, something different, something innovative out there. We had a lot of new ideas, a lot of new concepts, such as our sugar piece. The way it was designed and suspended was very different. Our entire cold table was very different. We had stuff on the edges of plates, which you're not supposed to do. Today in hot food we did petits fours, but not traditional petits fours. We did little dishes, we did spoons, things that are a little more cutting-edge like we do in the U.S. We took a big risk. I've won gold before, and the medals are great, but the thing is about learning, trying to push the bar a little bit. That's always what happens when you put new stuff out there. Everyone hates it the first year, but you know that next time, everyone will be doing it."

Apparently not everyone hated Team USA's efforts, evidenced by the gold medal in hot food. Indeed, of seven international pastry teams, Team USA, with its cold-food silver, placed second worldwide after Germany.

But even if America had not placed among the top-three-scoring teams, it was crucial that the United States was at the IKA this year (only the second time pastry teams competed in the Olympiade der Köche, or "Culinary Olympics," and the first for the U.S.A.), said Susan Notter, CEPC, one of the U.S. judges for the cold-buffet pastry category in regional-team competition.

"We have great pastry chefs in the U.S., and if you look at other competitions, the Coupe du Monde in Lyon and now the pastry-team competition in Las Vegas, for instance, America is in the forefront in pastry. So it's important that we are here and that we support this show."

For their hot-food showing, Aoyama and Pell presented a "Raspberry Star" gâteau consisting of raspberry mousse, passion-fruit sauce, pistachio biscuit, vanilla custard and vanilla-bean sable; several friandises; and as a cold dessert, "Cosmic Citrus," consisting of citrus mousse, lime-biscuit tower, strawberry sorbet, minted citrus, strawberries and mango, and strawberry sauce.

Despite the team's success in Erfurt, Aoyama believes it's the sheer experience of the IKA that counts—not which medals are won. "How many people actually have the opportunity to be an Olympian, in culinary or sports?" he said. "The spirit of the competition is to come here and interact with people, to learn, bring that back to the States, share that with people at your property. That's what it's about ultimately."

Scrapping Plans, Yet Placing Third in the World

Although a handful of regional U.S. teams competed in the cold-buffet category at this year's IKA, the United States fielded one regional team under the ACF Culinary Team USA 2004 banner. That team placed third in the world among 53 regional teams. (Team Ontario placed second, and Switzerland's chefs' association team placed highest of all.)

2004 ACF Culinary Team USA Pastry

Darrin Aoyama, CEPC
(captain),
executive pastry chef,
River Oaks Country Club,
Houston, Texas

Roy Pell,
executive pastry chef,
The Ritz-Carlton, Phoenix, Arizona

Gilles Renusson
(coach),
pastry chef/instructor,
Grand Rapids Community College,
Grand Rapids, Michigan

Chef Aoyama enjoys the challenges of just being an Olympian.

USA pastry celebrates their overall success.

2004 ACF Culinary Team USA Regional

Scott Fetty, chef/instructor, Pennsylvania Culinary Institute, Pittsburgh, Pennsylvania

Heather Hurlbert, executive pastry chef, Duquesne Club, Pittsburgh, Pennsylvania

Jamie Keating, CCC, executive chef, Milliken & Company, LaGrange, Georgia

Craig Peterson, Hallbrook Country Club, Leawood, Kansas

Kevin Zink, CCC, executive chef, Summit Food Service Management, Albuquerque, New Mexico

Charles Carroll, CEC, AAC, (coordinator) executive chef, River Oaks Country Club, Houston, Texas

Fritz Gitschner, CMC, AAC, (coach) executive chef, Houston Country Club, Houston, Texas

Chris Northmore, CMPC, (pastry coach) executive pastry chef, Cherokee Town & Country Club, Atlanta, Georgia

Simplicity proves to be a winner as the team USA regional celebrates.

Interestingly, ACF's regional team finished among the top three teams without the benefit of a captain—a philosophy that team coordinator Charles Carroll, CEC, AAC, instituted early in the team's training more than a year ago. "I wanted all team members to be equally responsible for our success," he says. And, the team's focal buffet platter, which had been developed and fine-tuned for 11 months, was scrapped less than two months before the IKA. Instead, Carroll and coach Fritz Gitschner, CMC, suggested a statelier, simpler direction, and the team started over from scratch. Despite the abrupt change, it proved the right choice, Carroll said.

"In September I said to all the guys, 'Look, what was one of the greatest platters of the 1988 team?' And right away they named the platter. What about the '92 team? They named it right away. What about 2000? And they named that buffet platter. Platters set the standard for the table. I can tell if it's going to be beautiful from 20 feet away. The platter we were working on was not one of those platters, and I wanted us to develop a platter that's memorable, so that five years from now, someone can say, 'Do you remember that table?' That's what we tried to achieve."

The result: a lobster platter produced by team member Jamie Keating. "The only reason that platter happened was Jamie's heart," says Carroll, who credits Keating with working on the new concept night and day to have it ready for Erfurt within the short time frame. "I received ten to 15 e-mails a day from this guy, with pictures. He probably worked harder on that lobster platter in seven weeks than in the prior 11 months on the original one."

Borrowing antiques from a large warehouse in Houston, where both Carroll and Gitschner are based, and focusing with excruciating clarity on a simple-but-elegant approach with its entries, Culinary Team USA's regional team took a gold in each of the three categories of the cold-food division. And they did it on a shoestring budget that team members augmented with fund-raising.

Carroll is a veteran of past "Culinary Olympics," having served as a regional-team member twice and, in 1993, as a member of the U.S. national team competing in Basel and in 2000 as a member of the U.S. national team competing in Erfurt. He says that former CIA president Ferdinand Metz, CMC, AAC, who managed the 1980, 1984 and 1988 U.S. culinary teams, and current CIA president L. Timothy Ryan, CMC, AAC, who captained the 1988 team, impressed upon him years ago that simplicity combined with elegance would win the day.

"One of our displays at my club [River Oaks Country Club] is on a beautiful antique cherry-finished wood table. For Erfurt, we didn't want any moving parts or trains, just simple and elegant. If you walked into your grandmother's dining room, what would you see? That's where the concept started." Indeed, Carroll worked with a Houston craftsman to build the team's table from rich wood for "little to nothing." Elegance of the regional team's display was communicated by silver and, suspended above the table, a three-dimensional Van Gogh-esque arrangement of flowers within an empty gilded frame. The food, says Carroll, spoke for itself.

Carroll believes the sheer commitment and enthusiasm of the regional team's members—Keating, Scott Fetty, Heather Hurlbert (pastry chef), Craig Petersen and Kevin Zink, CCC, plus pastry coach Christopher Northmore, CMPC—are what earned the team success in Germany. "We were a very young team, and the guys gave me 120%," Carroll says. "To score third overall in the world is a great tribute to their hard work. That was literally their first big show. For some of them it was one of the few shows they'd ever done. In the van riding back from the awards ceremony, these guys were asking, 'How can we do this again? When's the next show?'"

"I've been on teams that had the A players, but we had more problems with some of those gentlemen. With these guys, there's no question that this team was hungry and dedicated. The work that Heather put into it the last six months at the Duquesne Club, for instance, was probably worth three years of experience. Where her work came from and where it ended up is unbelievable, but it came because she worked on it day in and day out. I enjoyed these guys. They were a really great team."

Students Judged on Skills, as Well as Work

The U.S. youth team competed in cold food on the second day of the IKA, and won a bronze for its entries—two different restaurant platters or dishes serving two and a single portion of two different desserts. The team's platters consisted of roast rack of lamb with a mustard-seed/black-pepper crust, braised lamb-shank charlotte, and glazed root vegetables; and Alaska king salmon with fresh-herb crust, with shellfish stew and lobster/potato croquettes. Individual desserts were a vanilla/orange bavarian, carrot/orange gelée, hazelnut/chocolate florentine and currant/vanilla sauce; and apple/cinnamon baked Alaska with apple tartlet and vanilla/citrus sauce.

The team competed in the hot kitchen two days later against formidable talent. Having already won a hot-food gold medal in international competition earlier this year at the World Association of Cooks Societies Congress in Dublin, expectation for the U.S. team's hot-food performance in Erfurt was high. Unlike its fellow, professional teams from the United States, however, all national youth teams performed in an extra category, that of skills evaluation, known as the "culinary studio." Because of that extra requirement, only one course, as opposed to three, was required in the hot kitchen, said team manager Steve Jilleba, CMC, CCE, AAC. Team USA's hot-food entry consisted of eggplant-wrapped roasted loin of lamb with shiraz-braised shredded lamb shoulder.

In the studio, each team member who competed in the hot kitchen in the morning devoted 30 minutes in the afternoon to preparing a menu for two. Team tasks were to clean, butcher and portion out a "salmon trout" (a hybrid trout species popular in Germany) and prepare two individual portions of cold hors d'oeuvre; prepare a salmon-trout cream soup and a salmon-trout forcemeat (farce); prepare a main course featuring salmon trout; and prepare three dessert plates. Because students pulled tasks from a hat, no individual student would know in advance which of the tasks he or she would perform, so proficiency in all was paramount. Krystal Weaver, for example, drew the soup task.

Set up as four tabletop cooking stations before bleachers filled with roaring, flag-waving spectators, the youth-team culinary studio was a heady experience in which everyone—student competitors, judges and ecstatic fans—was slave to the sweeping hands of the clock. Nations cheered as young people from their countries performed the required tasks, and the United States was no different.

While U.S. youth-team member Kim Lex performed her skills test, coach Thomas Macrina, CEC, AAC—who has spent more than a year working with the young Americans who make up the team—sat in the front row among spectators, directly in front of Lex, muttering under his breath throughout. "You're going to burn it," he mumbled almost inaudibly, referring to the sauté pan that grew hot awaiting the fish. As if reading his mind, Lex dropped in the fish with tongs. "Beautiful, beautiful," Macrina whispered.

2004 ACF Culinary Team USA Youth

Scott Campbell
cook,
Westchester Country Club
Rye, New York

Chad Durkin
(pastry),
cook,
Susanna Foo Chinese Cuisine,
Philadelphia, Pennsylvania

Kim Lex,
cook,
Hartefeld National Golf Club,
Avondale, Pennsylvania

Krystal Weaver,
cook,
Piazza's Bakery,
Levittown, Pennsylvania

Lou Yocco,
cook,
Hartefeld National Golf Club,
Avondale, Pennsylvania

Steven Jilleba, CMC, CCE, AAC,
(Manager)
corporate executive chef,
Unilever Foodsolutions,
Lisle, Illinois

Thomas Macrina, CEC, AAC,
(Coach)
chef,
Desmond Hotel & Conference Center, Malvern, Pennsylvania

Sponsors of ACF Culinary Team USA 2004

Grand Platinum

Unilever Foodsolutions

Silver

Chef Revival

Fortessa

Kraft Foodservice

Tyson Foods

Westchester Country Club

Bronze

Chef's Hat

Club Managers Association of America

Team USA National celebrates with a strong showing.

As the Culinary Olympics close, Chefs Buchner and Leonard revel in team USA's achievements.

Ultimately, ACF Culinary Team USA's youth team won a gold medal in the hot-food portion of the competition, and with its cold-food bronze, placed sixth in the world among 16 youth teams.

As ACF Culinary Team USA 2004 captain Edward G. Leonard, CMC, AAC, told all five teams before they departed for Germany: "It is when we commit ourselves fully to the task and objectives at hand that all sorts of things flourish, and great things become reality and we all succeed." Indeed, we did.

The Final Scores

The closing ceremony of the IKA is as special as the opening. The final medals for the national teams, student teams, pastry teams and military teams are presented. The awards and standings for the regional teams are given, as well. When a team wins a championship, the national anthem of the respective country is played, and all in the hall stand to salute excellence.

On October 21, the final day of the 2004 IKA, awards for national teams were announced last. Just prior, the results of performance of the other teams under the ACF Culinary Team USA 2004 banner were announced:

- Student team: gold in the hot kitchen, bronze in the cold program, resulting in sixth overall
- Regional team: one gold and third overall among 42 countries
- Military team: two gold medals and second place overall among 11 teams
- Pastry team: one gold, one silver and second place among seven teams

The U.S. national team waited as the medals were awarded and the championships in Categories A, B and C of the cold-buffet program were announced. Sweden won Category A and beat the USA in Category C by less than a half-point. Canada won Category B.

Finally, placements in the coveted Category R were announced, with a gold medal and the world hot-food championship going to ACF Culinary Team USA 2004! The hall erupted; members of the U.S. team were full of many emotions as they walked to the stage for the grand-prize gold medal and U.S.A.'s national anthem played.

Sixteen years since the U.S.A.'s last major win at the IKA is a long time, and Team USA 2004, with its back against the wall, not only won one of only four gold medals in hot food, but took the hot-food championship, as well.

All in all in 2004, the teams making up ACF Culinary Team USA 2004 won six gold medals, three silvers, one bronze and a special gold medallion for the highest possible score on a single entry.

Sweden did a remarkable thing and won the overall championship for the second time, keeping its 2000 title. Team USA's win placed the United States third in the world behind Sweden and Switzerland, respectively, resulting in the best finish at the IKA since the 1988 team tied for the world championship. Character and legacy... Yes, Team USA 2004 showed its stuff and left its mark in a little town called Erfurt.

As I told the teams upon departing the United States for Germany, "Leaving our legacy in the history of ACF culinary teams awaits us. If we succeed at our goal and achieve our objectives, the legacy of American cuisine is in our hands." Indeed, the American legacy of professional cooking and world-class cuisine lives on, thanks to a handful of U.S. chefs who showed the world what America is capable of.

Meet the ACF Culinary Team USA 2004 Captain and ACF President

Edward G. Leonard, CMC, AAC

Edward G. Leonard, CMC, has held virtually every cooking and management position in virtually every segment of the food-service industry. Today, he is executive chef of Westchester Country Club, ranked 15th nationwide among all private clubs, in Rye, N.Y. In 1997, he passed the grueling 10-day exam of skills and knowledge to become certified as a master chef—one of only 59 in the nation—by the American Culinary Federation (ACF).

As president of ACF from 2001 to 2005, Leonard created a new strategic direction for the 20,000-member organization that included increasing membership, expanding the organization's respected certification program, promoting cultural diversity and advancement in the workplace, and raising awareness of America's professional cooking force. Indeed, as the leader of the largest professional organization of chefs in the United States, Leonard served as the de-facto spokesperson for all U.S. chefs for four years, and effectively extended the influence of the federation over governmental, workplace and food-safety issues and increased ACF's stature in the eyes of the global cooking community. Until 2009, he will continue to lead ACF as past president on the federation's board of directors.

Since 2003, Leonard has also served as vice president of the 71-nation, 8-million-member World Association of Cooks Societies, a position he will hold through early-2007.

A passionate, avid member of ACF since 1982, Leonard's vision and leadership have been instrumental in raising the standards of excellence of the federation and the profession. In recognition of his guidance, he received ACF's Chef Professionalism Award for the Northeast (1994) and the national ACF Leadership Award (2000).

Leonard has guided ACF Culinary Team USA to championships at international culinary competitions since 1998. Under his leadership at the 2000 International Culinary Exhibition, or "Culinary Olympics," in Germany, the U.S. team dominated several categories and committed its best showing since 1988. After only five months of practice, ACF Culinary Team USA 2004 took home a gold medal in the hot-food competition and a silver medal in cold food at the Expogast Culinary World Cup in Luxembourg in November 2002. In 2003, Leonard led Culinary Team USA to victory at the American Culinary Classic in Chicago, at which the U.S. team scored highest in cold-buffet and hot-food competition among 11 international teams.

Thanks to Leonard's successful management of Culinary Team USA and the prestige that the team has earned for American chefs and American cuisine worldwide, ACF's Foundation unanimously named Leonard captain of ACF Culinary Team USA 2008, which will hold tryouts for team-member selection in mid-2006.

Leonard is the author of *Tastes and Tales of a Chef: The Apprentice's Journey* (Pearson Prentice Hall, 2005), a compendium of recipes, culinary history, personal anecdotes and cooking and career advice. He is currently working on two additional publishing projects. The chef is married to Ariadna Leonard, and has three children, Edward, Giancarlo and Cosette. The credo that guides his life and career as a professional culinarian: "One must live to cook, not cook to live."

Edward G. Leonard, CMC, AAC

Team Captain, ACF Culinary Team USA 2004

President, American Culinary Federation

Meet ACF Culinary Team USA 2004 Members

Joachim Buchner, CMC

Richard Rosendale, CC

Daniel Scannell, CMC

Russell Scott, CMC

Patricia Nash

Joachim Buchner, CMC

Joachim Buchner is executive chef of Chevy Chase Country Club in Chevy Chase, Md. He completed his apprenticeship under Fischkuche Pirckheimer in Nuremberg, Germany. He earned certified master chef certifications from both the Industrie-und Handelskammer Nuremberg and ACF. He previously served as executive chef at the Dusseldorf Hilton in Germany, and at the Sheraton Premier Hotel in Tyson's Corner, Va.

Richard Rosendale, CC

Richard Rosendale is the sous chef at the exclusive Greenbrier resort in White Sulphur Springs, W.Va. He studied culinary arts in northern Italy, and completed apprenticeships under three ACF-certified master chefs. Rosendale has won several ice-carving and ACF medals at numerous competitions. He also served as regional-team assistant at the IKA International Culinary Arts Competition in 2000.

Daniel Scannell, CMC

Daniel Scannell is executive chef of Cherry Hill Country Club in Denver, Colorado. He is known internationally as a serious culinary medal- and trophy-winner, having brought home many top cooking awards from other nations. Scannell previously served as executive chef at Oak Hill Country Club in Rochester, N.Y. He has a bachelor's degree in foodservice management and an associate's degree in baking and pastry arts from Johnson & Wales University in Providence, R.I.

Russell Scott, CMC

Russell Scott is executive chef of Isleworth Country Club in Windemere, Fla. Until recently, he was a lecturing instructor in culinary arts at The Culinary Institute of America (CIA) in Hyde Park, N.Y. He captained the CIA's Culinary Team in 2000 and the California Culinary Olympic Team in 1996. Scott is a graduate of the Community College of Allegheny County in Pittsburgh and Johnson & Wales University. He has previously served as executive chef at Perspectives and the Hotel Nikko in Los Angeles, and at the Virginia Country Club in Long Beach, Calif.

Patricia Nash

Patricia Nash is the executive pastry chef at the Westchester Country Club in Rye, N.Y. Nash served as an apprentice at the IKA International Culinary Art Competition in 2000. Prior to her current position, Nash served as a pastry cook at Trump Plaza Casino and Hotel in Atlantic City, N.J. and before that, as a pastry cook at Showboat Casino-Hotel in Atlantic City. She is a 1997 graduate of the Academy of Culinary Arts at Atlantic Cape Community College in Mays Landing, N.J.

Cooking with America's Championship Team

Competition Recipes

Alaskan King Crab Terrine

Yields: 20 terrines

Alaskan King Crab Terrine:

8 pounds halibut or leftover dover sole
2 pounds raw scallops
24 each large egg yolks
3 each large eggs
14 1/2 ounces unsalted butter, room temperature
Kosher salt and ground white pepper to taste
Pinch cayenne
3 cups heavy cream, lightly whipped
2 pounds crab trimmings
60 pounds king crab legs
7 cups blanched spinach leaves (garnish)

Salsify:
Yields: 300 portions

30 pounds salsify
3 gallons milk
1 1/2 gallons water
9 each lemons

Blanc:
Yields: 6 gallons

5 gallons water
10 ounces flour
9 each lemons
3 pounds white onions
1 1/2 pounds carrots
1 1/2 pounds celery
Salt to taste
3 Sachets to include per sachet
  20 each parsley stems
  1/2 bunch chives
  1/2 bunch chervil
  25 cracked peppercorns
  5 each bay leaves
  3 each cloves

Orange Segments:
Yields: 300 portions

40 each blood oranges

To Make the Alaskan King Crab Terrine:

- Place halibut and scallop meat in food processor bowl and process until smooth.
- Add egg yolks and whole eggs, one at a time, and process after each to combine.
- Add butter and pulse to incorporate. Season with salt, white pepper, and cayenne.
- Place mixture in stainless steel bowl and gently fold in whipped cream followed by the crabmeat. Assemble the terrines.

To Make the Salsify:

- Peel the salsify and plunge into the milk, water and lemon solution. Keep the salsify submerged with a thin sheet of cheesecloth.

To Make the Blanc:

- Whisk the flour and water together in order to remove any lumps. Small dice the aromatics and add to the Blanc. Also add the lemons, sachet, and the salt to taste.
- After all the salsify has been peeled and placed into the Blanc, place a piece of cheesecloth over the salsify to keep it submerged during cooking. Gently simmer the salsify till just tender, but not falling apart. Set aside for plating.

To Make the Orange Segment:

- Section the blood oranges and use for garnish.

Foamed Aïoli

Yields: 3 quarts

Foamed Aïoli:
21 each yolks
3 cups whole eggs
4 each lemon juice
3 tablespoons sherry vinegar
12 teaspoons Kosher salt
12 tablespoons Dijon mustard
3 cups olive oil
Tabasco as needed
6 cups vegetable oil

To Make the Foamed Aïoli

- Whisk the eggs lightly. Add all the ingredients except for the oil. After all the ingredients have been mixed, slowly incorporate the remaining oil to create an emulsion.
- Add the aïoli to a charged ISI frother and shake vigorously before use.

CHEF'S TIP:

- The foamed aïoli is used to garnish the alaskan king crab terrine.

She Crab Bisque

Yields: 9 Gallons

She Crab Bisque:
9 pounds blonde roux
25 pounds blue crabs, live
3 pounds clarified butter
2 pounds minced onions
1 1/2 pounds minced celery
2 pounds minced leeks
30 cloves minced garlic
2 1/2 pounds tomato paste
2 ounces Hungarian paprika
1 1/2 quarts brandy
6 gallons chicken stock
6 gallons fish stock
3 each sachet
(see page 20 for recipe)

Finish and Serve:
1 1/2 gallons heavy cream, heated
8 pounds blue crabmeat, cleaned
Salt and pepper to taste
3 ounces Worcestershire sauce
3 ounces Tabasco sauce
3 cups dry sherry
1 1/2 cups fresh thyme leaves

To Make the She Crab Bisque:

- Start the roux.
- Rinse, split and clean the crabs thoroughly.
- Heat the butter in a soup pot over medium-high heat. Add the crabs and cook, stirring occasionally, until they are bright red, about 10 to 12 minutes. Add the onions, celery and leeks and cook over medium heat, stirring occasionally, until they are a light brown, 5 to 6 minutes. Add the garlic and continue to cook until the aroma is apparent, about 1 minute.
- Add the tomato paste and paprika and cook over medium heat, stirring occasionally, for 3 to 4 minutes. Add the brandy and stir well to deglaze the pan. Continue to cook until the brandy is almost completely cooked away.
- Add the stock. Bring to a boil, then reduce the heat to establish an even, gentle simmer. Add the roux and simmer for 45 minutes, skimming the surface occasionally.
- Purée the solids until smooth. Strain the puréed soup through a fine wire-mesh sieve. The soup is ready to finish for service.

Finish and Serve:

- Add the hot cream, then the crabmeat and roe. Bring to a simmer. Taste the soup and adjust seasoning with salt, pepper, Worcestershire sauce and Tabasco sauce. Finish with the sherry, fresh thyme leaves and profiteroles.

Breaded Crab Leg

Yields: 300 portions

Breaded Crab Legs:

300 1-ounce pieces crab leg
6 pounds flour
60 each eggs
3 cups milk
12 pounds Japanese bread crumbs
Oil for frying as needed

To Make the Breaded Crab Legs:

- Dry the crab legs. The crab legs should be cut into 1-inch-long pieces. Pass the crab legs through the standard breading procedure.
- Fry the breaded crab legs in hot fat at 350 degrees F. until golden brown.

Warm Shallot & Pancetta Dressing for Spinach Salad

Yields: 300 servings

Warm Shallot & Pancetta Dressing:

5 cups pancetta
12 cups sliced shallots
6 tablespoons minced garlic
9 cups quality virgin olive oil
3 cups + sherry vinegar
5 tablespoons minced chives
5 tablespoons parsley
Salt and pepper to taste
2 cups scallions

Finish and Serve:

36 pounds spinach

To Make the Warm Shallot & Pancetta Dressing:

- Render the pancetta and reserve the fat. Sweat the shallots and the garlic in the bacon fat and some of the olive oil.
- Remove the mixture from the heat and let it cool slightly at room temperature.Whisk in the remaining ingredients. Adjust the seasoning as needed.

Finish and Serve:

- Toss the spinach with the dressing for service.

Orange Juice Reduction

Yields: 5 cups

Orange Juice Reduction:

40 each blood oranges (juiced)
2 cups orange blossom honey
3 cups good port

To Make the Orange Juice Reduction:

- Combine all the ingredients together in a sauce pot and reduce to a syrup consistency.

Venison Loin

Yields: 125 portions

Apple Syrup:
Yields: 2 cups
1/2 gallon apple juice
2 each cinnamon sticks
2 each bay leaves
1 cup honey
1 cup sugar
1/2 cup champagne vinegar
1/2 cup white wine
Vanilla bean (optional)

Venison Loin:
7 loins venison (about 25 pounds)
1 case apple smoked bacon
2 cups apple syrup
Salt and pepper to taste
Clarified butter as needed

To Make the Apple Syrup:

- Reduce all the ingredients together in a heavy stainless steel pot until the liquid forms a syrup. Strain and brush on the venison.

To Make the Venison Loin:

- Wrap the venison loins in the bacon and sear in the hot clarified butter.
- Season, and cook the loins until medium rare. Let the meat rest before cutting.

Braised Red Cabbage

Yields: 100, 1/2-ounce servings

Red Cabbage:
8 pounds red cabbage, peeled, cored and finely shredded
2 cups red wine
2 cups red wine vinegar
2 cups sugar
6 ounces red currant jelly
Salt and black pepper to taste
3 each cinnamon sticks
5 each cloves, whole
12 each juniper berries
6 each bay leaves
1 pound onions, sliced 1/8"
4 each apples, peeled and sliced
8 ounces bacon, rind removed, small dice

To Make the Red Cabbage:

- Marinate the cabbage as follows 1 day before it is needed for service: Cut the cabbage into thin wedges. Place into a cryo bag with all ingredients except the bacon, onions and apples. Mix well, seal and refrigerate overnight.
- Small dice the bacon and julienne the onions.
- In a rondeau, render the bacon until crisp, then add the onions and sweat until soft.
- Drain the marinated cabbage from the marination liquid and reserve the liquid.
- Slice the cabbage thin and sauté it in the bacon fat. Add the apples. Add the marination liquid, cover and cook slowly on top of the stove or in a 300 degree F. oven until tender. Stock or water may need to be added during the cooking process if the mixture becomes dry. Check the seasonings and balance of sweet and tart flavors.

CHEF'S TIP:

- If needed, bind the red cabbage with a little slurry of potato starch or cornstarch.

Braised Venison Neck Dumpling

Yields: 110 portions

Venison Neck:

12 pounds bone-in venison neck
16 ounces clarified butter
2 pounds onions
1 pound celery
1 pound carrots
1/2 pound leeks
2 ounces mushroom trimmings
2 ounces shallots
2 ounces tomato paste
1 bottle red wine
6 ounces port
2 ounces flour
2 gallons fortified venison stock
2 ounces aged balsamic
2-4 ounces butter
Salt and pepper to taste

Sachet to Include:

15 parsley stems
8 each thyme
3 each rosemary
3 each bay leaf
10 each juniper berry
4 each sage
5 each dried mushroom (crushed)
1 bunch chives
20 cracked black peppercorns

Butter Sauce:
Yields: About 2 quarts.

1 cup water or flavored wine reduction
4 pounds butter
Salt and white pepper to taste
5 each lemons for juice
1 pound grain mustard
8 ounces white truffle oil
8 ounces fine cut chives

To Make the Venison Neck:

- Cut the venison neck into sections.
- In a large heavy bottom rondeau, heat the clarified butter and sear the neck sections. After the neck has well browned, remove from the rondeau and set aside. Add into the rondeau the mirepoix and caramelize. About halfway through the browning process of the mirepoix add the leeks and the mushrooms.
- Next, stir in the shallots and then the tomato paste. After the tomato paste has cooked out add the red wine little by little. Form a glaze on the surface of the rondeau with the wine and then add the port. Reduce the liquid by 1/2. Singer the reduction with the flour and add the venison neck back to the rondeau.
- Add the venison stock and the sachet to the rondeau. Cover the liquid with a sheet of parchment and also a lid. Bring the braising liquid up to a steady simmer and place in a 350 degree F. oven for 2 1/2 hours.
- After the venison is tender, strain the braising liquid and place on the stove in a medium sauce pot. Adjust the seasoning with salt, pepper, aged balsamic vinegar, and some whole butter. The braised venison is now ready for use in the filling.

To Make the Butter Sauce:

- Over low heat stir the butter into the liquid.
- Season with salt pepper and lemon juice.
- Add the mustard, truffle oil and chives.

Braised Venison Neck Dumpling (continued)

Bread Crumb Topping:

3 pounds sweet onions finely sliced
1 quart milk
2 pounds seasoned flour
ChefNique chef spice and salt as needed
Frying fat as needed
2 each white loaf bread (crusts removed)
2 pounds butter

Dumplings:
Yields: 110 portions

24 pounds russet potatoes
2 pounds kosher salt
2 pounds semolina or cream of wheat
2 pounds flour
8 ounces potato starch
4 ounces salt
10 eggs
20 egg yolks

Dumpling Filling:
Yields: 125 portions

8 ounces butter
12 ounces onions (small dice)
5 ounces celery root (small dice)
5 ounces carrot (small dice)
5 ounces leek (small dice)
4 pounds braised venison neck (small dice)
2 quarts venison sauce (braising liquid), hot
2 ounces aged balsamic vinegar
2 teaspoons gelatin
1 ounce fresh chopped herbs
1 tablespoon ChefNique pâté spice
Salt to taste

To Make the Bread Crumb Topping:

- Immerse the onion in the milk. Drain off the milk and dust the onions with flour.
- Fry the onions in hot oil until they are crisp. Drain over a rack and let cool.
- Crush the onions, and chop the bread in a food processor.
- Toast the bread in melted butter until golden brown. Mix the bread crumbs and the crushed onions together.

To Make the Dumplings:

- Wash the potatoes and place on kosher salt to bake.
- Remove potato skins and put through a ricer onto a work surface; level and let cool.
- Add the semolina, flour, potato starch, 2 ounces of salt, eggs and egg yolks. Mix well.

To Make the Filling:

- Sauté the onions in the butter until translucent. Next, add the celery, carrot, leeks, and cook until they are slightly tender.
- Add the venison neck, sauce and the balsamic vinegar. Sprinkle in the gelatin and stir well; add fresh herbs and ChefNique spice.
- Bring the filling to a boil and let cool in a shallow pan or a flex mold.
- Fill the dumplings with the cold meat mixture.
- Bring a large pot of water to a boil and season with salt to taste. Lower the boiling salt water to a simmer and cook the dumplings for 15 minutes.
- Roll in grain mustard butter sauce and top with fried bread crumbs.

Smoked Chestnuts

Yields: 110

Chestnuts:
110 each blanched chestnuts (peeled)
3 cups wood dust

To Make the Chestnuts:

- Smoke the chestnuts until a nice color and flavor is achieved.

Mushroom Medley

Yields: 125 Portions

Mushroom Medley:
8 ounces whole butter
8 ounces peanut oil
8 ounces shallots
1 ounce minced garlic
6 pounds assorted mushrooms
2 each lemon juice
Salt and pepper to taste
1 cup chopped fresh herbs (marjoram, parsley, and very little rosemary)

To Make the Mushroom Medley:

- Heat the butter and oil together. Add the shallots, garlic, and mushrooms together.
- Add the lemon juice, and season with salt and pepper. Finish with the fresh herbs.

Savory Caraway Tuile

Yields: 1 1/2 pounds

Caraway Salt:
Yields: 1 1/2 pounds
16 ounces Kosher salt
8 ounces dry caraway

Caraway Tuile:
18 ounces AP flour
6 ounces 10x sugar
16 each egg whites

To Make the Caraway Salt:

- Grind the ingredients together until a uniform mixture is achieved and sift.

To Make the Caraway Tuile:

- Sift the flour and the sugar together. In a stainless steel bowl add the egg whites to the dry ingredients. Mix until a smooth batter forms.
- The batter is now ready to spread on a template. Spread the batter over the template and bake just until the batter starts to set. Remove from the oven without browning.
- After the tuiles have rested for about 10 minutes, place back in the oven to brown. Remove from the oven and let rest.
- Dust the tuiles with the caraway salt before serving.

Parsnip Purée

Yields: 120 portions

Parsnip Purée:

15 pounds parsnips
1 1/2 gallons heavy cream
6 tablespoons Kosher salt
3 teaspoons white pepper
1 cup Pernod
4 tablespoons unsalted butter

To Make the Parsnip Purée:

- Peel the parsnips and cut in medium dice. Cover them with cream, salt, pepper, and Pernod, in a medium sauce pot. Bring the mixture to a simmer.
- After the parsnips are tender, strain and place in a vita blender. Purée the parsnips until very smooth. Adjust the consistency with some of the reserved cream.
- Finish the purée with the whole butter and check the seasoning.

Vegetables

Yields: 125 portions

Vegetables:

10 pounds haricot vert or small green beans
10 pounds baby carrots (120 each)
Salt and pepper to taste
5 quarts vegetable stock
1 quart butter sauce
1 ounce ChefNique (taste of Naples)
1 ounce chopped fresh herbs

To Make the Vegetables:

- Cook the carrots and green beans in vegetable stock.
- Drain well and season with salt and pepper. Toss in the butter sauce, ChefNique (Naples spice) and chopped fresh herbs.

Autumn Flavors Terrine

Yields: 110 portions

Hazelnut Cake:

5 pounds butter
5 pounds sugar
32 each eggs
1 pound, 14 ounces cake flour
5 pounds toasted hazelnut flour, cool
1 1/2 ounces cinnamon

Milk Chocolate Cinnamon Ganache:

1 tablespoon ground cinnamon
1 quart heavy cream
2 pounds, 8 ounces milk chocolate cut in small chunks

Apple Jelly:

34 each gala apple, divided
2 quarts apple juice or cider, divided
1 pound sugar
1 ounce cinnamon
22 each gelatin sheets use gold or platinum

To Make the Hazelnut Cake:

- In a mixer, at medium speed, whip butter and sugar, until all the sugar is dissolved and the butter looks airy, white and creamy.
- Slowly add eggs, 2 to 3 at a time, occasionally stop the mixer scraping down the side of the bowl.
- In a seperate bowl mix the cake flour, toasted hazelnut flour, and cinnamon.
- Reduce the speed of the mixer to slow. Add the flour mix; continue to mix until all the flour is well incorporated. Check the bottom of the mixing bowl, to assure a well mixed cake batter. The cake will not bake correctly if the flour mix is not thoroughly incorporated.
- Spread 1 pound 12 ounces, of cake mix on to a greased parchment paper lined, 13"x18", baking pan, and spread evenly over the pan.
- Bake in a 350 degrees F. oven for 8-9 minutes, or until the cake starts to pull away from the side of the pan and is lightly browned at the edges.
- Set aside until needed.

To Make the Milk Chocolate Cinnamon Ganache:
(Thin layer on hazelnut cake before spreading the apple jelly)

- Heat the milk and cinnamon, in a stainless steel pot until just ready to boil, remove from heat.
- Stir in the chocolate, whisk gently until all the chocolate is melted.
- Remove from pot and place in a bowl, refrigerate until needed.

To Make the Apple Jelly:

- Peel, remove the core, and dice, into large chucks, 24 of the apples. In a sauce pot heat 1 1/2 quarts of the apple juice and add the apple chunks. Continue to cook over low heat until the apples are soft. Remove apples from the liquid and puree in a food processor.
- Peel and remove the core of the remaining apples and dice small. In a sauce pot reheat the liquid from the first cooked apples and the remaining apple juice; add half of the sugar and all of the cinnamon. Bring to a boil, reduce the heat to low and add the diced apples.
- Simmer for 3 to 4 minutes, remove from heat, add the apple purée and the softened gelatin sheet. Adjust sweetness by adding more sugar if desired. Spread onto baking pan and refrigerate until firm.

CHEF'S TIP:

- To soften the galantin sheet submerge in cold water for 5 minutes, drain well and squeeze out all the water.

Autumn

Autumn Flavors Terrine (continued)

Yields: 110 portions

Pumpkin Custard:

3 quarts heavy cream
2 pounds, 8 ounces sugar
3 each vanilla beans split in half
2 pounds, 12 ounces yolks
3 pounds, 8 ounces Libby's pumpkin purée
1 1/4 ounces pumpkin spice

Vanilla Bean Mousse:

1 quart, 1/2 cup milk
4 each vanilla bean seeds
4 tablespoons vanilla extract
15 ounces sugar
3 ounces cornstarch
3 cups yolks
10 ounces butter
3 pounds, 1 ounce heavy cream
24 each gold gelatin sheets

Caramel Glaze:

3 pounds, 12 ounces sugar
3 pounds, 8 ounces water
3 ounces cornstarch
3 pounds, 8 ounces heavy cream
10 each gold gelatin sheets

To Make the Pumpkin Custard:

- In a stainless steal sauce pot heat, heavy cream, sugar, and vanilla beans. Reduce the heat and keep the mixture just below the boiling point for 5 minutes.
- In a speared mixing bowl combine egg yolks, pumpkin purée and pumpkin spice.
- Add in the hot heavy cream mix slowly 1 cup at the time. Strain through a sieve.
- Pour into a greased half round terrine mould and bake in a 310 degrees F. oven water bath, for 15 minutes or until set. Remove from the water bath and cool or freeze.

To Make the Vanilla Bean Mousse:

- In a heavy bottom sauce pot heat the milk, vanilla bean seeds, and vanilla extract simmer for 3 minutes and remove from heat.
- In a speared mixing bowl combine egg yolks, sugar and cornstarch.
- Whisking constantly, add slowly the hot milk to the eggs.
- Return the mix to the sauce pot and place over medium heat.
- Stirring constantly bring the mix back up to heat; continue to cook until the mixture thickens.
- Remove from heat, whisk in butter and the soften gelatin sheets, let cool.
- Whip heavy cream to soft peak and fold the whipped cream into pastry cream (cooked milk and egg mixture).
- Pour into desired mould.

To Make the Caramel Glaze:

- In a heavy sauce pan combine, sugar, water, and cornstarch, heat over medium flame and cook until the sugar is melded and start to browned.
- Remove from heat and add heavy cream. Add soften gelatin sheets.
- Strain and let cool.

To Assemble the Terrine:

- Spread a thin layer of the chocolate milk chocolate cinnamon ganache onto the hazelnut cake. Cut into strips the size of the pâté mould. It would be best to use a collapsible pâté mould.
- On the bottom of the mold, place the hazelnut cake, top with a 1/8 layer of the apple jelly, and top with one more layer of the cake.
- Place the baked pumpkin custard over the cake; assure that the custard is centered.
- Add the vanilla bean mousse into the pâté mold and completely cover the pumpkin custard.
- Refrigerate until all ingredients are set.
- Remove from the mold and cover the top of the pâté with the caramel glaze.
- Slice to desired portion.

CHEF'S TIP:

- If the caramel glaze is too thick, you may add water to adjust.

Apple Cider Sorbet

Yields: 110 portions

Apple Cider Sorbet:

1 gallon Zeigler's apple cider
4 each cinnamon sticks
15 each whole cloves
1 each orange, zest only
3 ounces dark rum
8 ounces sugar
4 ounces corn syrup
1 1/2 ounces sorbet base (from Rose's)
2 tablespoons honey

To Make the Apple Cider Sorbet:

- In a stainless sauce pot, combine apple cider, cinnamon sticks, orange zest, dark rum, sugar, corn syrup, sorbet base and honey and bring to boil.
- Reduce heat to a simmer and continue to simmer and reduce by 1/3.
- Strain through a fine strainer and chill.
- To freeze the sorbet follow the direction on your ice cream freezer.
- Transfer the frozen sorbet into small containers and store in freezer until needed.

Praline Feullitine Crunch

Yields: 110 portions

Praline Feullitine Crunch:

2 cups feullitine crunch or lightly crushed corn flakes
10 ounces white chocolate (couverture)
6 ounces praline paste

To Make the Praline Feullitine Crunch:

- Melt the chocolate in a bowl (double boiler) over hot water. Add praline paste and stir until smooth.
- Toss the feullitine or corn flakes with the melted chocolate mix.
- Spread on parchment lined baking pan, place another piece of parchment on top and gently roll to flatten.
- Refrigerate the crunch for 5 minutes or until lightly set, but still soft.
- Remove the top sheet of parchment paper and place on cutting board.
- Cut into desired shape. Set aside until needed.

CHEF'S TIP:

- It would be easier to serve from refrigerator however, it will loose crunch if left in refrigerator for too long.
- The amount of white chocolate/praline paste mix will determine the 'brittleness' of the crunch.

Cranberry Sauce

Yields: 110 portions

Cranberry Sauce:

2 pounds cranberry
2 each vanilla beans
1 quart orange juice
8 ounces sugar
1/2 cup Riesling wine
1 cup caramel glaze

To Make the Cranberry Sauce:

- In a sauce pot combine the cranberry, vanilla beans, orange juice, sugar and wine.
- Heat over medium heat and simmer for 5 minutes.
- Remove from heat and strain through a fine sieve.
- Add caramel glaze to adjust seasoning.

Cinnamon Tuile Batter

Yields: 110 portions

Cinnamon Tuile Batter:

4 ounces all-purpose flour
4 ounces sugar
4 ounces egg whites
4 ounces melted butter

To Make the Cinnamon Tuile Batter:

- In a small bowl combine the flour and sugar mix well.
- Add the egg whites and melted butter and whisk until well combined.
- Chill and let rest for 3 hours or more.
- Spread the batter, onto a silicon pad, into the desired shape, you may use a template, cut outs or pipe with a pastry bag.
- Bake for 4 minutes in a 350 degrees F. oven, remove from oven and let cool.
- After the cookies are completely cooled finish baking the cookies until golden about 4 more minutes.

Cooking with America's Championship Team

Recipes

Pacific Seafood Chowder with Wakame Pesto

Chef Russell Scott, CMC
Serves 4 (1 quart)

Wakame Pesto:

1/4 cup peanut oil
1 teaspoon minced shallot
1/2 teaspoon minced garlic
1/2 ounce dulse seaweed, crumbled
3/4 cup warm water
1 tablespoon chopped toasted peanuts or toasted sesame seeds
1/2 cup olive oil
Salt and pepper to taste

Soup:

1 cup dry white wine
1 clove garlic, minced
2 tablespoons fresh ginger, cut into very fine strips
2 cups clam juice
4 cups coconut milk
1 cup heavy cream
3 stalks lemongrass, split
3 kaffir lime leaves (tied in cheesecloth)
1 tablespoon red curry paste
Juice from half a lemon
2 1/2 tablespoons cornstarch
Salt and pepper to taste

Snapper and Shrimp:

4 ounces snapper fillet, skinned, medium dice
4 ounces shrimp, peeled, medium dice
Clarified butter as needed

Finish and Serve:

1/4 cup very finely diced celery, blanched
1/4 cup very finely diced carrot, blanched
1/4 cup very finely diced leek, blanched
1 cup small dice potato (Yukon gold, russet, purple Peruvian, or a combination), cooked in salted boiling water until tender
1/4 cup scallions (green parts only), very thinly sliced on the bias

To Make the Wakame Pesto:

- In a small saucepan, heat the peanut oil over medium heat. Add the shallot and garlic and cook until just soft. Set aside.
- In the container of a blender, crumble the dried seaweed and blend with warm water until smooth. Add the garlic and shallot and the peanuts. Blend until smooth. With the motor running, slowly pour in the olive oil. Season with salt and pepper and set aside.

To Make the Soup:

- In a large non-reactive pot, combine the wine, garlic and ginger and bring to a boil. Add the clam juice, coconut milk and cream and return to a boil. Add the lemongrass and lime leaves (sachet). Stir in the curry paste and lemon. Simmer until a rich flavor is developed.
- Mix the cornstarch with a little stock and stir into the soup. The soup should have a medium thickness. Bring to a simmer, stirring. Remove the sachet and strain. Season to taste with salt and pepper.

To Make the Snapper and Shrimp:

- Sauté the diced snapper and shrimp in clarified butter until just cooked through.

Finish and Serve:

- Divide the snapper and shrimp between four soup bowls. Top with the cooked celery, carrot, leek and potatoes. Ladle hot soup into the bowls and garnish with scallions and wakame pesto.

Giancarlo's Chili

Chef Ed Leonard, CMC
Serves 4

Chili:

10 ounces minced beef chuck
10 ounces minced pork butt
8 ounces minced veal shoulder
2 teaspoons kosher salt
5 tablespoons olive oil
1/2 cup finely diced onion
1/4 cup finely diced carrot
2 cloves garlic, finely sliced
3 tablespoons tomato paste
2/3 cup red wine
4 peeled, seeded plum tomatoes
2 to 3 tablespoons ChefNique Chili Spice
1 teaspoon dried oregano
1 teaspoon red pepper flakes
2 cups beef or chicken broth
Kosher salt and ground black pepper to taste
1 cup cooked white cannellini beans
4 tablespoons cold butter, diced
2 tablespoons extra-virgin olive oil

Finish and Serve:

Kosher salt and ground black pepper to taste

To Make the Chili:

- Pat meat dry with paper towels and sprinkle with kosher salt. Heat 3 tablespoons of the olive oil in a heavy skillet over high heat. Cook beef, pork and veal until browned, 2 to 3 minutes. Remove meat with a slotted spoon, leaving oil and juices in the skillet. Reserve meat.
- Add the remaining 2 tablespoons olive oil to the skillet. Cook onion, carrot and garlic until caramelized, 3 to 4 minutes. Mix in tomato paste and cook 1 to 2 minutes more. Pour in wine, scrape up any bits from the bottom of the pan, and cook until most of liquid has evaporated. Remove from heat and transfer to a large pot.
- Add tomatoes, chili spice, oregano and pepper flakes to the pot. Stir in broth, salt and few grindings of black pepper. Place pot on the stove, add the meats and bring to a simmer. Partially cover pot and simmer until meat is tender, about 1 hour.
- Remove chili from heat and fold in beans, butter and extra-virgin olive oil.

Finish and Serve:

- Season to taste again with salt and pepper and serve.

CHEF'S TIP:

- Serve chili in a bowl with some shredded aged cheddar cheese and a dollop of sour cream.

Seared Sea Scallop and Clam Chowder

Chef Ed Leonard, CMC
Serves 4

Clams:

32 Manila clams, scrubbed and rinsed well
1 small shallot, diced
4 tablespoons unsalted butter
1 tablespoon extra-virgin olive oil
1 teaspoon chopped parsley
1/2 cup white wine

Soup:

2 tablespoons unsalted butter
1 tablespoon grape seed oil
3 ounces diced fat back or smoked bacon
1/3 cup diced onion
1/4 cup diced celery
2 tablespoons all-purpose flour
2 1/2 cups clam broth
8 ounces medium Yukon gold potatoes, peeled and diced small
1/2 cup heavy cream
1 tablespoon unsalted butter
1 teaspoon chopped fresh thyme

Scallops:

1 tablespoon extra-virgin olive oil
4 large sea scallops
2 teaspoons Spice de Cosette
Juice from one lime

Finish and Serve:

2 tablespoons grape seed or vegetable oil
8 ounces baby spinach
1/4 cup chicken broth or water

To Make the Clams:

- In a stainless steel pot with tightly fitting lid, combine all ingredients. Place over medium heat and steam until all clams open, 2 to 3 minutes.
- Remove clams from pot, take meat out of shells and return meat to liquid left in pot. Set aside.

To Make the Soup:

- In a 2-quart stainless-steel pot, combine butter, oil and fatback. Place over medium heat and cook until fat back starts to render its fat, 1 to 2 minutes. Add onion and celery and cook, stirring, 2 to 3 minutes.
- Stir in flour and cook 1 minute. Whisk in 1 1/2 cups of the clam broth, whisking until smooth. Adjust heat and simmer.
- Meanwhile, combine potatoes and remaining cup broth in a saucepan. Bring to a boil, adjust heat and simmer until potatoes are fork tender. Add potatoes to soup mixture.
- Add the cream to the reserved clams and bring to a simmer. Stir in butter and thyme and mix well. Pour into soup.
- Simmer soup 3 to 5 minutes. Season to taste with salt and pepper if needed.

To Make the Scallops:

- In a nonstick skillet, heat oil over high heat. Season scallops with spice and sear until browned, 2 to 3 minutes on each side. Remove from pan and keep warm.

Finish and Serve:

- Add baby spinach and the broth to the skillet the scallops cooked in and cook quickly 1 to 2 minutes. Distribute spinach between four large soup bowls. Top each bed of spinach with a scallop and ladle 3/4 to 1 cup of soup around each scallop.

CHEF'S TIP:

- Chef Leonard notes a that drizzle of lemon or herb olive oil is a nice touch and flavor booster for this dish.

Real Pasta and Bean Soup

Chef Ed Leonard, CMC

Serves 4

Pasta and Bean Soup:

2 tablespoons olive oil
1 small onion, cut into small dice
1 carrot, peeled and diced
1 stalk celery, peeled and diced
1 cup Borlotti beans
4 cups chicken broth
6 tablespoons cold unsalted butter
1 teaspoon sea salt, plus more to taste
1/2 cup extra-virgin olive oil
2 cloves garlic, thinly sliced
1 teaspoon crushed red pepper flakes
3/4 cup diced, seeded plum tomatoes
1 tablespoon chopped parsley
1 cup fresh rigatoni pasta, cut into pieces

Finish and Serve:

1/4 cup grated Reggiano Parmesan
4 tablespoons extra-virgin olive oil

To Make the Pasta and Bean Soup:

- Heat olive oil in a heavy bottomed saucepan set over medium heat. Add onion and carrot and cook for 2 to 3 minutes. Add celery, beans and broth to the pot and bring to a boil. Cover the pot and simmer until the beans are tender, about 2 hours.
- Remove half the beans and place in a blender, food mill or food processor. Add butter to the blender and purée. Add of salt and reserve.
- In another pot, heat olive oil over low heat and add garlic and pepper flakes. When garlic is tender add tomatoes and parsley. Cook 1 to 2 minutes, add bean purée and cook for 2 to 3 minutes.
- Add this mixture to the whole beans and chicken broth. Season with salt. Stir well, add pasta and cook 3 to 5 minutes.

Finish and Serve:

- Divide soup between four bowls, sprinkle with Parmesan, drizzle with extra-virgin olive oil and serve.

CHEF'S TIP:

- A simple soup, but one with hearty flavors. Serve with red wine and fresh Italian bread and you have the ultimate comfort meal.

Team USA's Roasted Tomato Soup

Chef Ed Leonard, CMC

Serves 4

Soup:

4 tablespoons extra-virgin olive oil
2 pounds ripe Roma tomatoes, halved
1 small sweet onion, thinly sliced
4 garlic cloves
2 teaspoons honey
1 teaspoon brown sugar
8 blanched basil leaves
Sea salt and ground pepper to taste
Pinch crushed red pepper flakes
2 cups chicken broth
1 cup tomato purée
4 tablespoons diced cold butter
2 tablespoons aged balsamic vinegar

Finish and Serve:

4 tablespoons fresh ricotta cheese
4 small slices Italian bread, toasted or grilled
4 tablespoons extra-virgin olive oil
12 peeled cherry tomatoes
4 basil leaves

To Make the Soup:

- Preheat oven to 360 degrees F. Pour oil into a small roasting pan and heat in the oven until oil is very hot. Take pan out of the oven and carefully add tomatoes and toss. Add the onion and garlic and toss again. Drizzle with honey, sprinkle with sugar and top with the basil leaves. Sprinkle with sea salt and pepper and roast until skins are lightly browned, 20 to 25 minutes, stirring a couple of times during cooking.
- In a stainless-steel pan, bring broth and tomato purée to a boil. Adjust heat and simmer for 20 minutes
- Add the roasted tomatoes to the broth along with all juices from the roasting pan. Simmer 10 minutes.
- A cup at a time, transfer the soup to a blender and purée. Strain soup through a sieve into a stainless-steel pot. Whisk in the butter and vinegar. Season with salt if needed.

Finish and Serve:

- Place a dollop of ricotta onto each bread slice and put one in each of four soup bowls.
- Heat the olive oil in a sauté pan. Sauté tomatoes for 1 to 2 minutes. Pour soup into bowls, garnish with tomatoes and basil leaves and serve.

CHEF'S TIP:

- Chef Leonard notes that the key to this soup—or any dish—is the freshness and quality of the ingredients. Use the finest quality butter, extra-virgin olive oil, ripe tomatoes, fresh hand-beaten ricotta and fragrant basil.

Mushroom, Beef and Barley Soup

Chef Louis Yocco (photo page 47)
Serves 4

Soup:
2 1/2 pounds beef short ribs
Salt and pepper to taste
2 tablespoons olive oil
5 shallots, minced
3/4 pound button mushrooms, sliced
1/2 pound shiitake mushrooms, stems discarded, caps sliced
1 teaspoon cumin
1 teaspoon chili powder
1/2 cup barley, rinsed and drained
2 sprigs fresh thyme, chopped fine
1/2 cup dry red wine
5 cups beef broth
1 bay leaf
2 cups Italian plum tomatoes, crushed
1 tablespoon balsamic vinegar
2 tablespoons finely chopped flat-leaf parsley

Finish and Serve:
Sour cream for garnish

To Make the Soup:

- Season ribs liberally with salt and pepper. In a large, heavy pot, heat 1 tablespoon of the oil over high heat. Working in two batches, sear the ribs on both sides until golden brown. Remove ribs from pan and set aside.
- Drain excess fat from the pot, then add another 1/2 tablespoon oil and place over medium high heat. Set about a third of the mushrooms aside for garnish. Sauté the shallots and remaining mushrooms until browned, about 5 minutes. Add the cumin, chili powder, barley, and thyme; sauté until spices are aromatic and barley smells nutty.
- Pour in the wine and simmer until liquid is reduced by half. Add the broth, bay leaf, tomatoes and the ribs; bring to a boil, reduce heat and simmer, covered, for 1 1/2 hours, or until the meat falls from the bone.
- Remove ribs from the soup. Remove meat from bones and shred. Add meat to soup.
- Heat remaining 1/2 tablespoon oil in a small sauté pan over medium heat. Add reserved mushrooms and cook until tender. Add vinegar to pan and cook until evaporated. Season with salt and pepper and stir in 1/2 tablespoon of the parsley.
- Skim off and discard fat from the top of the soup. Remove and discard the bay leaf. Stir in remaining 1 1/2 tablespoons parsley.

Finish and Serve:

- Season the soup with salt and pepper and serve garnished with sour cream and the sautéed mushrooms.

Louis Yocco competes for the youth team in the hot-food division, for which it won gold.

Mushroom, Beef and Barley Soup (pg 46)

Broccoli, Beer and Bacon Soup with Wisconsin Cheddar (pg 48)

Award-Winning Peoples Choice Red Chili (pg 49)

Chilled Tomato Water with Avocado and Asiago Olive Crisp (pg 50)

Broccoli, Beer and Bacon Soup with Wisconsin Cheddar

Chef Russell Scott, CMC (photo page 47)

Serves 4

Soup:

4 strips smoked bacon, diced
1⁄2 cup diced celery
1⁄2 cup diced onion
2 tablespoons minced garlic
4 tablespoons all-purpose flour
2 cups chicken stock
1 sachet (see Chef's Tip)
12 ounces (1 1/2 cups) beer
1 tablespoon Tabasco sauce (optional)
2 tablespoons Worcestershire sauce
1 cup heavy cream, scalded
3/4 cup grated Wisconsin cheddar cheese
Salt and pepper to taste

Finish and Serve:

1/4 cup small broccoli florets, blanched
1/4 cup cooked wild rice
1/4 cup grated Wisconsin cheddar cheese
1/4 cup croutons

To Make the Soup:

- In a soup pot, cook bacon over low heat until it is crisp and has rendered its fat, stirring often to promote even cooking. Remove crisp bacon with a slotted spoon and set aside to garnish the soup.
- Add celery, onion and garlic to the fat in the pot and cook, stirring, just soft. Remove the vegetables from the pot with a slotted spoon and reserve. Sprinkle the flour over the fat in the pan and stir to make a roux. Cook for 5 minutes.
- Add stock to the pan, blending with a hand-held blender or whisking vigorously to remove any lumps. Simmer for 10 to 15 more minutes to remove any starchy flavor.
- Add the vegetables back to the pan along with the sachet and bring to a simmer. Add the beer, Tabasco and Worcestershire and cook for 10 minutes.
- Add the scalded cream and cheese. Simmer and stir long enough to melt the cheese. Season to taste with salt and pepper.

Finish and Serve:

- Place reserved bacon, broccoli and wild rice in the bottom of four soup bowls. Top with soup. Sprinkle with cheese and croutons just before serving.

CHEF'S TIP: Herb Sachet

- Chef Scott makes his sachets by tying 2 chopped parsley stems, 1 bay leaf, 1/4 teaspoon cracked black peppercorns, and a 1/4 teaspoon dried thyme loosely in a piece of cheesecloth.

Award-Winning Peoples Choice Red Chili

Chef Dan Scannell, CMC (photo page 47)

Serves 4

Red Chili:

1/2 cup olive oil
1/2 cup minced onion
1 minced poblano pepper
1/2 cup minced garlic
1 teaspoon crushed red pepper
1 teaspoon kosher salt
1 teaspoon ground black pepper
1 pound skirt steak, grilled and minced
2 cups canned crushed plum tomatoes
1/2 cup tomato juice
1 tablespoon tomato paste
2 tablespoons chopped cilantro leaves
1 teaspoon ground coriander
1 teaspoon ground cumin
1 teaspoon sugar
13 bay leaves
1 teaspoon sherry vinegar
1 tablespoon ancho chili powder
1 smoked or fresh jalapeño pepper, minced
1 tablespoon chipotle chile pepper paste
5 dashes Tabasco Sauce

Finish and Serve:

1 tablespoon chopped cilantro leaves
1 tablespoon chopped parsley leaves
1 teaspoon chopped thyme leaves
1 cup shredded cheddar cheese
4 sage leaves, chopped
4 tablespoons sour cream
1 ripe avocado, peeled and chopped

BEVERAGE RECOMMENDATION

Ice-cold beer

For the Red Chili:

- In a 2-quart stockpot, heat oil over medium-high heat and sauté onion and poblano until the onion is lightly browned. Add garlic, red pepper, salt and black pepper. Add skirt steak and sauté for a few minutes. Add all remaining ingredients and bring to a boil. Reduce heat and simmer for 1 hour.

Finish and Serve:

- Stir herbs into chili. Transfer chili to a casserole, sprinkle with cheese, and bake in a 350 degree F. oven until cheese is golden brown. Serve with sour cream and fresh avocado.

Chilled Tomato Water with Avocado and Asiago Olive Crisp

Chef Richard Rosendale, CC (photo page 47)

Serves 4

Tomato Water:

5 large ripe tomatoes
1 tablespoon sugar
1 teaspoon salt
1 sprig fresh basil, plus 4 nice leaves for garnish
20 saffron threads (optional)

Avocado:

1 avocado

Asiago Olive Crisp:

6 pitted kalamata olives
2 tablespoons grated Asiago cheese

Finish and Serve:

4 grape or baby tomatoes
4 pitted kalamata olives
1 tablespoon extra-virgin olive oil

To Make the Tomato Water:

- Combine the tomatoes, sugar and salt in a food processor. Process until tomatoes are liquefied. Line a strainer with cheesecloth and suspend the strainer over a large bowl. Pour the tomatoes into the strainer. Set in the refrigerator and allow to strain overnight.
- Discard the tomato solids in the cheesecloth. Measure out 1 cup of the tomato water. In a small saucepan, bring the tomato water to a gentle simmer. Add the basil sprig and the saffron and steep 20 minutes, then return this liquid back to the remaining tomato water. Place the tomato water in the refrigerator until ready to use.

To Make the Avocado:

- Remove the skin and pit from the avocado and cut the avocado into four equal portions. Place in ice water until ready to use.

To Make the Asiago Olive Crisp:

- Mince the olives and dry them off very well.
- Melt a quarter of the Asiago cheese (in a single layer) in a small non-stick skillet and sprinkle a quarter of the chopped olives over the cheese. When the cheese is crisp and golden brown, turn the crisp out onto a cutting board to cool. Repeat until all the cheese and olives are used and you have four crisps.

Finish and Serve:

- Cut the grape tomatoes and olives into quarters. Set aside.
- Place a piece of the fresh avocado in each of four shallow serving bowls. Divide the quartered tomatoes and quartered olives among the bowls. Ladle in the chilled tomato water and garnish each bowl with a cheese crisp, basil leaf and a drizzle of olive oil and serve.

CHEF'S TIP:

- The amount of tomato water you get will depend on the ripeness of the tomatoes you use. Very ripe tomatoes will give you the maximum yield.

White Onion Soup Soubise with Crispy Onion Straws

Chef Dan Scannell, CMC (photo page 53)
Serves 4

Onion Soup:
4 tablespoons extra-virgin olive oil
1 tablespoon unsalted butter
2 large Spanish onions, chopped
2 teaspoons minced garlic
1/2 cup white wine
1 cup canned chicken broth
1 quart heavy cream
1 cup whole milk
2 teaspoons kosher salt
1 teaspoon ground white pepper
2 teaspoons truffle oil
1/4 teaspoon freshly ground nutmeg (optional)

Onion Straws:
2 cups vegetable oil
1 medium Spanish onion, sliced very thin
1 cup all-purpose flour
Salt

To Make the Onion Soup:

- Heat a 2-quart stockpot over medium heat. Add oil and butter. Add onions and gently sauté until the onion is translucent (don't allow it to brown). Add the garlic.
- Add the wine to the pot and simmer until about half the liquid has evaporated. Add broth, cream and milk. Reduce heat and simmer gently until liquid is reduced by one third, about 30 minutes. Cool.
- Working in three batches, purée the soup in a blender until very smooth. Stir in salt, pepper and truffle oil.

To Make the Onion Straws:

- Place oil in a large saucepan and heat to 350 degrees F. Dredge onion slices in flour and shake off excess flour. Fry until golden brown. Drain on a plate covered with paper towels to absorb excess oil. Season with salt.

Finish and Serve:

- Ladle the hot soup into 4 bowls, top with crispy Onion Straws and serve.

Leek, Corn and Oyster Stew Baked in Puff Pastry

Chef Richard Rosendale, CC (photo page 53)
Serves 4

Stew:

1 tablespoon unsalted butter
1 small shallot, minced
1 clove garlic, minced
1/4 cup diced celery root or celery
1 cup sliced leek
1 cup fresh corn kernels
1/2 cup oyster mushrooms
1/4 cup chardonnay
1 cup oyster liquor (juice from the oysters) or chicken stock
3/4 cup heavy cream
Salt and white pepper to taste
1 cup fresh oysters
1/2 teaspoon chopped dill

Pastry:

1 sheet puff pastry
All-purpose flour
1 large egg yolk, lightly beaten
1/2 teaspoon sea salt

To Make the Stew:

- In a saucepan over medium heat, melt the butter. Add the shallot, garlic, celery, leek, corn and mushrooms and cook until tender. Add the wine and reduce by half. Add the oyster liquor and reduce by half again. Add the heavy cream and simmer until the stew is thick enough to coat the back of a spoon.
- Season the stew with salt and white pepper. Stir in the oysters and dill. Set aside to cool. When cooled, divide between four 8-ounce soufflé dishes or oven-proof bowls.

To Make the Pastry:

- Roll the puff pastry out to a thickness of 1/8 inch, using a small amount of flour to keep it from sticking to your surface or rolling pin. Cut out four circles that are each a little larger than the circumference of the soufflé dishes. Brush a little egg yolk around the lip of the soufflé dishes and place a circle of puff pastry on top of each dish. Press the pastry onto the edges of the dishes to seal. Brush the surface of the pastry with the egg yolk and sprinkle a little sea salt on the dough.
- Preheat oven to 400 degrees F. Bake until the pastry is golden brown.
  Serve immediately.

CHEF'S TIP:

- Leftover puff pastry scraps can be cut into shapes and decorations with cookie cutters or a paring knife and used to decorate the tops of these stews. Simply adhere your decorations to the pastry with a little egg wash.

White Onion Soup Soubise with Crispy Onion Straws (pg 51)

Leek, Corn and Oyster Stew Baked in Puff Pastry (pg 52)

Cream of Sunchoke Soup with Parmesan Froth (pg 54)

Goulash Soup (pg 55)

Cream of Sunchoke Soup with Parmesan Froth

Chef Richard Rosendale, CC (photo page 53)

Serves 4

Soup:

1 tablespoon unsalted butter
1/2 cup diced onion
1/4 cup diced celery
1 pound sunchokes (Jerusalem artichokes), peeled and sliced
1 clove minced garlic
1 shallot, minced
1/4 cup dry white wine
2 cups chicken stock
1 cup heavy cream
Salt and white pepper to taste

Froth:

1 cup 2% milk
5 each cracked peppercorns
1 sprig rosemary
1 cup grated Parmesan cheese
1 cup heavy cream
2 teaspoons salt

Finish and Serve:

Fresh sliced chives

To Make the Soup:

- Melt the butter in a heavy-bottom soup pot over medium heat. Add the onion and celery and cook, covered, until the vegetables are translucent. Add the sunchokes and stir. Add the garlic and shallot. Cook for 2 minutes.
- Pour in the white wine and then the chicken stock. Simmer until the sunchokes are tender, about 30 minutes. Transfer to a blender and blend until silky smooth. Add back to a clean pot and add the heavy cream. Bring to a simmer and adjust the seasoning with salt and pepper.

To Make the Froth:

- In a small saucepan, combine the milk, peppercorns and rosemary. Heat over medium heat until bubbles just form around the edges of the pan. Remove from the heat and whisk in the cheese. Let the milk sit at room temperature for about half an hour. Strain out the cheese, peppercorns and rosemary and discard. Whisk in the heavy cream and the salt. Place the milk in a frother and charge with two CO_2 cartridges. Place in the refrigerator until ready to use.

Finish and Serve:

- Reheat the sunchoke soup.
- Divide between four soup bowls and top with foam and fresh chives.

CHEF'S TIP:

- A frother can be purchased at gourmet shops or on-line. However, you can also whip the heavy cream and then gently fold it into the strained milk.

Goulash Soup

Chef Joachim Buchner, CMC (photo page 53)

Serves 4

Goulash:

1/4 cup vegetable oil
3 ounces lean beef, cut into 1/4-inch cubes
1/2 cup onion, cut into 1/4-inch dice
1 clove garlic, sliced
Pinch whole caraway seeds
1 tablespoon mild paprika
2 tablespoons all-purpose flour
6 cups beef broth or bouillon
1 cup 1/4-inch cubes peeled, diced potato
1/2 red bell pepper, cut into 1/4-inch cubes
1/2 yellow bell pepper, cut into 1/4-inch cubes
1/2 green bell pepper, cut into 1/4-inch cubes
1 teaspoon grated lemon zest
1 tablespoon lemon juice
Salt and pepper to taste

Finish and Serve:

Chopped scallions (optional)
Chopped chives (optional)
Hot sauce (optional)

BEVERAGE RECOMMENDATION

German dark beer

To Make the Goulash:

- In a large heavy soup pot, heat the oil over high heat. Add beef and sauté until lightly browned. Add onion and continue to sauté for 5 minutes, stirring often.
- Reduce heat to medium and add garlic, caraway and paprika; continue to cook for 3 minutes. Sprinkle in flour, stir, and add beef broth. Turn up the heat to high. Bring to a boil, reduce heat, and simmer soup for 10 minutes.
- Add potato and simmer for 10 more minutes. Add bell peppers and continue to simmer for 5 minutes or until potato and beef are tender.
- Add lemon zest and lemon juice. Season with salt and black pepper.

Finish and Serve:

- Add hot sauce if you would like the soup spicy. Garnish with scallions and chives and serve.

CHEF'S TIP:

- This hearty soup can be served either as a starter or as a meal on its own.
- Accompany it with freshly toasted garlic bread or crusty bread.

Hailey Salad

Chef Kevin Zink, CCC
Serves 4

Dressing:
1/4 cup white balsamic vinegar
2 shallots, finely minced
1 teaspoon lemon zest
3/4 cup olive oil
2 tablespoons finely sliced chives
Dash Worcestershire sauce
Dash Tabasco
Pinch sugar
Sea salt and freshly cracked pepper

Salad:
4 3/4-inch-thick slices from a head of iceberg lettuce
4 3/4-inch-thick slices from a head of romaine lettuce
4 3/4-inch-thick slices tomato
Sea salt and pepper to taste
Olive oil
Chopped chives

Parmesan Disk:
1/2 cup finely grated Parmesan cheese

Finish and Serve:
8 baby carrots, peeled
1/4 cup snipped lettuce sprouts or other sprouts or micro greens
1/4 cup finely crumbled Gorgonzola cheese

To Make the Dressing:

- Combine vinegar and shallots; let sit for 15 minutes. Add lemon zest. Slowly whisk in olive oil. Stir in remaining ingredients and season to taste with salt and pepper.

To Make the Salad:

- With a 3-inch biscuit cutter, cut the iceberg and romaine lettuce and tomato slices into perfect rounds. Season the lettuce rounds with a dab of the dressing. Sprinkle tomato disks with salt, pepper, olive oil and chives and set aside.

To Make the Parmesan Disk:

- Heat a non-stick skillet over medium-high heat. Sprinkle parmesan into skillet and let cook until golden brown. Remove cheese disk from pan and, while still warm, cut out cheese disks with the 3-inch cutter.

Finish and Serve:

- Marinate the baby carrots in a small amount of dressing. Toss the sprouts with a small amount of dressing.
- Place a romaine disk in the center of each of four salad plates and spoon on a bit of dressing. Top with a romaine disk with Gorgonzola crumbles, then with tomato and iceberg. Spoon on some more dressing. Top with Parmesan disk and finish with marinated carrots and sprouts. Drizzle dressing around the plates and serve.

CHEF'S TIP:

- Chef Zink named this salad after his daughter. It is a fun dish that they enjoy preparing together.

Jersey Tomato and Onion Salad

Chef Krystal Weaver (photo page 59)

Serves 6

Tomato and Onion:

1/2 cup extra-virgin olive oil
2 tablespoons balsamic vinegar
1 bunch fresh basil leaves, chopped
2 cloves garlic, finely chopped
3 jumbo beefsteak tomatoes, cored and cut into wedges
1 extra large sweet onion, cut into long julienne strips
4 cups mixed field greens
1 tablespoon chopped oregano leaves
Salt and freshly ground black pepper to taste

To Make the Jersey Tomato and Onion Salad:

- In mixing bowl, whisk together oil, vinegar, basil and garlic. Add tomato and onion and let sit for 2 hours.
- When ready to serve, add greens and oregano and toss well. Season to taste with salt and pepper.

Taco Salad

Chef Krystal Weaver (photo page 59)

6 to 8 servings

Salad:

1 pound ground beef
3 ounces taco seasoning
1 head iceberg lettuce, chopped
1 cup shredded cheddar cheese
1 cup shredded Monterey Jack cheese
2 tomatoes, diced
1 red onion, diced
1/2 green bell pepper, diced
1/2 orange bell pepper, diced
Coarsely chopped cilantro
8 ounces sliced and pitted Greek olives
16-ounce bag tri-color tortilla chips

Dressing:

1/2 cup sour cream
1/4 cup lemon juice
2 tablespoons taco seasoning
1 8-ounce jar salsa

To Make the Salad:

- In a medium skillet, brown ground beef, breaking up pieces of meat with a spoon or spatula. Stir in taco seasoning and cool.
- In large serving bowl, combine remaining salad ingredients. Add cooled beef and chips.

To Make the Dressing:

- Whisk together sour cream, lemon juice, taco seasoning and salsa.

Finish and Serve:

- Toss the dressing with salad and serve.

Jersey Tomato and Onion Salad (pg 58)

Taco Salad (pg 58)

Wedge of Boston Lettuce with Heirloom Tomato Salad and Cucumber-Buttermilk Dressing (pg 60)

Contemporary Caesar Salad (pg 61)

Wedge of Boston Lettuce with Heirloom Tomato Salad and Cucumber-Buttermilk Dressing

Chef Russell Scott, CMC (photo page 59)

Serves 4

Cucumber-Buttermilk Dressing:

1 cucumber, seeded but not peeled
2 cups mayonnaise
1/2 cup buttermilk
1/4 cup red wine vinegar
1/2 cup thinly sliced scallions
1 teaspoon celery seeds
1 tablespoon onion powder
1 tablespoon coarsely chopped fresh dill
1 ounce finely grated Parmesan cheese
Tabasco sauce to taste
Salt and pepper to taste

Basil Dressing:

1/2 cup white balsamic vinegar
1/2 cup olive oil
1/2 cup vegetable oil
1 tablespoon minced shallot
1/4 cup thinly sliced basil leaves
Sugar to taste
Salt and pepper to taste

Salad:

8 ripe heirloom tomatoes

Finish and Serve:

2 heads Boston lettuce, stem end trimmed, heads halved
1/2 cup thinly sliced scallions

To Make the Cucumber-Buttermilk Dressing:

- Combine cucumber, mayonnaise, buttermilk, vinegar, scallions, celery seeds and onion powder in a blender and blend until smooth. Pour into a bowl and stir in dill and Parmesan. Season to taste with Tabasco, salt and pepper. Refrigerate 1 day before serving; makes approximately 4 cups.

To Make the Basil Dressing:

- Place vinegar in a medium stainless-steel bowl. Slowly whisk in oils. Whisk in shallot and basil and season to taste with sugar, salt and pepper. Makes about 2 cups.

To Make the Salad:

- Slice tomatoes into 1/4-inch-thick slices. Marinate in Basil Dressing for approximately 30 minutes at room temperature.

Finish and Serve:

- Blot off any excess dressing and divide tomato slices between four chilled 10-inch plates. Place a wedge of lettuce directly on top of the tomatoes and dress each with about a quarter cup Cucumber-Buttermilk Dressing. Sprinkle each with scallions and serve.

CHEF'S TIP:

- Chef Scott serves this salad with fried cornbread (see page 229).

Contemporary Caesar Salad

Chef Richard Rosendale, CC (photo page 59)

Serves 4

Lettuce:

1 large head of romaine lettuce

Parmesan Cheese Disks:

1/4 cup grated Parmesan cheese

Crouton:

4 slices white bread

Olive oil, salt and pepper to taste

Dressing:

1/4 teaspoon minced garlic

1/2 teaspoon Worcestershire sauce

2 teaspoons Dijon mustard

2 large egg yolks

Juice of 1/2 lemon

1/4 cup grated Asiago cheese

1/2 cup olive oil

1 cup canola oil

1/4 cup red wine vinegar

1/2 teaspoon cracked black pepper

Salt to taste

Finish and Serve:

Cherry, baby or grape tomatoes, quartered, for garnish (optional)

Micro greens for garnish

To Make the Lettuce:

- Slice off the bottom end of the lettuce and discard. Remove the leaves, keeping them whole. Rinse, dry and set aside.

To Make the Parmesan Cheese Disks:

- Heat a non-stick skillet set over medium-low heat. Sprinkle 2 teaspoons of the grated cheese into the pan and cook until it starts to melt and turn brown. Turn the cheese out onto a cool surface to cool. Repeat this step three more times until you have four cheese disks.

To Make the Crouton:

- Preheat oven to 275 degrees F. Using a cookie cutter or a paring knife and a jar, cut a 3-inch circle from each piece of bread. Season the bread with salt and pepper and drizzle with olive oil. Toast in the oven until golden brown. Place a circle on each of four salad plates.

To Make the Dressing:

- In a blender, combine minced garlic, Worcestershire, mustard, yolks, lemon juice and cheese and blend for 1 minute. Next, with the motor running, add the olive oil and the canola oil a little at time, alternating with additions of vinegar. Blend in the pepper and season to taste with salt.

Finish and Serve:

- Place the romaine leaves in a large bowl and toss with the dressing. Transfer the leaves to a sheet of plastic wrap and roll the leaves up into a cylinder. Twist the two ends tightly. Cut the romaine into four portions. Unwrap and place one in the center of each bread circle. Place the cheese disk on top of the romaine and serve garnish with tomatoes, micro greens and any leftover dressing.

Asparagus Salad the Italian Way

Chef Ed Leonard, CMC

Serves 4

Asparagus Salad:

34 spears medium asparagus, 1/2 inch trimmed off the bottom

1 shallot, peeled and finely minced

1/2 cup 12-year-old balsamic vinegar

8 basil leaves

2 tablespoons chopped parsley

1 tablespoon grated lemon zest

1 1/2 cups extra-virgin olive oil

1/2 cup mayonnaise

Coarse sea salt to taste

Ground black pepper

2 medium Yukon Gold potatoes, cooked and sliced

2 to 3 teaspoons black or white truffle oil

Kosher salt to taste

Finish and Serve:

4 medium hard-boiled eggs, peeled and pushed through a sieve or chopped fine

8 shaved slices Parmigiano-Reggiano cheese

4 very thin truffle slices

To Make the Asparagus Salad:

- Bring a large saucepan of salted water to a boil. Blanch asparagus until just tender, 3 to 4 minutes. Drain and plunge into cold water to stop the cooking. When cool, dice ten of the spears.
- In a stainless-steel bowl, combine shallot and vinegar. Stir to combine and let sit for 15 minutes.
- In a food processor, combine diced asparagus spears, basil, parsley, lemon zest and 1/2 cup of the oil and process until smooth. Transfer to a large bowl and whisk in remaining oil. Whisk in mayonnaise, vinegar and shallot and season with salt and pepper.
- Toss potatoes with the truffle oil and season with kosher salt.

Finish and Serve:

- Arrange six asparagus spears on each of four plates with tips facing one way. Top spears with potatoes. Drizzle dressing over the potatoes and asparagus. Garnish with chopped hard-boiled egg, Reggiano and truffle slices.

Watermelon Salad with Mâche, Cotija Cheese and Ginger Dressing

Chef Russell Scott, CMC (photo page 65)

Serves 4

Ginger Dressing:

1/2 cup champagne vinegar

1 tablespoon fresh ginger, finely minced

Juice and zest from 1 orange

1 1/2 cups grape seed oil

Salt and pepper to taste

Salad:

4 half-inch thick slices red watermelon

2 half-inch-thick-slices yellow watermelon

1/4 cup sliced red onion, rinsed under cold running water

Finish and Serve:

2 bunches mâche (lamb's lettuce), rinsed, roots removed, leaves left in clusters

1/2 ounce crumbled cotija cheese

To Make the Ginger Dressing:

- One day before serving, whisk together the vinegar, ginger, orange juice and zest. Very slowly whisk in the oil. Season to taste with salt and pepper and refrigerate for at least 24 hours.

To Make the Salad:

- Cut a rectangle 2 inches by 4 inches form the center of each slice of red watermelon. Set aside the rectangles. Cut the remaining flesh from the red melon slices into small dice. Cut the flesh of the yellow melon slices into small dice.
- Marinate the melon rectangles in ginger dressing. Separately, marinate the diced melon (both the red and yellow) together with the sliced onion in ginger dressing.

Finish and Serve:

- Place a red melon rectangle in the center of each of four chilled 10-inch each plates. Top each with a quarter of the diced melon and onion. Top with a quarter of the mâche. Sprinkle with the cheese, drizzle with some of the leftover dressing, and serve.

Lobster Soufflé and Baby Greens

Chef Dan Scannell, CMC (photo page 65)

Serves 4

Lobster Soufflé:

2 8-ounce rock lobster tails, split in half

1 large egg white

1 1/2 cups heavy cream

2 teaspoons sea salt

1/2 teaspoon ground white pepper

2 tablespoons softened, unsalted butter

2 teaspoons Old Bay Seasoning

Finish and Serve:

2 cups baby mâche lettuce

Extra-virgin olive oil

Lemon juice

Salt and pepper to taste

To Make the Lobster Soufflé:

- Place food processor bowl and blade in the freezer. Remove the lobster meat from the shells and trim the red membrane from the meat to expose just the white of the lobster. Set shells aside and place the lobster meat into the well-chilled food processor. Pulse 15 seconds. Add the egg white and continue to pulse until incorporated. Slowly add the heavy cream and pulse until smooth. Do not over mix.
- Press the lobster mousse mixture through a fine tamis or sieve. Season with salt and pepper and set aside.
- Preheat oven to 400 degrees F. Brush the lobster shells with the softened butter and spoon lobster mousse into the shells, filling each evenly.
- Place the filled lobster tails into an oven-proof baking dish with a little water on the bottom. Sprinkle with Old Bay Seasoning. Bake until lightly browned, about 10 minutes.

Finish and Serve:

- Toss mâche with olive oil, lemon juice, and salt and pepper to taste. Serve with the warm lobster tails.

Watermelon Salad with Mâche, Cotija Cheese and Ginger Dressing (pg 64)

Lobster Soufflé and Baby Greens (pg 64)

Sautéed Baby Artichoke and Fava Bean Salad (pg 66)

Roasted Yellow Beets and Summer Truffle Salad (pg 67)

Sautéed Baby Artichoke and Fava Bean Salad

Chef Joachim Buchner, CMC (photo page 65)
Serves 4

Artichokes:
8 baby artichokes
1/4 cup lemon juice
1 tablespoon kosher salt

Fava Beans:
1 1/2 cups shelled fava beans

Dressing:
2 tablespoons white balsamic vinegar
Salt and white pepper to taste
Sugar to taste
4 tablespoons olive oil

Finish and Serve:
4 tablespoons olive oil
6 small porcini mushrooms, halved
3 cloves garlic, sliced
1/2 cup thin strips red onion
1/2 cup sun-dried tomatoes
1 teaspoon chopped tarragon
2 bunches arugula
Extra-virgin olive oil

BEVERAGE RECOMMENDATION
Farmingham, Marlborough, 2000 Chardonnay

To Make the Artichokes:
- Trim the bottoms of the artichoke stems and peel tough skin away from the remaining stems. Remove the outer, darker leaves by bending them back until they snap. You should have only the inner, pale-green leaves left.
- Bring 5 quarts of water to a boil in a large pot and add the lemon juice and salt. Add the artichokes and cover them with a clean kitchen towel to keep them submerged in the water. Simmer for 25 minutes. Remove from heat and let cool in cooking water.
- After artichokes are cooled, cut each in half and scoop out and discard the hairy choke. Set artichokes aside.

To Make the Fava Beans:
- In another pot of boiling water, cook the fava beans for 5 minutes. Remove from the boiling water and submerge in ice water to stop the cooking. Slip the tough outer skin off each bean. Set aside.

To Make the Dressing:
- In a glass mixing bowl, whisk together the vinegar, salt, pepper and sugar. Slowly whisk in the olive oil. Set dressing aside.

Finish and Serve:
- Heat a large sauté pan over high heat and add the olive oil. Add the artichokes and the porcinis and sauté until golden. Reduce heat and add the garlic and the onion. Cook for 2 minutes. Add the tomatoes and fava beans; continue cooking until the beans are warm. Remove pan from heat and mix in the dressing and the tarragon.
- Place arugula on a platter or divide among four plates. Top with vegetables, drizzle with extra-virgin olive oil and serve.

CHEF'S TIP:
- This is a perfect salad for spring, full of bright colors and bold flavors. Serve it with grilled focaccia.

Roasted Yellow Beets and Summer Truffle Salad

Chef Joachim Buchner, CMC (photo page 65)

Serves 4

Roasted Yellow Beets and Summer Truffle Salad:

16 baby yellow beets, tops reserved
1/2 cup olive oil
Sea salt to taste
1/2 cup water
1 red bell pepper
1/8 teaspoon Dijon mustard
2 tablespoons aged sherry vinegar
Pinch kosher salt
Pinch sugar
Freshly ground white pepper
1/4 teaspoon white truffle oil
1 diced shallot
1 teaspoon finely sliced chives
2 sliced scallions
8 ounces baby lettuce

Finish and Serve:

2 1-ounce black summer truffles, thinly sliced.

BEVERAGE RECOMMENDATION

Weingut Kurt Hain, Piespoter Goldtropfchen, Kabinett, Germany 2001

To Make the Roasted Yellow Beets and Summer Truffle Salad:

- Preheat oven to 375 degrees F. Trim the beets, removing and reserving the green tops separately. Wash beets well and dry. Toss beets with 1/4 cup of the olive oil and sea salt. Place in a small baking dish with the water and cover with foil. Roast until beets are tender, 20 to 30 minutes.
- Cool beets. Rub off and discard the skin of the beets. Halve and set aside.
- Meanwhile, brush bell pepper with oil and roast alongside the beets, uncovered, until the skin is bubbling or browned. Place it in a plastic bag and cool. Rub off skin, remove seeds, and cut flesh into small dice. Set aside.
- In a mixing bowl, whisk together the mustard, vinegar, kosher salt, sugar and white pepper. Slowly whisk in truffle oil and 4 tablespoons of the olive oil. Add diced roasted pepper, shallot, chives, scallions and beets. Let marinate at room temperature for 30 minutes.
- Remove beets from marinade. Use half of the marinade left in the bowl to toss with the baby lettuce and beet greens. Reserve the other half of the marinade for finishing.

Finish and Serve:

- Arrange greens on four plates. Top with beets and thinly sliced truffle, drizzle with the reserved dressing and serve.

CHEF'S TIP:

- This flavorful salad with sweet beets and fragrant summer truffles goes well with grilled seafood or a thick steak.
- Check your local gourmet food store for truffle availability.

Crispy Potato and Goat Cheese Salad with Basil Oil and Aged Balsamic Vinegar

Chef Richard Rosendale, CC
Serves 4

Potatoes:
1 large Idaho potato, peeled and sliced paper-thin on a mandolin
Olive oil

Goat Cheese:
1 8-ounce log of goat cheese
1 bunch fresh chives, very thinly sliced

Mushrooms:
2 Portobello mushroom caps

Basil Oil:
1 bunch fresh basil
1/2 cup canola oil
Salt to taste

Finish and Serve:
2 bunches baby greens (like frisée, micro greens, or alfalfa sprouts)
1/4 cup aged balsamic vinegar
Pepper to taste

To Make the Potatoes:

- Preheat oven to 275 degrees F. Cover a sheet pan with oiled parchment paper and lay the potato slices out on the paper. Place a second sheet of parchment on top of the potatoes and another sheet tray on top of the first one. Bake at 275 degrees F. until potatoes are golden brown and crisp, about 40 minutes.

To Make the Goat Cheese:

- Cut the goat cheese in half length wise and roll the goat cheese into a two long cylinders. Roll the goat cheese in the chives and set aside at room temperature.

To Make the Mushrooms:

- Preheat a grill or broiler. Remove the black gills from the Portobello mushrooms and discard. Rub the mushrooms with olive oil and season with salt and pepper. Grill or broil the mushrooms 2 1/2 minutes on each side. Refrigerate until ready to serve.

To Make the Basil Oil:

- Blanch the basil in boiling salted water for 10 seconds. Plunge the basil into ice water to stop the cooking. Squeeze water out of basil. Place basil in a blender with the canola oil and a little salt. Purée until liquefied. Line a strainer with cheesecloth and strain the basil oil through the cheesecloth. Set aside.

Finish and Serve:

- Slice the mushrooms and divide them between four plates. Slice the cheese into 12 1/4-inch slices and place three slices on top of the mushrooms on each plate. Place a potato crisp in between each slice of the goat cheese. Toss the greens with the balsamic vinegar and all but a tablespoon or so of the basil oil. Season with salt and pepper. Divide the greens between the plates. Drizzle the remaining basil oil around the plate and serve.

Roasted Celery and Celery Root Salad with Lobster Tail, Mango and Vanilla Dressing

Chef Joachim Buchner, CMC

Serves 4

Celery:

12 3-inch-long pieces celery
2 tablespoons vegetable oil
1 teaspoon sea salt
1 small celery root
Kosher salt and freshly ground white pepper to taste
Juice of 1/2 lemon
2 tablespoons mayonnaise
1 tablespoon soft goat cheese
1 tablespoon sliced parsley leaves

Lobster:

2 1 1/2-pound lobsters, cooked

Mango and Vanilla Dressing:

1/4 cup milk
1/4 vanilla bean
1/2 cup fat-free yogurt
Juice of 1/2 lemon
Kosher salt and freshly ground white pepper to taste

Finish and Serve:

2 mangoes, peeled, seeded and cut into thin slices
24 celery leaves
12 whole chives

BEVERAGE RECOMMENDATION

Louis Sipp, Alsace, 2000 Riesling

To Make the Celery:

- Preheat the broiler. Peel celery, removing tough strings. Place in a baking pan, brush with oil and season with sea salt. Broil until soft and brown. Let cool.
- Peel the celery root and cut it into thin, even strips. Place in a mixing bowl and season with salt and white pepper. Add the lemon juice, the mayonnaise, goat cheese and parsley and mix well. Set aside to let flavors combine.

To Make the Lobster:

- Cut lobsters in half and remove lobster tail meat. Break open claws and remove meat. Refrigerate until ready to serve.

To Make the Vanilla Dressing:

- In small saucepan, warm milk and let vanilla bean steep for 5 minutes. Remove vanilla bean, split it open and use the tip of a knife to scrape the small black seeds into the milk. Set aside to cool.
- Add the cooled vanilla milk to the yogurt, season with salt and the lemon juice.

Finish and Serve:

- Fan mango slices out on four plates. Top with roasted celery. Cover celery with the celery root salad. Arrange the lobster tail on top of the celery root salad and spoon the yogurt dressing over. Garnish with celery leaves and chives and serve.

CHEF'S TIP:

- A refreshing salad made from two kinds of celery and sweet lobster meat. Serve this with crisp sesame crackers or with freshly baked potato buns.

Cured Salmon with Black Pepper Crust

Chef Jamie P. Keating, CCC
Serves 4

Radish Salad:

1 cup white vinegar
2 cups water
2 tablespoons sugar
1/2 teaspoon kosher salt
12 radishes
2 tangerines, peeled, segmented and seeded
1/4 cup peeled, diced cucumber
2 scallions, chopped

Artichoke Purée:

1/4 cup pureéd artichoke bottoms
1/4 cup pitted black olives, chopped in the food processor
2 cloves garlic, coarsely chopped
2 tablespoons extra-virgin olive oil

Salmon:

1/4 cup black peppercorns
1 pound skinless salmon fillet
2 cups kosher salt, plus more to taste
1 1/2 cups sugar
2 sprigs dill

Sauce:

1 shallot, finely chopped
1 cup orange juice
1 cup white balsamic vinegar
1 teaspoon Dijon mustard
1 teaspoon honey
2 1/2 cups grape seed oil
Leaves from 2 sprigs thyme, chopped
Kosher salt to taste

Finish and Serve:

4 bunches hydroponic mâche greens
Saltine crackers
8 tablespoons white balsamic vinaigrette

BEVERAGE RECOMMENDATION

Laetita, Brut Rose, 2000 California

To Make the Radish Salad:

- Combine the vinegar, water, sugar and salt in a small saucepan. Heat just until the salt and sugar dissolves. Remove from heat, add radishes, and allow to cool to room temperature. Transfer radishes and liquid to a jar, cover and refrigerate until needed.
- Slice pickled radishes. Gently toss tangerines, radishes, cucumber and scallions. Set aside.

To Make the Artichoke Purée:

- In separate bowl, mix artichoke purée, olives, garlic and olive oil. Cover and refrigerate until needed.

To Make the Salmon:

- In a small heavy skillet over medium heat, toast peppercorns, shaking pan frequently, until fragrant. Transfer them to a spice grinder or peppermill and coarsely grind. Coat salmon with the pepper and refrigerate.
- Mix the 2 cups salt, sugar and dill in a stainless-steel bowl. Layer half the salt mixture into a glass baking dish. Place salmon fillet into baking dish and sprinkle with remaining salt mixture. Cover with plastic wrap and refrigerate for 4 1/2 hours.

To Make the Sauce:

- Using a food processor, pulse together the shallots, orange juice, white balsamic, mustard and honey. With the motor running, slowly drizzle in the grape seed oil and continue to process for 30 seconds. Stir in thyme and season to taste with salt.

Finish and Serve:

- Divide the radish salad between four plates. Remove salmon from pan and dust off salt mixture. Cut three thin slices per plate and rest the slices on top of the radish salad. Place mâche greens toward top of plate. Drizzle with 2 tablespoons of the white balsamic vinaigrette, top with 1 tablespoon of the olive mixture and a cracker and serve.

CHEF'S TIP:

- You can substitute any mild, young lettuce greens for the mâche in this recipe.

Salmon Cakes with Creole Mayonnaise

Chef Louis Yocco
Serves 4

Creole Mayonnaise:

1 cup mayonnaise
1 teaspoon Worcestershire sauce
Dash Tabasco
2 teaspoons whole-grain mustard
Salt and pepper to taste

Salmon Cakes:

1 1/2 pounds Idaho potatoes, baked, then pressed through a sieve
1 pound cooked, flaked salmon
2 tablespoons melted unsalted butter
2 teaspoons whole-grain mustard
1 tablespoon finely chopped Italian parsley
1 tablespoon finely chopped dill
Juice and zest of 1 lemon
Salt and pepper to taste
1/4 cup all-purpose flour
1 large egg, beaten
1 cup dried breadcrumbs

Finish and Serve:

Peel of 1 lemon, removed in one strip with a sharp paring knife
4 pieces frisée lettuce
1 sprig dill
1 teaspoon red wine vinegar
1 1/2 tablespoons extra-virgin olive oil
1 red bell pepper
1/4 cup olive oil

To Make the Creole Mayonnaise:

- Combine the mayonnaise, Worcestershire, Tabasco and 2 teaspoons mustard in a bowl and season with salt and pepper; refrigerate until serving.

To Make the Salmon Cakes:

- In a mixing bowl, combine potatoes, salmon, butter, mustard, parsley, dill and lemon zest and juice. Season with salt and pepper. Divide mixture into eight equal portions, form each into a ball and flatten into a disk.
- Place the flour, egg and breadcrumbs separately in shallow bowls. Dip each salmon cake first in the flour, then in egg, and finally dredge them in the breadcrumbs, making sure that they are evenly coated; refrigerate for 30 minutes.

Finish and Serve:

- Divide the lemon peel in four sections. Using the strips of peel, tie together four bundles each with a piece of frisée and dill sprig.
- Combine the vinegar and the extra-virgin olive oil, season with salt and pepper and set aside. Cut just the outer flesh of the pepper into eight diamond shapes and set aside.
- Heat olive oil in a sauté pan over medium-high heat. Working in two batches if necessary, add the salmon cakes and cook on both sides until evenly brown; drain on a paper towels.
- Serve cakes warm with the mayonnaise, garnishing each plate with a pepper diamond and a frisée bundle drizzled with the vinegar-and-oil mixture.

Grilled French Bread with Salt-Cured Olive Tapenade, Saffron Onions, White Beans and Pesto

Chef Dan Scannell, CMC

Serves 4

French Bread:

12 slices of grilled French bread
Olive oil
Salt and pepper

Olive Tapenade:

2 cups salt-cured olives
1 teaspoon ground black pepper
3 tablespoons grated Parmigiano-Reggiano cheese
2 teaspoons minced roasted garlic
2 teaspoons lemon juice
1/2 cup extra-virgin olive oil
2 teaspoons snipped fresh chives

White Beans and Basil:

2 cups cooked navy beans
2 tablespoons extra-virgin olive oil
1 teaspoon kosher salt
1/4 teaspoon ground black pepper
2 tablespoons chopped basil leaves
2 teaspoons lemon juice
2 tablespoons chopped tomatoes

Saffron Onions:

2 tablespoons melted unsalted butter
2 tablespoons olive oil
1 teaspoon saffron threads
2 cups sliced Spanish onions
1 teaspoon kosher salt

Pesto Sauce:

6 to 8 ounces fresh basil leaves
1 clove garlic
1 teaspoon lightly toasted pine nuts
2 teaspoons grated Parmesan cheese
1/2 cup extra-virgin olive oil

Finish and Serve:

12 slices grilled zucchini, thinly sliced
1 cup peeled diced tomatoes
2 cups field greens of baby romaine
Lemon juice

To Make the French Bread:

- Brush bread with olive oil and season with salt and pepper. Grill until slightly charred.

To Make the Olive Tapenade:

- In a food processor, combine olives, pepper, cheese, garlic and lemon juice. Pulse for 15 seconds or until well chopped. With the motor running, slowly drizzle in the olive oil. Remove from food processor and mix in chives.

To Make the White Beans and Basil:

- Combine all ingredients and mix well. Refrigerate.

To Make the Saffron Onions:

- Place a medium sauté pan over medium low heat. Add butter, oil and saffron. Cook until heated. Add onions and gently sauté until the onions are tender, about 5 minutes. Sprinkle with salt

To Make the Pesto Sauce:

- Blanch basil leaves in boiling water. Drain and pat dry. Place in a food processor with the remaining ingredients and process until smooth. Set aside.

Finish and Serve:

- Top 4 slices with 1 cup of the White Beans and Basil, 4 slices with 1 cup of the Olive Tapenade, 4 slices with 1 cup of the Saffron Onions and 4 slices with grilled zucchini. Mix greens with diced tomatoes and dress greens with lemon juice and more olive oil and serve with pesto and bread.

Pan-Seared "Summer Style" Foie Gras

Chef Russell Scott, CMC
Serves 5

Foie Gras:

1 1-pound fresh foie gras lobe
Salt and pepper

Vegetables:

3/4 cup thinly sliced cauliflower
3/4 cup sliced shallots
1/4 cup corn kernels
1/4 cup peas, cleaned and blanched
1/4 cup green seedless grapes, split in half
3 tablespoons slightly sweet white wine
Zest from 1 orange
2 tablespoons unsalted butter
Salt and pepper to taste

Verjus Caramel:

1 cup red or white verjus
1 1/2 cups water
1/2 cup raisins
1 cup heavy cream

Finish and Serve:

1 ounce pea shoots
5 slices baguette, 1/4-inch-thick, toasted

To Make the Foie Gras:

- Slice foie gras into five 1/2-inch-thick medallions. Season with salt and pepper on both sides. Heat a skillet and sear the foie gras (without adding fat to the pan) until it is a rich brown color on both sides and cooked to medium doneness.

To Make the Vegetables:

- Using 2 tablespoons of the rendered foie gras fat or clarified butter, sauté the cauliflower and shallots in a second skillet. Add the corn, peas and grapes to the vegetables. Add the wine and orange zest. Cook until most of the liquid has evaporated. Swirl butter into pan and toss until melted. Season to taste with salt and pepper.

To Make the Verjus Caramel:

- In a heavy saucepan, combine the verjus, water and raisins. Bring to a simmer and reduce until the liquid is syrupy and resembles honey. (Over cooking this will cause the sauce to get dark and take on a caramelized flavor.)
- Heat the heavy cream and strain it into the verjus syrup. Continue to reduce the mixture back to a syrupy consistency. Strain and cool to room temperature.

Finish and Serve:

- Spoon the vegetables into the center of five 10-inch plates. Drizzle the verjus caramel around the vegetables on the plates. Place the toasted baguette slices on top of the vegetables. Place a piece of seared foie gras on top of each baguette slice and garnish the top of the foie gras with pea shoots. Serve immediately.

CHEF'S TIP:

- Verjus is an unfermented grape juice. It is tart and makes a great substitute for vinegar.

Asparagus and Morels in Flaky Pastry

Chef Russell Scott, CMC

Serves 4

Pastry:

1 sheet partially thawed puff pastry

1 egg, lightly beaten

Whole fennel seeds

Coarse salt

Asparagus:

16 asparagus spears

Mushroom Sauce:

2 cups heavy cream

4 tablespoons unsalted butter, diced

2 ounces morels, cleaned and cut into uniform pieces

1 tablespoon minced shallot

1/2 teaspoon minced garlic

4 tablespoons fresh whole tarragon leaves

Salt and pepper to taste

To Make the Pastry:

- Preheat oven to 375 degrees F. Brush partially thawed puff pastry evenly with egg. Cut into strips 4 inches long and 1 1/2 inches wide. Sprinkle with fennel seeds and salt. Transfer to a parchment-lined sheet pan and bake until golden.

To Make the Asparagus:

- Blanch asparagus in salted boiling water. Immediately plunge spears in ice water until cold. Drain and refrigerate until ready to serve.

To Make the Mushroom Sauce:

- In a small saucepan, simmer heavy cream until reduced by half.
- Place a small sauté pan over medium heat and melt the butter. Cook the morels briefly, then add the shallot and garlic and cook until softened. Add the tarragon leaves, toss briefly and add reduced heavy cream. Season to taste with salt and pepper and keep warm.

Finish and Serve:

- When ready to serve, preheat oven to 325 degrees F. Place asparagus spears on sheet pan with puff pastry and place in the oven until very hot.
- Remove the asparagus and pastry from the oven. Cut the pastry in half length wise and place one half in the center of each of four 10-inch plates. Place a quarter of the asparagus on top of each. Spoon the mushroom sauce over the asparagus. Top each stack with the remaining halves of pastry and serve.

Crab-Stuffed Morels, Grilled White Asparagus, Foamed Aïoli and Ruby Grapefruit

Chef Dan Scannell, CMC
Serves 4

Mushrooms:

10 ounces snow crabmeat or lump crabmeat
1 cup mayonnaise
1 tablespoon minced shallot
1 teaspoon minced garlic
2 teaspoons minced red bell pepper
1 tablespoon whole-grain mustard
2 teaspoons dry mustard powder
1 large egg, beaten
10 dashes Tabasco sauce
4 dashes Worcestershire sauce
1 teaspoon Old Bay seasoning
2 teaspoons chopped cilantro
2 teaspoons chopped parsley
2 teaspoons kosher salt
1 teaspoon ground black pepper
8 large fresh morel mushrooms or rehydrated dried morels

Foamed Aïoli:

2 tablespoons fresh egg yolk or pasteurized egg yolk
1/4 cup whole fresh egg or pasteurized egg
1 tablespoon fresh lemon juice
1 teaspoon sherry vinegar
1 teaspoon kosher salt
1 1/2 teaspoons Dijon mustard
1/4 cup extra-virgin olive oil
1/2 cup vegetable oil
4 drops Tabasco
Pinch cayenne pepper

Finish and Serve:

12 white asparagus spears, peeled, blanched in salted water and grilled
12 ruby grapefruit segments
Chive or chili oil

To Make Mushrooms:

- Combine the crabmeat, mayonnaise, shallot, garlic, bell pepper, mustards, egg, Tabasco, Worcestershire, Old Bay, cilantro, parsley, salt and pepper and mix well. Chill well.
- Clean mushrooms and stuff with the crab mixture. Grill or bake in a 400 degree F. oven until the mushrooms are hot, about 10 minutes.

To Make the Foamed Aïoli:

- In a stainless-steel bowl, whisk together yolk, whole egg, lemon juice, vinegar, salt and mustard. Pouring in a very thin stream and whisking constantly, whisk in olive and vegetable oils. Whisk in Tabasco and cayenne.
- Pour the mixture into a commercial whip-cream canister. Screw top on tightly and fill with the gas cartridge. Aïoli can be keep in the refrigerator for up to four days.

Finish and Serve:

- Divide the asparagus between 4 plates. Shake canister well and foam aïoli over asparagus. Top with mushrooms. Serve garnished with ruby grapefruit segments and chive or chili oil.

CHEF'S TIP: Foam Canister

- Foam canisters can be purchased at gourmet food stores. If you don't have one, simply drizzle the foamed aïoli over the dish.

Grilled Dublin Bay Prawns with Red Pepper Rouille

Chef Dan Scannell, CMC
Serves 4

Dublin Bay Prawns:
4 Dublin Bay prawns
4 wooden skewers, soaked in water for 20 minutes
1 tablespoon melted unsalted butter
Kosher salt and ground black pepper
1 tablespoon olive oil
4 cooked, blanched artichoke bottoms
1/4 cup white wine
2 teaspoons fresh lemon juice
1 tablespoon cold unsalted butter
1 tablespoon fresh minced chives

Red Pepper Rouille:
8 ounces canned pimentos, drained
6 tablespoons extra-virgin olive oil
2 teaspoons kosher salt
1/2 teaspoon ground white pepper
2 tablespoons mayonnaise
2 teaspoons sherry vinegar
4 dashes Tabasco
1/4 teaspoon cayenne pepper

Finish and Serve:
12 toast points

To Make the Dublin Bay Prawns:

- Preheat a grill or, to bake the prawns, preheat the oven to 375 degrees F. Clean and peel the prawns. Thread each on a soaked skewer lengthwise. Brush with melted butter and sprinkle with salt and pepper. Grill or bake until cook through.
- While the prawns are cooking, heat the olive oil in a skillet and sauté the artichoke bottoms until warmed through. Add the wine and lemon juice to the pan and cook until liquid is reduced by half. Swirl in the cold butter and fresh chives. Season with salt and pepper.

To Make the Red Pepper Rouille:

- Place the pimentos in a blender and pulse to chop. With the motor running, slowly pour in the olive oil. Add salt, pepper, mayonnaise, vinegar, Tabasco and cayenne. Continue to purée until smooth. Chill before serving.

Finish and Serve:

- Place the artichokes in the center of warmed plates and fill each with 1 tablespoon Red Pepper Rouille. Top with a grilled prawn and serve with toast points.

CHEF'S TIP:

- Dublin Bay prawns are also known as langostinos, scampi and lobster dainties. You may substitute very large shrimp or lobster tail meat in this recipe.

Creamy Lobster Risotto with Clam and Vermouth Jus

Chef Richard Rosendale, CC

Serves 4

Risotto:

2 1/2 cups lobster or chicken stock
1 tablespoon olive oil
1 tablespoon minced white onion
1 cup Carnaroli or Arborio rice
1/4 cup dry white wine
1/2 cup diced lobster meat, either raw or cooked
3 tablespoons grated Asiago cheese
2 tablespoons unsalted butter
1 tablespoon chopped basil
Juice of 1 lemon
Salt and white pepper to taste

Clams:

20 littleneck clams, scrubbed and rinsed
1 tablespoon minced garlic
1 teaspoon minced shallot
10 sprigs fresh thyme
1/4 cup vermouth
3 tablespoons unsalted butter
1 tablespoon chopped parsley
Salt and white pepper to taste

Finish and Serve:

4 small basil sprigs for garnish

To Make the Risotto:

- Put stock in a small pot and keep just below boiling. Heat the oil in a medium, heavy bottom saucepan over medium heat. Add the onion and cook until softened. Stir in the rice. Pour in the wine. When most of the liquid has evaporated, add one ladle at a time of stock to the risotto, stirring until all the stock has absorbed. This will take about 15 minutes.
- Remove from the heat and stir in the lobster meat, Asiago and butter. Stir in basil and lemon juice and season with salt and white pepper.

To Make the Clams:

- Place the clams in a saucepan. Add the garlic, shallot, thyme and vermouth. Cover and bring to a simmer. Cook, covered, until the clams open. Swirl in the butter and parsley. Adjust the seasoning with salt and white pepper to taste.

Finish and Serve:

- Mound risotto in four shallow bowls or on four plates. Place five clams on each serving and drizzle with some of the liquid from the pot. Garnish each serving with a basil sprig and serve.

CHEF'S TIP:

- If you are using fresh lobster for this recipe and find some green lobster roe in the body of the lobster, save it: You can mash it together with the butter used to finish the risotto; it will turn a beautiful red color when cooked.

Sea Scallop Rossini with English Pea Purée

Chef Richard Rosendale, CC
Serves 4

Crouton:
4 2-inch rounds white bread cut from 1/8-inch-thick slices
Olive oil as needed

Spinach:
1 teaspoon unsalted butter
1 tablespoon minced shallot
1 handful fresh spinach leaves

Pea Purée:
1/2 cup fresh peas
1/2 cup chicken stock
2 tablespoons heavy cream
1 cup pea tendrils or spinach
Unsalted butter to taste
Salt and white pepper to taste

Sea Scallops:
4 sea scallops
Olive oil to taste
Salt and pepper to taste
Juice of 1 lemon

Foie Gras:
1/4 pound foie gras, cut into 4 slices

Finish and Serve:
4 slices black truffle
4 chervil sprigs

To Make the Crouton:

- Brush the bread rounds with olive oil and toast in a 300 degree F. oven until golden brown. Set aside.

To Make the Spinach:

- In a sauté pan over medium heat, cook the shallots in butter until translucent and add the spinach. Cook until just wilted and vibrant green. Season with the salt and white pepper.

To Make the Pea Purée:

- In a medium saucepan, combine the peas, stock and cream. Bring to a simmer and cook until the peas are tender. Let the peas cool for about 5 minutes and place with their cooking liquid in a blender along with the fresh spinach. Blend until silky smooth. Blend in the butter and adjust the seasoning with salt and white pepper. Keep the pea purée warm.

To Make the Scallops:

- Rinse the scallops and remove the side muscle and discard. Sear the scallops in a hot sauté pan with a little olive oil until a nice brown crust is achieved, 1 to 2 minutes on each side. Season with salt and pepper on both sides and squeeze the lemon juice over them.

To Make the Foie Gras:

- Heat another sauté pan over high heat. When hot, add the foie gras to the pan without adding any fat or oil. Cook 1 minute per side. It will be very soft when cooked and nicely browned.

Finish and Serve:

- Place a spoonful of the pea purée on each of four plates. Top purée with toasted bread round. Set a scallop on each crouton and a slice of foie gras on each scallop. Garnish each with a slice of truffle and a sprig of chervil and serve.

CHEF'S TIP:

- You can use a small hand blender to purée the peas instead of a large blender. Or just double the amount for the purée to make it simpler to prepare in a standard blender.

Black Angus Beef Tartar with Toasted Brioche and Fried Quail Egg

Chef Richard Rosendale, CC
Serves 4

Beef:
1/2 pound Angus beef filet
1 large egg yolk
1/2 tablespoon chopped gherkins
1/2 tablespoon chopped capers
1 teaspoon chopped red onion
1/2 tablespoon chopped parsley
Splash Tabasco
Splash Worcestershire sauce
Splash brandy
Salt and freshly cracked pepper to taste

Brioche:
4 slices brioche bread (1/4-inch thick)
1 tablespoon unsalted butter

Finish and Serve:
4 quail eggs
Olive oil as needed
1 head frisée
5 slices bresaola or prosciutto, cut into thin strips
1/4 cup extra-virgin olive oil
Juice of 1 lemon

To Make the Beef:

- With a sharp knife, chop the beef very finely. Mix in the egg yolk. Mix in gherkins, capers, red onion and parsley. Season with the Tabasco, Worcestershire, brandy and salt and pepper to taste. Set aside.

To Make the Brioche:

- Heat the butter in a large skillet over medium-high heat. Fry the brioche until golden brown on both sides.

Finish and Serve:

- Using ring molds, form the tartar into four equal cylinders and place one on each of the brioche slices, or simply place in a mound on the brioche.
- Fry the quail eggs in a little olive oil and place one on top of each tartar. Toss the frisée, bresaola, olive oil and a squeeze of lemon juice in a bowl. Adjust the seasoning with salt and pepper. Place a pile of the frisée and bresaola salad next to each of the tartars and serve.

CHEF'S TIP:

- The quail egg can be omitted, but it's certainly a nice touch.

Crab and Spinach Dip

Chef Kim Lex

Makes 2 cups

Crab and Spinach:

1 tablespoon olive oil
1 clove garlic, thinly sliced
4 scallions, thinly sliced
8 ounces crabmeat
1 cup white wine
1/2 cup sour cream
4 ounces Boursin cheese
Juice of half a lemon
2 cups spinach leaves, rinsed and dried
1/2 teaspoon kosher salt
1/4 teaspoon freshly ground pepper

Finish and Serve:

Bread bowl or crackers for serving

To Make the Crab and Spinach:

- In a large skillet over medium-low heat, combine the oil, garlic and all but 1 tablespoon of the scallion. Cook, stirring, until the vegetables are softened, about 2 minutes. Add the crabmeat and sauté for 1 minute. Pour in wine and cook until evaporated.
- Stir in the sour cream, cheese and lemon juice and cook until cheese is melted. Add the spinach; cover, reduce heat to low, and cook until the spinach is just wilted. Stir in salt and pepper and mix well.

Finish and Serve:

- Serve hot with bread or crackers.

CHEF'S TIP:

- Chef Lex likes to serve this dish in a bread bowl. Cut the top off of a bread round, remove the bread inside and fill with crab and spinach dip.

When the youth team completes its hot-food entry, Kim Lex will perform a task in the culinary studio by picking a skill out of a hat. Her assignment: to sauté a fish perfectly.

Brine-Cured Pork Kabobs with Jalapeños and Pineapple

Chef Kim Lex

Serves 8

Spicy Molasses Glaze:

2 tablespoons dark molasses
3 cloves garlic, minced
2 Serrano chiles or jalapeños, seeded and minced
1-inch piece fresh ginger, peeled and grated
1/2 teaspoon crushed red pepper flakes
3/4 cup extra-virgin olive oil
Salt and pepper to taste

Pork Kabobs:

6 cups cold water
1/4 cup sugar
3 tablespoons kosher salt, plus more for seasoning
2 bay leaves
1 tablespoon whole black peppercorns
1 tablespoon whole allspice berries
3 cloves garlic, chopped
1 3/4 pounds pork loin, cut into 1 1/2-inch cubes
1/2 pineapple, peeled, cored and cut into 1 1/2-inch chunks
16 medium jalapeños, cut in half lengthwise, seeds scraped out and discarded
Freshly ground black pepper
2 tablespoons extra-virgin olive oil

To Make the Spicy Molasses Glaze:

- Whisk together the molasses, garlic, chiles, ginger, pepper flakes and oil in a small bowl. Season with salt and pepper to taste. Set aside.

To Make the Pork Kabobs:

- Combine the water, sugar, salt, bay leaves, peppercorns, allspice and garlic in a bowl. Add the pork, cover, and refrigerate for at least 4 hours or overnight. Drain.
- Thread pork onto 8 skewers, alternating with pineapple chunks and jalapeño halves. Brush with glaze and season with salt and pepper.
- Heat a grill to high heat. Grill skewers, brushing with more glaze and the olive oil, until the pork is cooked through but still juicy in the center, about 12 minutes. The pineapple and peppers should be soft and lightly charred.

Finish and Serve:

- Serve with more spicy molasses glaze on the side.

Maui Shrimp Cocktail

Chef Ed Leonard, CMC
Serves 4

Shrimp:

1 cup chicken broth
2 cans coconut milk
2 tablespoons peeled, sliced fresh ginger
1/4 cup light soy sauce
1/2 cup pineapple chunks, with core and skin still on
1 stalk celery, chopped
16 jumbo shrimp, peeled and deveined

Finish and Serve:

4 dehydrated pineapple disks (optional)
Coconut Cocktail Sauce (see recipe below)

To Make the Shrimp:

- In a saucepan, combine broth, coconut milk, ginger, soy sauce, pineapple, and celery. Bring to a boil, adjust heat and simmer 15 minutes. Add shrimp. Remove pan from the heat when liquid comes back to a boil. Remove shrimp from liquid and place in a dish. Cool at room temperature for 10 minutes, then refrigerate until chilled.

Finish and Serve:

- Serve chilled shrimp with coconut cocktail sauce (see recipe below), and garnish with a dehydrated pineapple disk (optional).

CHEF'S TIP:

- Strain this cooking liquid and refrigerate or freeze to use again for cooking shrimp, or as a marinade for seafood.
- Chef Leonard likes to garnish this dish with a dehydrated pineapple disk.

Coconut Cocktail Sauce

Chef Ed Leonard, CMC
Makes 2 cups

Cocktail Sauce:

1/2 cup chili sauce
3/4 cup Heinz Ketchup
Juice of 1 lime
2 tablespoons Frank's Red Hot or other hot sauce
2 tablespoons sesame oil
1/4 cup prepared horseradish
4 tablespoons shredded coconut
1/2 cup cream of coconut
1/4 cup soy sauce
1/2 cup minced sweet pineapple
1 tablespoon finely chopped parsley
1 tablespoon finely chopped sage leaves

To Make the Cocktail Sauce:

- Mix all ingredients together and chill. Serve with Maui shrimp cocktail.

Tomato Tart Tartin

Chef Ed Leonard, CMC
Serves 4

Melted Onions:
1 tablespoon olive oil
1 tablespoon unsalted butter
8 ounces thinly sliced onions
1 tablespoon brown sugar
5 tablespoons red wine
1 teaspoon minced tarragon
Salt and pepper to taste

Pesto Sauce:
6 to 8 ounces fresh basil leaves
1 clove garlic
1 teaspoon lightly toasted pine nuts
2 teaspoons grated Parmesan cheese
1/2 cup extra-virgin olive oil

Tomatoes:
8 large plum tomatoes, peeled and quartered
1/2 cup extra-virgin olive oil
2 tablespoons sugar
Kosher salt and ground black pepper to taste

Tart Pans:
Softened butter
1 tablespoon sugar
1 teaspoon kosher salt

Pastry:
Four 4-inch circles puff pastry
1 teaspoon beaten egg
1 teaspoon vegetable oil

Cheese Mousse:
2 tablespoons extra-virgin olive oil
6 ounces fresh goat cheese, at room temperature
6 ounces fresh Ricotta cheese
1 large egg white
2 tablespoons heavy cream
1 tablespoon honey
3 tablespoons pesto sauce

To Make the Melted Onions:
- Heat olive oil and butter in a skillet set over medium heat. Add onions and sauté until soft, about 5 minutes. Add brown sugar and cook until onions are nicely browned, about 10 minutes.
- Add wine to pan and cook until liquid is almost evaporated. Stir in tarragon, season to taste with salt and pepper and set aside.

To Make the Pesto Sauce:
- Blanch basil leaves in boiling water. Drain and pat dry. Place in a food processor with the remaining ingredients and process until smooth. Set aside.

To Make the Tomatoes:
- Toss tomatoes with olive oil and sugar. Season with salt and pepper and let sit for 5 minutes.

To Prepare the Tart Pans:
- Preheat oven to 260 degrees F. Have ready four 4-inch round tart pans with removable bottoms. Rub the bottoms of the pans with butter and sprinkle with sugar and salt. Layer eight tomato pieces into each tart.
- Bake the tarts until tender, 30 to 45 minutes. Set aside.

To Make the Pastry:
- Preheat oven to 400 degrees F. Place pastry circles on a parchment-lined sheet pan and refrigerate for 20 minutes.
- Remove pastry from refrigerator and pierce all over with a fork. In a cup, whisk together egg and oil. Using a pastry brush, brush pastry circles with the egg and bake until lightly browned. Set aside.

To Make the Cheese Mousse:
- Combine all ingredients and mix well.

Finish and Serve:
- Preheat oven to 360 degrees F. Spread cheese mousse over tomatoes in the tart pans. Top cheese with onions. Bake until warmed, 6 to 8 minutes. Invert each tart pan onto the center of a dinner plate. Garnish with more pesto and serve.

CHEF'S TIP:
- Garnish these tarts with some dressed mixed baby greens or frisée salad for an extra touch.

Open Scallop and Crab Ravioli with Citrus Butter Sauce

Chef James Decker
Serves 4

Scallop and Crab Ravioli:

1 1/4 cups flour, plus extra for kneading the dough and dusting the scallops
1 medium egg
1/2 teaspoon salt
1 teaspoon vegetable oil
2 tablespoons unsalted butter
1/4 cup finely chopped shallot
1/2 teaspoon minced garlic
12 large scallops, each sliced into three disks
12 pieces jumbo lump crabmeat
Zest and juice of one lemon
Zest and juice of one lime
2 tablespoons white wine
1 tablespoon finely diced parsley
Salt and pepper to taste

Finish and Serve:

1 tomato, peeled, seeded and diced
Dill sprigs for garnish

BEVERAGE RECOMMENDATION

Santa Margarita Pinot Grigio

As sous chef to Team USA national, James Decker (r.) assists national-team member Russell Scott.

To Make the Ravioli:

- Place 1 1/4 cups of the flour in a food processor. Whisk together the egg, salt and vegetable oil. With the motor running, slowly add the wet ingredients to the flour. Process until the dough comes together in a ball and then process for 1 minute to knead the dough. Turn out on a floured surface and continue to knead by hand for one more minute.
- Feed the dough through a pasta machine until very thin---1/32 of an inch or less. Use a round 3-inch cutter and cut a total of 12 pasta rounds from the dough.
- Just before serving, cook the pasta rounds in generous amount of rapidly boiling salted water until done, about 2 minutes. Remove from water and let drain until needed.
- In a large sauté pan, melt the butter over medium heat. Add the shallot and garlic and sweat until translucent. Dredge scallops in flour and add to the pan. Cook the scallops until each side becomes lightly browned. Add the crab and heat for 30 seconds. Add the zests and juices, wine and parsley. Simmer 30 seconds more. Season with salt and pepper to taste

Finish and Serve:

- Place a pasta round on the bottom of a dinner plate or shallow soup bowl. Lay three slices of scallop and one piece of crab on top of the pasta. Spoon on a small amount of the sauce. Next, add another layer of pasta, 3 more scallops and another piece of crab. Top with a bit more sauce. Cover with a final pasta round and garnish with diced tomato and fresh dill. Repeat to make three more servings.

Shrimp Tempura Roll

Chef James Decker
Serves 4

Shrimp Tempura Roll:

1/2 cup sushi rice
1/2 cup water
1 tablespoon rice wine vinegar
1/2 teaspoon salt
1 teaspoon sugar
1 egg
1 cup ice water
1 cup all-purpose flour, plus more for dredging the shrimp
4 cups vegetable oil
4 large shrimp, peeled (leave the tail section on) and deveined
2 soy paper wrappers, cut in half diagonally to form triangles
1 avocado, pitted, peeled and cut into 1/4-inch-wide strips
4 ounces cream cheese, cut into 4 strips each a 1/4 inch wide and 2 inches long
4 teaspoons tobiko (flying fish roe)
1 teaspoon wasabi powder, mixed with a small amount of water to form a paste, plus more for serving

Finish and Serve:

Pickled ginger for serving
Soy sauce for serving

BEVERAGE RECOMMENDATION

Asahi Super Dry (Japanese beer)

To Make the Shrimp Tempura Roll:

- Put the rice in a strainer and rinse under running water until the water runs clear, about 3 minutes. Place the rice in a colander and drain for 15 minutes. Combine rice and water in a medium pot with a thick bottom. Cook the rice, covered, for approximately 5 minutes on high heat; lower the heat to medium and cook 10 minutes. Do not remove the cover of the rice or stir during the cooking.
- When done there should be no liquid in the pan and the rice should have some bite but no crunch. Let sit covered for 10 minutes. Transfer the rice to a bowl and cool 5 minutes. Stir together the vinegar, salt and sugar. Fold the vinegar mixture into the rice and adjust seasoning as necessary.
- Beat egg in a bowl. Whisk in ice water and then the 1 cup of flour. Whisk the batter briefly and set aside. Heat oil in a medium, heavy bottom saucepan to 350 degrees F. Skewer the shrimp on bamboo skewers up the center of the tail so that they cook straight. Dip the shrimp in a little flour and then into the batter. Shake off any extra batter and fry shrimp until golden brown. Remove from oil and place on paper towels to drain.
- Place a piece of the soy paper on a bamboo rolling mat and spread 1/4 inch of rice over the bottom three-quarters of the triangle. Remove the skewers from the shrimp and place a shrimp in the center of the rice with the tail pointing up to the tip of the soy paper that has no rice on it. Place some avocado, one cream cheese strip, 1 teaspoon tobiko and 1/4 teaspoon wasabi next to the shrimp. Using the mat as a guide, roll the soy paper around the rice and other ingredients to form a roll about 1 1/2 inches across. Repeat with the remaining ingredients.

Finish and Serve:

- Slice each roll into 4 pieces and serve with pickled ginger, soy sauce and wasabi.

CHEF'S TIP:

- All of the special ingredients and equipment called for in this recipe can be found at some Asian specialty grocery stores or at Sushi Foods Company in San Diego, (888) 817-8744 and online at www.sushifoods.com.

Herb Grilled Shrimp, Curry Spiced Apples and Sweet-and-Spicy Orange Dressing

Chef Joachim Buchner, CMC

Serves 4

Herb Grilled Shrimp:

2 tablespoons chopped shallots
Juice of 2 lemons
1/2 teaspoon chopped garlic
1/4 teaspoon chopped thyme
1/4 teaspoon chopped marjoram
2 tablespoons chopped parsley
1/4 cup olive oil
Kosher salt and freshly ground pepper to taste
12 large or jumbo shrimp, peeled and deveined

Curry Grilled Apples:

2 Granny Smith apples
1/3 cup vegetable oil
1 tablespoon curry powder

Sweet-and-Spicy Orange Vinaigrette:

2 shallots, cut in quarters
1 clove garlic
1 jalapeño, halved and seeds removed and discarded
2 tablespoons freshly squeezed orange juice
2 tablespoons frozen orange juice concentrate
1 teaspoon grated orange zest
2 tablespoons cider vinegar
1/4 cup olive oil

Mixed Lettuce Salad:

8 ounces seasonal mixed baby lettuce, well rinsed and spun dry
2 oranges, peeled (all white pith removed)
Salt, ground white pepper, and cayenne to taste

To Make the Herb Grilled Shrimp:

- In large glass or ceramic mixing bowl, combine shallots, lemon juice and garlic. Mix well using a rubber spatula, pressing down to crush the garlic and the shallots. Add thyme, marjoram, parsley and olive oil and combine. Season with salt and pepper and add shrimp. Let shrimp marinate for several hours.
- Preheat a charcoal or gas grill until very hot. Remove shrimp from marinade and let drain. Grill the shrimp, basting with the marinade, until just cooked through, about 2 minutes per side. Remove shrimp from grill and keep warm.

To Make the Curry Grilled Apples:

- Peel apples, cut them in half and core. Slice each apple half into 7 slices and discard the two end pieces of each half. You should have 20 slices in total.
- Preheat a charcoal or gas grill until very hot. In a mixing bowl, combine vegetable oil and curry and stir well. Brush apple pieces with curry oil and grill 20 seconds on each side. Keep warm.

To Make the Sweet-and-Spicy Orange Vinaigrette:

- In a blender, combine shallots, garlic, jalapeño, orange juice, concentrated orange juice, orange zest and cider vinegar. Blend at medium speed until puréed. Turn speed to low and, with the motor running, drizzle in the olive oil.
- Transfer to a mixing bowl and stir in salt, pepper and cayenne. Refrigerate until needed.

To Make the Mixed Lettuce Salad:

- In a large bowl, toss greens with enough of the Sweet-and-Spicy Orange Vinaigrette to lightly coat. Cover and set aside.
- Using a paring knife, cut just between the membrane of each orange section to release the segment. Set aside.

Finish and Serve:

- Fan out three to five pieces of the grilled apple on each of four plates. Set shrimp next to the apples and garnish with baby lettuce and orange segments. Drizzle some of the vinaigrette over shrimp and apples and serve.

CHEF'S TIP:

- This is one of Chef Buchner's favorite starters, combining sweet, tangy and spicy flavors. It works well in summer and in early fall.

BEVERAGE RECOMMENDATION

Livio Felluga "Terra Alte," Fruili 2000

Baked Chanterelles with Parmesan Cheese

Chef Joachim Buchner, CMC
Serves 4

Chanterelles:

3 cups chanterelle mushrooms
3 tablespoons sunflower seed oil
3 tablespoons unsalted butter
3 tablespoons minced shallots
1/4 teaspoon minced garlic
Juice of 1 lemon
1/4 cup white wine
2 cups heavy cream
1 tablespoon sliced chives
1/4 teaspoon ChefNique Taste of Roma Spice Rub
1/2 tablespoon chopped chervil
Salt to taste
Ground white pepper to taste
2 tablespoons softened unsalted butter
1 cup grated Italian aged Parmesan

Finish and Serve:

12 slices baguette
4 tablespoons extra-virgin olive oil
Sea salt to taste

BEVERAGE RECOMMENDATION

Pighin Fruili, 2002 Pinot Grigio

To Make the Chanterelles:

- Clean and cut chanterelles into quarters or halves depending on size. In a large stainless-steel sauté pan, heat the sunflower oil over high heat until very hot. Add mushrooms and sauté. Add butter, shallots and garlic and cook for 2 minutes. Reduce heat and add lemon juice and wine. Simmer until all liquids have evaporated.
- Meanwhile, in a separate saucepan, simmer the cream over medium heat, stirring occasionally, until reduced to 1 cup.
- Preheat the oven to 375 degrees F. When the mushrooms are cooked, add the reduced cream to the pan. Add chives, spice rub and chervil. Season with salt and pepper. Butter small baking dishes with the softened butter and divide the mushroom mixture between them. Top with Parmesan cheese and bake until the cheese is melted and golden, about 15 minutes.

Finish and Serve:

- Toast the baguette, brush with olive oil, and sprinkle with sea salt. Serve alongside the baked mushrooms.

Sautéed Sea Scallops with Asparagus Tips and Wheat Berry Salad

Chef Joachim Buchner, CMC
Serves 4

Wheat Berry Salad:
4 tablespoons olive oil
1 tablespoon diced shallot
1 tablespoon sliced celery
1/2 cup cooked wheat berries
1 teaspoon chopped parsley
1 teaspoon finely sliced mint leaves
1 scallion, sliced
1 tomato, peeled and cut into small dice
Salt and pepper to taste
2 tablespoons lemon juice

Asparagus:
12 stalks medium-thick asparagus, trimmed to 5 inches long
1 tablespoon vegetable oil
1 teaspoon grated lemon zest
Salt and white pepper to taste
1 teaspoon finely sliced chives

Sea Scallops:
8 large sea scallops
Kosher salt
Freshly ground white pepper
1/4 cup olive oil
1 tablespoon lemon juice

Finish and Serve:
Extra-virgin olive oil for garnish
Chives for garnish

BEVERAGE RECOMMENDATION
Chalone Vineyards, Pinot Blanc, Monterey 2000

To Make the Wheat Berry Salad:

- Heat a 10-inch sauté pan over high heat. When very hot, add 2 tablespoons of the olive oil and reduce heat to medium. Add shallot and celery and cook until the vegetables are tender. Let cool.
- Transfer the shallot and celery into a large glass mixing bowl. Add cooked wheat berries, parsley, mint, scallion and diced tomato. Season with salt, pepper and lemon juice. Add the remaining 2 tablespoons olive oil. Let rest for 15 minutes and add more salt and pepper if needed. Set aside.

To Make the Asparagus:

- Bring a large pot filled with salted water to a boil. Cook the asparagus until tender, about 4 minutes.
- In a 10-inch sauté pan, warm oil over low heat. Add the lemon zest and the cooked asparagus. Season with salt and pepper and continue to cook gently for 2 more minutes. Add chives. Keep warm.

To Make the Sea Scallops:

- Pat scallops dry and season with salt and white pepper. Heat a 10-inch sauté pan over high heat until very hot. Add olive oil to the pan. Wait 15 seconds, then set the sea scallops into the hot oil. Reduce heat to medium and cook scallops on both sides until golden, approximately 2 minutes on each side.
- Remove scallops from pan and place on a warm plate. Brush lemon juice over scallops.

Finish and Serve:

- Arrange three asparagus stalks in the center of each of four plates. Drizzle with the lemon zest oil left in the pan. Spoon wheat berry salad next to the asparagus and set two sautéed scallops on top of the salad on each plate. Drizzle extra-virgin olive oil over the scallops, garnish with chives and serve.

Buttermilk Fried Chicken with Succotash and Mustard Pan Gravy

Chef Russell Scott, CMC
Serves 4

Mustard Pan Gravy:

1 1/2 pounds chicken bones
8 strips finely diced slab bacon
1/2 cup onions, chopped
1/4 cup leeks, chopped
1/4 cup carrot, chopped
1/4 cup celery, chopped
2 parsley stems
1 bay leaf
1/4 teaspoon cracked black peppercorns
1/4 teaspoon dried thyme
6 tablespoons all-purpose flour
3 cups chicken stock, hot
2 tablespoons whole-grain mustard
Salt and pepper to taste

Buttermilk Chicken:

1 3-pound chicken, cut into 8 pieces
2 cups buttermilk
1 tablespoon dried oregano
Salt to taste
2 teaspoons ground pepper
1/2 cup plus **2 tablespoons** Old Bay seasoning
2 cups all-purpose flour
Oil for deep frying

Succotash:

2 tablespoons unsalted butter
1/4 cup finely diced onion
1/4 cup finely diced red bell pepper
3/4 cup butternut squash, diced and blanched
3/4 cup fresh sweet corn kernels
3/4 cup blanched fava beans
Salt and pepper to taste
1 tablespoon chopped flat-leaf parsley

To Make the Mustard Pan Gravy:

- Roast chicken bones in a 325-degree F. oven until lightly browned.
- In a medium pot, cook bacon until crispy and fat is rendered. Remove bacon with a slotted spoon and set aside. Add the onion, leek, carrot and celery to the pot with the hot fat and cook until lightly browned. Add the parsley, bay leaf, peppercorns and thyme and continue to cook for a few more minutes.
- Sprinkle the flour over the vegetables and cook and stir for a few minutes. Add the hot stock and stir until smooth. Simmer for 20 to 30 minutes, strain, stir in mustard and adjust seasoning.

To Make the Chicken:

- Combine the chicken with the buttermilk, oregano, salt, pepper and the 2 tablespoons of the Old Bay. Mix well, cover, and marinate for 24 hours and up to two days but no more than three days.
- When ready to cook the chicken, heat a large pot of oil to 350 degrees F. and preheat oven to 350 degrees F. Combine the flour and the remaining 1/2 cup Old Bay. Mix well.
- Remove chicken from buttermilk and let excess drip off. Dredge the chicken in the flour mixture and let sit several minutes. Dredge the chicken in the flour again and then deep fry just until crisp and light golden brown. Transfer to a roasting rack set on a sheet pan and bake until chicken reaches an internal temperature of 160 degrees F., about 20 minutes.

To Make the Succotash:

- Melt butter in a medium skillet and cook onion and bell pepper until soft. Add squash, corn and fava beans and heat through. Season to taste with salt and pepper. Stir in parsley and serve.

Finish and Serve:

- Place 2 pieces of fried chicken on each plate; spoon succotash and Braised Swiss Chard onto plate and drizzle the plate with gravy.

CHEF'S TIP:

- Chef Scott serves this dish with braised swiss chard (see page 234).

Chicken French

Chef Dan Scannell, CMC
Serves 4

Chicken French:

1 cup all-purpose flour
2 teaspoons kosher salt
1 teaspoon freshly ground black pepper
4 boneless, skinless half chicken breasts, gently pounded
3 large eggs, lightly beaten
1/4 cup extra-virgin olive oil
1/4 cup white wine
1 tablespoon fresh lemon juice
2 tablespoons unsalted butter
2 tablespoons chopped assorted fresh herbs (parsley, chives, tarragon, thyme)

Finish and Serve:

2 tablespoons finely grated Parmigiano-Reggiano cheese

To Make the Chicken French:

- Preheat oven to 350 degrees F. and place a large sauté pan over medium heat. Combine flour, salt and pepper on a plate. Dredge the chicken in the flour mixture and then coat in the beaten eggs.
- Add the oil to the pan. When the oil is very hot, gently add the chicken and sauté, turning once, until chicken is lightly browned.
- Transfer chicken to an ovenproof pan and place in the oven. Bake until the chicken is cooked through (it should register 165 degrees F. on an instant-read thermometer), about 5 to 7 minutes.
- Return the pan you sautéed the chicken in to medium heat. Add wine and lemon juice. Cook, scraping up any browned bits from the bottom of the pan, and simmer until the liquid is reduced by half. Remove from the heat and swirl in the butter and herbs. Season to taste with salt and pepper if needed.

Finish and Serve:

- Pour sauce over cooked chicken breasts and sprinkle with cheese. Serve immediately.

CHEF'S TIP:

- This is a regional favorite in the Rochester area and at the Oak Hill Country Club.
- Chef Scannell likes to serve this dish with assorted sides such as orzo and broccoli rabe.

Roasted Chicken "Pot Pie" with Mashed Carrots and Parsnips

Chef Richard Rosendale, CC

Serves 4

Chickens:

2 young chickens or game hens, rinsed and patted dry

1/4 cup softened unsalted butter

Salt and pepper to taste

1 bunch fresh thyme

1 lemon, halved

Pie:

1 tablespoon unsalted butter

1/4 cup diced white onions

1/2 cup diced celery

1 cup sliced mushrooms

1/2 cup partially cooked fresh peas

1 tablespoon all-purpose flour

1 cup chicken stock

1/4 cup milk

1 teaspoon chopped fresh thyme

Salt and pepper to taste

4 3-inch baked pie shells

Carrots and Parsnips:

1 cup peeled carrots cut into 1/2-inch slices

1 cup peeled parsnips cut in 1/2-inch slices

1 1/2 cups heavy cream

1 tablespoon Pernod

Salt and pepper to taste

1 teaspoon unsalted butter

1 teaspoon chopped parsley

To Make the Chicken:

- Preheat oven to 400 degrees F. Rub chickens all over with the butter. Season the outside and inside of the birds with salt and pepper. Stuff half the thyme and half the lemon in each of the cavities. Roast until the juices run clear. Remove the thigh meat from the birds after they have rested and dice it. Reserve.

To Make the Pie:

- Melt the butter in a skillet over medium heat. Add the onions, celery and mushrooms and cook until tender. Stir in the peas and then the flour. Stir in the stock and milk. Let the filling simmer until thickened, about 10 minutes. Season with thyme and salt and pepper. Stir in the diced thigh meat from the chickens.
- Fill the pie shells with the hot filling.

To Make the Carrots and Parsnips:

- Place the carrots in salted water and bring to a boil. Cook until just tender.
- In a small saucepan, combine the parsnips, cream, Pernod and some salt. Simmer until the parsnips are tender. Once cooked, mash the carrots and parsnips together in a stainless-steel bowl and add some of the cream and the butter to adjust the consistency. Stir in parsley and salt and pepper to taste.

Finish and Serve:

- Carve breast meat off chickens. Serve each breast with a pie and some of the carrots and parsnips.

CHEF'S TIP:

- You can make one large pie instead of individual ones if you prefer.

Honey-Maple Breast of Duckling with Rosemary Polenta, Caramelized Pearl Onions, Port Wine Poached Pear, Sun-Dried Fruit Relish and Natural Duck Jus

Chef Craig Peterson

Serves 4

Duck:

2 tablespoons honey
1 tablespoon maple syrup
2 cups water
1 bouquet garni (thyme, garlic, leek, bay leaf, and parsley stems tied in cheesecloth)
1/8 teaspoon TCM (tinted curing mixture)
2 duck breasts, trimmed

Caramelized Pearl Onions:

1 tablespoon unsalted butter
12 pearl onions, peeled and blanched
1/4 cup chicken stock

Poached Pear:

2 cups port wine
2 cups sugar
1 Bosc pear, peeled, quartered, and cored

Rosemary Polenta:

1/2 cup milk
1 teaspoon chopped roasted garlic
1 tablespoon chopped leek
1 ounce cornmeal
1 ounce grated Parmesan cheese
1/8 teaspoon chopped rosemary
2 tablespoons unsalted butter

Duck Jus:

4 cups rich duck or veal stock
1 tablespoon chopped shallot
1 clove garlic, crushed
1 sprig of thyme
2 tablespoons port wine
2 tablespoons unsalted butter, cut into chunks
Salt and pepper to taste

To Make the Duck:

- Combine the honey, syrup, water, bouquet garni and TCM in a small saucepan and bring to a boil. Cool over an ice bath. When cold, submerge duck breasts in the mixture, cover and refrigerate overnight.
- Remove duck from marinate, blot dry and allow to air dry for 4-6 hours.
- Heat a heavy, medium skillet over medium heat. Add the duck, skin-side down, and cook until the fat of the skin is well rendered, pouring off excess fat as required. Turn and cook the other side until browned and the duck is medium-rare.
- Transfer duck to a cutting board. Let rest 10 minutes before slicing on the bias.

To Make the Caramelized Pearl Onions:

- In a small skillet over medium-low heat, melt the butter. Add the onions and cook, shaking the pan often, until the onions begin to brown and caramelize. Stir in chicken stock and cook until it is evaporated.

To Make the Poached Pear:

- In a small non-reactive saucepan, combine wine and sugar. Simmer until sugar is melted. Add pear, cover and poach on low heat until pear is fork tender. Cool pear in poaching liquid, cover and refrigerate.

To Make the Rosemary Polenta:

- In a small, heavy pot, bring milk, garlic and leek to a simmer. Slowly whisk in cornmeal. Cook, stirring, over low heat for 10 minutes. Sir in cheese and rosemary. Remove from heat and stir in butter. Keep warm.

To Make the Duck Jus:

- In a medium saucepan, combine stock, shallot, garlic and thyme and simmer until it is greatly reduced and syrupy.
- Stir in wine. Remove from heat and slowly whisk in butter one chunk at a time. Strain, discard the solids, and season jus with salt and pepper to taste.

Finish and Serve:

- Spoon the polenta in the center of each of four serving plates. Rest a poached pear resting to the side of it. Spoon the pearl onions to the opposite side of the pear, draping down the polenta. Allow the duck to rest for 10 minutes before slicing. Fan slices out over the lower center of the plates.
- Finish the plates with the chutney on top and sauce around the product.

CHEF'S TIP:

- Chef Peterson serves this with sun-dried fruit relish (see recipe page 233).
- TMC stands for tinted curing mixture, and is 94% salt, 6% potassium nitrite, and some red food coloring to turn it pink.

Grilled Chicken and Penne alla' Insalata

Chef Ed Leonard, CMC
Serves 4

Chicken:

3 tablespoons extra-virgin olive oil
Juice of 1 lime
2 teaspoons honey
1 teaspoon kosher salt
2 boneless, skinless chicken breasts, about 6 ounces each

Penne:

4 plum tomatoes, peeled, seeded and cut into quarters
16 pitted black olives
1 stalk peeled celery, sliced on the bias
1 red onion, sliced very thin
1/2 cup thin strips roasted red pepper
1 cup frisée lettuce
Juice of one lemon
1 cup plus 2 tablespoons highest-quality extra-virgin olive oil
6 tablespoons 25-year-old red wine vinegar
2 teaspoons minced basil leaves
1/2 teaspoon minced oregano leaves
Salt and pepper to taste
8 ounces baby penne pasta

Finish and Serve:

Shaved insalata ricotta slices

To Make the Chicken:

- Combine oil, lime juice, honey and salt. Add chicken, turn to coat and let sit 15 to 20 minutes.
- Preheat a gas or charcoal grill or a grill pan. Grill chicken until tender and just cooked through. Cool, then slice chicken on the bias. Reserve.

To Make the Penne:

- Gently toss together tomatoes, olives, celery, onion, peppers, frisée and lemon juice. Let stand 20 minutes at room temperature.
- Whisk together olive oil, vinegar, basil and oregano and season to taste with salt and pepper. Pour half of this dressing over tomato mixture and toss.
- Cook pasta in salted boiling water until al dente. Drain very well and immediately toss pasta with the remaining dressing. Toss with the tomato mixture.

Finish and Serve:

- Divide among four individual bowls. Lay chicken slices on top, spoon any remaining dressing over the chicken and garnish with shavings of ricotta insalata.

CHEF'S TIP:

- Ricotta insalata is a hard, dry cheese that is unlike fresh ricotta. It has a nice white color and a salty but sweet taste.

Smoked Quail Stuffed with Country Ham, Leeks and Quince

Chef Scott Fetty
Serves 4

Barbecue Sauce:

1/3 cup dark-brown sugar
1/4 cup cider vinegar
2 tablespoons Worcestershire sauce
1 tablespoon mustard
1 tablespoon chili powder
1/2 teaspoon ground cumin
1 teaspoon dried oregano
1/4 teaspoon cayenne pepper
1 1/2 teaspoons ground black pepper
1/4 teaspoon ground allspice
1/2 teaspoon ground ginger
1/4 cup yellow onion, diced small
1 quince, peeled, cored and diced small
2 tablespoons quince jelly
Salt to taste

Quails:

2 cups cold water
2 tablespoons brown sugar
2 tablespoons kosher salt
1 each cinnamon stick
1/4 teaspoon ground allspice
4 whole, boneless quail (request the butcher to bone the quails for you)
1 tablespoon unsalted butter
2 quince, peeled, cored and diced small (reserve the quince in lemon water to stop browning)
1 leek, white section only, cut into julienne strips
4 ounces Smithfield-style country ham, diced small
8 ounces ground pork
1 teaspoon minced sage
1 teaspoon minced thyme
Salt and cracked black pepper to taste
2/3 cup assorted fine hardwood smoking chips (such as mesquite, apple, pecan or hickory)

To Make the Barbecue Sauce:

- Combine all sauce ingredients in a medium saucepan. Place over low heat and simmer, uncovered, for 45 minutes, stirring occasionally.

To Make the Quails:

- Combine the cold water, brown sugar, kosher salt, cinnamon stick and allspice in a non-reactive pot and bring to a boil. Pour into a bowl large enough to hold the quails and cool. Refrigerate.
- Place quail in the cold brine and refrigerate for 2 hours. Dry the quail and refrigerate, uncovered, for 1 hour.
- Melt the butter in a large skillet over medium heat and add the quince, leek and ham. Cook, stirring, until the quince and leeks are soft. Cool this mixture for about 15 minutes. Combine the quince mixture with the ground pork, sage and thyme and blend well. Season with salt and pepper.
- Stuff the pork mixture into the cavities of the quails. Truss the quails with a thin band of aluminum foil.
- Place the wood chips in a stove-top smoker or a similar pan. Allow the chips to smolder over a low heat for 1 minute. Arrange the quail on a roasting rack and place in the smoking pan over the coals. Secure the lid and allow the quail to smoke for 5 minutes.
- Preheat oven to 350 degrees F. Transfer the quail to a roasting pan and place them in the oven. Roast the quail until they reach an internal temperature of 165 degrees F. Brush the quail with some of the barbecue sauce and keep warm.

Finish and Serve:

- Cut each quail in half, brush with more sauce, and drizzle some sauce around the plate.

CHEF'S TIP:

- This version of barbecue is delicious with quail, but could also be done with any type of game bird.
- Chef Fetty serves this dish with skillet cornbread (see page 232) and braised greens (see page 228). Other garnishes could include roasted corn, crisp sweet potatoes or a cabbage slaw.

Pan-Seared Duck Breast with Glazed Root Vegetables, Celery Root Purée and Orange Sauce

Chef Scott Campbell

Serves 4

Orange Sauce:

Zest of 3 large oranges
1/4 cup cold water
2 tablespoons sugar
3 tablespoons sherry vinegar
2/3 cup veal or duck stock
2 1/2 tablespoons unsalted butter, cut into chunks
Juice of 1/2 lemon

Celery Root Purée:

1 cup celery root, cut into large dice
2 large Idaho potatoes, cut into large dice
3/4 cup heavy cream, or as needed, heated
6 tablespoons unsalted butter, or as needed
Salt and white pepper to taste

Yellow Beets and Carrots:

1 large yellow beet, diced
1 large carrot, diced
1 tablespoon olive oil
2 tablespoons Rosemary Simple Syrup (see Chef's Tip)
Salt and pepper to taste
1 teaspoon chopped parsley

Duck:

1/2 cup sugar
1/2 cup kosher salt
4 cups water
4 duck breasts, skin scored deeply with a sharp knife
Salt and pepper to taste

Finish and Serve:

Orange segments

To Make the Orange Sauce:

- Place zest in small sauce pan. Add water and bring to a boil. Add sugar and cook until dissolved. Using a pastry brush dipped in clean water, wash down the sides of the pan to prevent crystallization.
- Add sherry vinegar and bring to a simmer and reduce. Add stock and reduce until thick and syrupy. Remove from heat and whisk in butter. Whisk in lemon juice. Keep warm.

To Make the Celery Root Purée:

- Place celery root in a large saucepan and cover by several inches with salted water. Bring to a boil and boil for 5 minutes. Add potatoes and boil until tender.
- Drain the vegetables and return them to the pan. Place over medium heat and cook, tossing the vegetables often, until all excess moisture is removed.
- Run potatoes and celery root through a ricer. Stir in heated cream and butter to the desired consistency. Season to taste with salt and pepper. Keep warm.

To Make the Yellow Beets and Carrots:

- Cook the beets and carrots in salted, boiling water until tender. Drain.
- Heat a sauté pan over medium heat. Add oil and cook vegetables until browned.
- Toss vegetables with syrup and parsley and season to taste with salt and pepper. Keep warm.

To Make the Duck:

- In a bowl, combine sugar, salt and water. Stir until crystals are dissolved. Add duck breasts, cover, and refrigerate for 2 hours.
- Remove duck from liquid and rinse. Pat dry. Season duck on both sides with salt and pepper. Place duck skin-side down in a cold cast-iron pan. Place pan over high heat. Cook until the duck breasts start to curl on the sides, then turn heat to low and let the fat fully render out of the skin.
- After skin is fully rendered and crisp, flip breasts and cook the other side until medium-rare, about 2 minutes. Let duck rest 5 minutes before slicing.

Finish and Serve:

- On a warm dinner plate place celery purée. Slice duck and lay slices in a half moon around the purée. Place beets and carrots in the center. Drizzle with orange sauce and garnish with orange segments.

CHEF'S TIP:

- To make rosemary simple syrup, bring 1 cup water and 1/2 cup sugar to a boil. Remove from heat, transfer to a container and add several sprig rosemary. Cool and refrigerate until ready to use.

Sweet Onion, Spinach and Feta Filled Chicken Breasts

Chef Joachim Buchner, CMC

Serves 4

Sweet Onions:

4 tablespoons olive oil

8 ounces sweet onion (Vidalia or Maui), thinly sliced

1/2 ounce sliced garlic (about 4 cloves)

1 teaspoon chopped oregano

1 teaspoon chopped parsley

1 pound spinach, well rinsed and dried

4 ounces feta cheese, diced

Salt and freshly ground black pepper to taste

Chicken Breasts:

4 7-ounce boneless, skinless chicken breasts

3 large eggs

1/2 cup milk

1 cup all-purpose flour

Salt and pepper to taste

1/2 cup vegetable oil

BEVERAGE RECOMMENDATION

Oliver Leflaive, Puligny, Montrachet, 2000

To Make the Sweet Onions:

- Heat a large sauté pan over high heat. Add the olive oil and onion and cook until onion is soft, about 3 minutes. Add garlic, oregano, parsley and spinach and continue to cook 1 more minute. Set aside and let cool.
- When cool, stir in feta cheese and season with salt and pepper.

To Make the Chicken Breasts:

- Rinse chicken breasts and pat them dry. Lay them on a cutting board. Season with salt and pepper. Divide the spinach and feta mixture over the four pieces, covering half of each breast. Fold the chicken breasts over. Refrigerate 20 minutes.
- Preheat oven to 350 degrees F. In a mixing bowl, whisk together eggs and milk. In another bowl, combine flour and salt and pepper to taste. Dredge each chicken breast in the seasoned flour, remove, shake off excess flour and dip in egg mixture. Dredge again in the flour and shake off excess.
- Heat a sauté pan over medium heat; add vegetable oil and the chicken breasts. Sauté on both sides for 5 minutes. Transfer to the oven and bake until chicken is cooked through, 8 to 10 minutes.

Finish and Serve:

- Remove from pan and serve.

CHEF'S TIP:

- This succulent chicken breast is filled with the bright flavors of sweet onion and feta cheese. Serve it with herb sautéed fingerling potatoes and olive oil poached plum tomatoes.

Espresso Rubbed Venison Tenderloin with White Corn Pudding

Chef Jamie P. Keating, CCC

Serves 4

Corn Pudding:

1 1/2 cups white sweet corn kernels
1 large egg
2 large egg yolks
1/3 cup heavy cream
1 tablespoon all-purpose flour
1 teaspoon kosher salt
1/2 teaspoon sugar
Cayenne pepper to taste
1 teaspoon finely chopped parsley
1 dash Tabasco sauce

Vegetables:

1 teaspoon unsalted butter
1 clove garlic, crushed
1 teaspoon extra-virgin olive oil
2 parsnips, peeled and cut into julienne strips
1 medium butternut squash, peeled and cut into julienne strips
Salt and pepper to taste
1/4 teaspoon nutmeg
1 teaspoon finely chopped rosemary

Venison:

1/4 cup freshly ground espresso
Kosher salt and cracked black pepper to taste
2 12-ounce venison tenderloins
2 tablespoons olive oil, plus more for tossing the tomatoes

Sauce:

1 teaspoon chopped shallot
1 teaspoon chopped garlic
1/4 cup Madeira wine
1 1/4 cups heavy cream
Kosher salt to taste

Finish and Serve:

1 cup currant tomatoes, halved

BEVERAGE RECOMMENDATION

Stoltman, Limestone Cuvee, California, 2001

To Make the Corn Pudding:

- Preheat oven to 350 degrees F. Butter four 6-ounce foil soufflé cups or ramekins. Combine the corn, egg, yolks and cream in food processor and pulse together. Add flour, salt, sugar and cayenne and blend for 10 seconds. Scrape into a bowl and stir in parsley and Tabasco.
- Fill cups with the corn mixture and cover each with foil. Set cups in a deep roasting pan. Add hot water to the pan to come half way up the sides of the cups. Bake for 30 minutes. Remove foil and bake until golden on top, about 5 more minutes.

To Make the Vegetables:

- In a medium skillet over medium heat, melt the butter and add the garlic and oil. Cook until the butter browns slightly and then add parsnips and squash. Cook until vegetables soften. Season with salt, pepper, nutmeg and rosemary. Set aside.

To Make the Venison:

- Combine espresso and salt and pepper. Roll the tenderloins in the mixture. Refrigerate until needed.
- Preheat oven to 350 degrees F. In large skillet set over medium heat, heat the olive oil. Add the tenderloins and brown on all sides. Transfer to a sheet pan, place in the oven, and roast to desired doneness, about 12 to 15 minutes for medium-rare. Remove from oven and allow tenderloins to rest at room temperature for 5 minutes before slicing.

To Make the Sauce:

- Place the same skillet the venison cooked in over medium heat. Add the shallot and garlic and cook until softened. Add the Madeira and cook until reduced by half. Add the cream and reduce by half again. Season with kosher salt. Froth sauce with a hand blender.

Finish and Serve:

- In a small bowl, toss currant tomatoes with just enough olive oil to coat and season lightly with salt. Set aside.
- Remove corn puddings from cups and cut each corn pudding in half. Place one half on each of four plates. Lean the other halves against each of the first halves. Slice the tenderloins on the bias. Divide between the plates, fanning around one side of the plate. Place a scoop of vegetables on the other side. Spoon sauce onto plate, spoon some tomatoes over corn pudding and serve.

CHEF'S TIP:

- Feel free to substitute pork tenderloin for the venison in this recipe.

Pecan Roast Bison Hanger Steak with Red Wine Reduction and Peruvian Mashed Potatoes

Chef Kevin Zink, CCC
Serves 4

Tomatoes and Asparagus:

1/4 cup salt
6 cups water
8 large asparagus spears, cut to about 3 1/2 inches and stems peeled
2 tablespoons olive oil
1 teaspoon chopped chives
1 teaspoon chopped parsley
1 teaspoon chopped thyme
2 teaspoons minced shallot
Sea salt and pepper to taste
4 1/2-inch slices tomato

Red Wine Reduction:

1/4 cup bison or beef trimmings
2 shallots, thinly sliced
3 cups red wine, preferably Bordeaux
2 sprigs thyme
2 cups rich veal stock
1 tablespoon white truffle oil
Unsalted butter to taste
Sea salt and freshly cracked pepper to taste

Hanger Steak:

4 5-ounce bison hanger steak portions
Sea salt and freshly cracked pepper to taste
4 slices apple-smoked bacon
1 tablespoon vegetable oil

Peruvian Mashed Potatoes:

5 purple potatoes
3 tablespoons softened, unsalted butter
1/2 cup hot milk
Salt and pepper to taste

To Make the Tomatoes and Asparagus:

- Bring salt and water to a boil in a small saucepan. Cook asparagus for 2 minutes. Drain and immediately plunge the asparagus into ice water. Drain and pat dry.
- Whisk together the olive oil, herbs and shallot. Season to taste with salt and pepper. Pour marinade over tomato and asparagus.
- Heat a gas or charcoal grill or grill pan until very hot. Grill tomato and asparagus until browned. Serve immediately.

To Make the Red Wine Reduction:

- Heat a saucepan over medium-high heat. Add trimmings and cook until browned. (Use a few teaspoons of oil to brown the meat if your trimmings aren't very fatty.) Add shallot and cook until lightly browned. Add wine. Simmer until wine is reduced to about a cup. Add thyme and stock and simmer until reduced and syrupy. Strain.
- Just before serving, reheat. Remove from heat and swirl in truffle oil and butter to taste. Season to taste with salt and pepper.

To Make the Hanger Steak:

- In a charcoal grill, light pecan wood and burn down to white coals. Season steak with salt and pepper and cook slowly over fire until pecan flavor is imparted to meat, 10 to 15 minutes.
- Preheat oven to 375 degrees F. Transfer meat to a roasting pan fitted with a rack and top the meat with bacon. Roast until steaks are medium rare and register 130 degrees F. with an instant-read thermometer. Remove from oven and let rest 10 minutes.

To Make the Peruvian Potatoes:

- In 2-quart saucepan, combine potatoes and cold water to cover. Simmer until potatoes are tender. Drain, let dry and then peel while they are still hot. Once peeled and while still hot, force the potatoes through a tamis or ricer into a clean warm saucepan.
- Whisk in butter and milk and season to taste with salt and pepper. Transfer the potatoes to a piping bag fitted with a plain round tip.

Finish and Serve:

- Pipe out 5 inches of potatoes in the center of each of four dinner plates. Spoon sauce along the bottom and top of the plate. Remove bacon from meat and save for another use. (Julienne the bacon and add to greens if you like.) Cut each piece of steak into five slices and transfer to the plates.

CHEF'S TIP:

- Chef Zink serves this dish with glazed carrots (see page 228).
- Bison hanger steak is available from Rocky Mountain Natural Meats in Denver, Colorado, (800) 327-2706. You can also substitute beef hanger steak or flatiron (top blade) steak for the bison.

Yankee-Style Pork Pot Roast

Chef Russell Scott, CMC
Serves 4

Pot Roast:

6 tablespoons vegetable oil
3 pounds pork shoulder, rolled and tied
Salt and pepper
8 ounces mirepoix (mixed rough cut carrot and onions)
2 tablespoons tomato purée
2 tablespoons flour
1 quart veal stock
1 sachet (see Chef's Tip)
Salt and pepper to taste

Vegetables:

8 Brussels sprouts, halved
1/4 cup finely diced carrot
1/4 cup diced turnips or celeriac
12 peeled pearl onions
12 mushrooms

Finish and Serve:

3 tablespoons unsalted butter
Salt and pepper to taste

To Make the Pot Roast:

- In large pot, heat oil over high heat. Season meat with salt and pepper and sear on all sides. Remove from pot and set aside. Add mirepoix to pot and cook until golden brown. Add the tomato purée and continue to cook for 5 minutes.
- Add the flour and cook 3-4 minutes. Add the stock and mix well. Bring to a boil and skim off and discard any foam that collects on the surface of the liquid.
- Transfer stock to a large braising pot with a tight fitting lid; place the meat into the liquid. Bring to a boil on the stovetop, skim again, and add the sachet. Cover, place in a 300 degree F. oven and cook until very tender, turning the meat every 15 minutes, 1 1/2 to 2 hours.
- Remove the meat from sauce and keep warm. Strain the sauce, season to taste with salt and pepper.

To Make the Vegetables:

- Cook the Brussels sprouts, turnips, onions and mushrooms separately in salted boiling water until just tender. Immediately plunge the vegetables into ice water to stop the cooking. Drain the vegetables and pat dry. Set aside or refrigerate until ready to serve.

Finish and Serve:

- In a sauté pan, melt the butter over medium heat. Add the cooked vegetables, season with salt and pepper, and cook gently until heated through.
- Slice the meat and top with sauce. Garnish with the vegetables and serve.

CHEF'S TIP:

- Chef Scott serves this pot roast with mac and cheese (see page 231).
- Chef Scott makes his sachets by tying 2 chopped parsley stems, 1 bay leaf, 1/4 teaspoon cracked black peppercorns, and a 1/4 teaspoon dried thyme loosely in a piece of cheesecloth.

Veal Chops with Grilled Belgian Endive and Polenta Fries

Chef Dan Scannell, CMC
Serves 4

Veal Chops:

4 10-ounce bone-in veal chops
4 tablespoons melted, unsalted butter
2 tablespoons ChefNique Steak Seasoning Spice

Polenta Fries:

4 1/2 cups water
2 teaspoons kosher salt, plus more for sprinkling on the fries
4 tablespoons unsalted butter
1 cup yellow cornmeal
1/2 cup grated Parmigiano-Reggiano cheese, plus more for sprinkling on the fries
2 cups flour
2 cups vegetable oil

Grilled Belgian Endive:

2 Belgian endive, split in half, core removed and discarded
2 tablespoons extra-virgin olive oil
2 teaspoons kosher salt
1 teaspoon black pepper
2 teaspoons fresh lemon juice

Mushroom Sauce:

2 tablespoons melted butter
2 teaspoons minced shallot
1 cup sliced mushrooms
1/4 cup quality brandy
1 cup demi-glace
1/2 teaspoon salt
1/2 teaspoon ground black pepper
1 teaspoon truffle oil
1 tablespoon unsalted butter
1 teaspoon chopped parsley
1 teaspoon chopped sage
1 teaspoon chopped tarragon

To Make the Veal Chops:

- Preheat the over to 350 degrees F. and place a large cast-iron skillet over medium heat. Brush the veal chops with melted butter and sprinkle with seasoning spice.
- When the skillet is very hot, sear chops until well browned on one side. Turn chops and continue to sear for about 5 minutes more. Transfer the skillet to the oven and cook until the chops reach the desired doneness, about 10 minutes for medium.

To Make the Polenta Fries:

- In a 2-quart stainless-steel saucepan, bring water and salt to a rolling boil. Add 2 tablespoons of the butter. Whisking constantly, very slowly whisk the cornmeal into the water.
- Once all the cornmeal has been incorporated, lower the heat to low and switch to a wooden spoon. Continue to cook, stirring, for 10 minutes. Remove from heat and stir in the remaining 2 tablespoons butter and the cheese.
- Line a baking sheet with parchment paper. Spread the polenta evenly over the parchment. Cover with plastic wrap and refrigerate for 2 hours.
- Using a sharp knife, cut the polenta into strips the size of French fries and gently flour the polenta. Heat oil to 350 degrees F. Working in batches, fry polenta until golden and crisp. Drain the fries, sprinkle with a little salt and grated parmesan cheese and serve hot. They are a wonderful garnish for all types of grilled or roasted meats.

To Make the Grilled Belgian Endive:

- Preheat a grill or broiler. Brush endive with oil and sprinkle with salt and pepper. Grill or broil until charred and cooked through. Sprinkle with lemon juice.

To Make the Mushroom Sauce:

- Heat the butter in a small skillet. Gently sauté the shallots and mushrooms for 2 minutes. Deglaze pan with brandy and reduce by half. Add demi-glaze and simmer for 2 minutes over medium heat. Season with salt and pepper.
- Gently swirl in the truffle oil and unsalted butter and finish the sauce with chopped fresh herbs.

Finish and Serve:

- Place a veal chop on a plate, drizzle with mushroom sauce and surround with polenta fries and a grilled endive half and serve.

CHEF'S TIP:

- Chef Scannell likes to serve this dish with bacon-wrapped green beans.

Braised Oxtails with Boursin Polenta

Chef Richard Rosendale, CC
Serves 4

Oxtails:

1/4 cup olive oil
5 pounds oxtails, cut by your butcher into 8 sections
1/4 cup diced carrot
1/4 diced celery
1/2 cup diced onion
Salt and pepper to taste
1 clove minced garlic
1/2 tablespoon tomato purée
1 1/2 cups merlot wine
1 tablespoon all-purpose flour
8 cups beef stock (preferably homemade)
1 sprig rosemary
2 sprigs parsley
2 bay leaves

Polenta:

1 cup chicken stock
1 cup milk
1 teaspoon chopped thyme
1 tablespoon grated Parmesan cheese
1 teaspoon salt
Pinch black pepper
1/2 cup cornmeal
1/2 wheel Boursin cheese

To Make the Oxtails:

- Preheat the oven to 350 degrees F. In a large pot over high heat, heat the olive oil. Brown the oxtails on all sides and remove from the pot. Add the carrot, celery and onion. Season with salt and pepper to taste. Cook until the vegetables are well browned, about 5 minutes. Add the garlic and cook for 2 more minutes.
- Add the tomato purée and stir until evenly distributed. In two additions, add the merlot, reducing the liquid by half both times. Sprinkle the flour over the pot. Add back the oxtails, along with the stock, rosemary, parsley and bay leaves. Bring to a simmer, cover, and place in the oven. Bake for 3 to 3 1/2 hours, skimming foam and oil off the top of the liquid every hour.
- Strain the braising liquid from the pan and season it with salt and pepper if necessary. (This will become the sauce.)

To Make the Polenta:

- Bring the stock, milk, thyme, Parmesan, salt and pepper to a simmer. Slowly whisk in the cornmeal. Simmer for 20 minutes on low heat, stirring frequently. Remove from the heat and stir in the Boursin cheese.

Finish and Serve:

- Spoon polenta on four plates and top with 2 pieces of oxtail. Drizzle some of the braising liquid over the oxtails, garnish with vegetables and serve.

CHEF'S TIP:

- Chef Rosendale serves this with fresh buttered vegetables like root vegetables or asparagus.

Pan-Roasted Veal Chop with Celeriac, Madeira and Wild Mushroom Cream Sauce

Chef Richard Rosendale, CC
Serves 4

Celery Root:

2 pounds celery root, peeled and cut into 1-inch cubes
2 cups heavy cream
2 cups chicken stock
1 tablespoon salt, plus more to taste
2 tablespoons unsalted butter
Pepper to taste

Veal:

4 6-ounce center-cut veal chops
Olive oil
2 sprigs rosemary, leaves chopped
Ground black pepper

Sauce:

1/2 pound assorted wild mushrooms, diced
1 small shallot, minced
1/2 cup Madeira
2 1/2 cups veal or chicken stock
1 cup heavy cream

Salad:

2 cups leaves from celery hearts
1 cup chervil leaves or other mild herb
Juice of 1 lemon
1 tablespoon olive oil
4 slices cooked, chopped pancetta
Salt and black pepper to taste

To Make the Celery Root:

- Rinse the celery root well under cold running water and place in a medium sauce pot with the cream, chicken stock and 1 tablespoon salt. Simmer until the celery root is tender. Strain and place in a food processor. Add 1/4 cup of the cooking liquid and process until smooth. Add the butter and adjust the seasoning with salt and pepper. Keep warm until ready to serve.

To Make the Veal:

- Coat the veal chops with olive oil, rosemary and black pepper. Set aside until ready to cook.
- Heat a sauté pan over high heat. Add 2 tablespoons of the olive oil and the veal chops. Cook until the chops are medium rare. Let the veal chops rest while you make the sauce.

To Make the Sauce:

- In the same pan that you cooked the veal in, cook the diced mushrooms and shallot over medium heat until nicely browned. Add the Madeira and simmer until reduced by half. Add the stock and reduce by half again. Add the heavy cream and reduce until the sauce coats the back of a spoon.

To Make the Salad:

- Toss the celery leaves, chervil, olive oil, lemon juice and bacon together. Season with salt and pepper to taste.

Finish and Serve:

- Place a veal chop and some puree and sauce on each of four serving plates. Garnish with salad and serve.

Naples Braised Beef with Pasta

Chef Ed Leonard, CMC
Serves 4

Beef and Pasta:

6 tablespoons olive oil
1 1/2 pounds diced boneless beef chuck or beef shoulder cut into 1/2-inch dice
Kosher salt and pepper to taste
6 tablespoons unsalted butter
1 onion, chopped
1 large clove garlic, minced
2 tablespoons tomato paste
1/3 cup red wine
2 teaspoons ChefNique Naples seasoning
1 cup Italian-style diced tomatoes
3/4 cup tomato sauce
1/2 cup beef broth
4 ounces rigatoni, cooked a la dente
1/4 cup grated Reggiano-Parmigiano cheese
1/2 teaspoon red pepper flakes
2 tablespoons chopped parsley
2 tablespoons extra-virgin olive oil

Finish and Serve:

Kosher salt and pepper to taste
Grated Reggiano-Parmigiano cheese to taste

To Make the Beef and Pasta:

- In a heavy stainless-steel pan, heat 2 tablespoons of the olive oil over medium heat. Season beef with salt and pepper. Add a third of the beef to the pan and cook until well browned. Transfer browned beef to a plate, add 2 more tablespoons oil to the pan, and cook half the remaining beef. Repeat until all the beef is browned. Set beef aside.
- Preheat oven to 260 degrees F. Add 2 tablespoons of the butter to the pan the beef cooked in. Add onion and garlic and cook over medium heat for 2 minutes. Add tomato paste and cook, stirring, 2 more minutes. Add wine and simmer until almost evaporated.
- Stir in seasoning, tomatoes, tomato sauce and broth and bring to a boil. Return beef to the pan, stir, and cover with a tightly fitting lid. Place in oven and cook until meat is very tender, about 1 1/2 hours, stirring occasionally.
- Remove pan from oven and stir in pasta and cheese. Place on the stove top over low heat and cook for 5 minutes.
- Dice the remaining 4 tablespoons butter and stir it into the beef. Stir in red pepper flakes, parsley and extra-virgin olive oil.

Finish and Serve:

- Season to taste with salt and pepper and serve with more Parmigiano on the side.

Filet of Beef Roasted in Coffee Beans with Velvet Chile Sauce

Chef Ed Leonard, CMC
Serves 4

Velvet Chile Sauce:

2 tablespoons olive oil
1 tablespoon puréed, roasted garlic
1/2 cup finely diced onion
2/3 cup chopped Ancho chiles
2 tablespoons tomato paste
1/2 cup strong brewed coffee
1/2 chopped roasted red peppers
1/2 cup chicken stock, plus more for thinning the sauce if needed
1 tablespoon chili powder
2 tablespoons high-quality cocoa powder
1/2 cup veal demi-glace
2 tablespoons cold unsalted butter, diced
Salt to taste

Beef:

4 tablespoons grape seed oil
2 tablespoons unsalted butter
4 5-ounce center-cut filet mignon steaks
Salt and pepper to taste
1 cup high-quality ground coffee

To Make the Velvet Chile Sauce:

- In a medium saucepan, heat oil over medium heat. Add the garlic, onion and chiles and cook, stirring, until softened. Add the tomato paste and cook 2 minutes. Add the coffee, stir, and simmer 2 to 3 minutes. Add the peppers, chicken stock, chili powder and cocoa and simmer 30 to 40 minutes.
- Transfer the chili sauce to a blender and blend until smooth. Stir in demi-glace and butter. Season to taste with salt. Add more chicken sauce if the sauce is too thick. Keep warm.

To Make the Beef:

- Preheat oven to 350 degrees F. In a large stainless-steel sauté pan, heat the oil and butter over medium heat. Season steaks with salt and pepper and roll in coffee to coat. Place in skillet and cook, turning once, until nicely browned, 2 to 3 minutes per side. (Be careful not to brown them too much or the coffee will become bitter.)
- Transfer skillet to oven and cook until the steaks reach the desired doneness. Remove from oven and let steaks rest for 2 minutes.

Finish and Serve:

- Transfer the beef to serving plates, coat the steaks with the warm sauce and serve.

CHEF'S TIP:

- For a real treat, Chef Leonard recommends serving this dish with rice and beans.

Grilled Guinness Marinated Sirloin Steaks

Chef Ed Leonard, CMC
Serves 4

Steak:

1 cup Guinness stout
1 1/2 cups beef broth or stock
4 tablespoons extra-virgin olive oil
2 sprigs thyme
1 teaspoon Worcestershire sauce
3 tablespoons ChefNique Master Steak seasoning
1 bay leaf
4 cloves garlic
2 sliced shallots
4 10-ounce sirloin steaks, trimmed

Sauce:

1/2 cup demi-glace or beef gravy
8 tablespoons unsalted butter, cut into 4 pieces

To Make the Steak:

- Whisk together the stout, broth, olive oil, thyme, Worcestershire, steak seasoning, bay leaf, garlic and shallots in a deep dish. Add the steaks (they should be totally covered by the marinade). Cover and refrigerate 8 hours.
- Prepare a gas or charcoal grill or heat a grill pan. Remove steaks from marinade and pat dry. Grill to desired doneness.

To Make the Sauce:

- Pour marinade into a pot and bring to a boil, skimming off foam that rises to the surface. Reduce the marinade by half. Stir in demi-glace. Remove from heat and strain
- Whisk in butter one piece at a time until it is totally incorporated into the sauce.

Finish and Serve:

- Serve sauce along with the steaks.

CHEF'S TIP:

- Dry-aged or free-range beef is best for this tasty dish.
- Chef Leonard suggests serving this with roasted potatoes and glazed carrots.

Seared Calf's Liver with Soft Polenta and Roasted Figs

Chef Ed Leonard, CMC
Serves 4

Polenta:
1 cup milk
1 1/4 cups chicken broth
4 tablespoons extra-virgin olive oil
10 tablespoons cold unsalted butter
1 teaspoon chopped sage
1 teaspoon kosher salt
2 tablespoons honey
1 cup polenta
1/4 cup grated Parmigiano-Reggiano cheese
Heavy cream as needed

Roasted Figs and Vinaigrette:
12 fresh figs
8 slices bacon
2 tablespoons brown sugar
2 tablespoons unsalted butter
1/3 cup chicken broth
1/2 cup extra-virgin olive oil
1/4 cup grape seed oil
1/4 cup balsamic vinegar
1/2 teaspoon sea salt

Liver:
1 1/2 pounds calf's liver
2 cups buttermilk
Flour
Salt and pepper to taste
2 tablespoons unsalted butter
2 tablespoons oil
1/3 cup brown gravy or demi-glace

To Make the Polenta:

- In a heavy bottom, stainless-steel pan, combine milk, broth, oil, 4 tablespoons of the butter, sage, salt and honey. Place over medium heat for 2 minutes. Begin to slowly sprinkle in the polenta, stirring briskly with a wooden spoon in one direction. Keep cooking, stirring constantly, until the polenta is very thick, 15 to 20 minutes.
- Remove from the heat and stir in the remaining 6 tablespoons butter and parmesan. Adjust seasoning with salt if needed and stir in cream for a creamier consistency. Keep warm.

To Make the Roasted Figs and Vinaigrette:

- Preheat oven to 365 degrees F. Wrap 8 of the figs in bacon slices and place in a small baking pan. Sprinkle with sugar, dot with butter and pour broth around figs. Roast 10 minutes.
- Remove figs and keep warm. Pour pan drippings into a small sauce pan. Cut remaining figs in half and scrap the flesh into the sauce pan. Add olive oil, grape seed oil, vinegar and salt. Using a hand-held blender, blend until smooth.

To Make the Liver:

- Trim liver of any membrane and vessels and soak in buttermilk overnight.
- Cut liver into four equal pieces. Sprinkle with sea salt or kosher salt. Dredge in flour seasoned with salt and pepper. Place butter and oil in a skillet set over medium-high heat. Place liver in hot pan and fry until liver is nicely browned, 2 to 3 minutes per side. Remove liver, add gravy to pan and bring to simmer.

Finish and Serve:

- Place polenta in middle of each of four plates. Top with liver, cutting each piece in half if desired. Place two figs on each plate. Top liver with pan gravy and drizzle the vinaigrette around each plate.

CHEF'S TIP:

- Venetians crave calf's liver, but it's less popular state-side than it should be. Try this version and you may find your family and friends requesting it.
- A parmesan cookie is a nice garnish for risotto. To make, just take an 8-inch skillet and wipe with some oil and place on low to medium heat. Place a 2- or 3-inch cookie cutter in the pan, sprinkle grated parmesan cheese inside the cookie cutter, remove cutter and repeat; you should be able to get three or four to a pan. Cook cheese until lightly brown and turn the cookie over using a spatula. Cook on the other side for an additional 1-2 minutes, remove and let rest on the counter.

Pan-Seared New York Strip Steaks with Garlic Mashed Potatoes, Spinach and Olive Oil Tomatoes

Chef Ed Leonard, CMC

Serves 4

Olive Oil Tomatoes:

4 plum tomatoes
2 cups extra-virgin olive oil
2 cloves garlic, peeled and smashed
4 basil leaves

Mashed Potatoes:

4 Idaho potatoes, peeled and cut into 1/2-inch pieces
3 tablespoons sea salt
1 cup heavy cream
6 tablespoons unsalted butter
6 cloves garlic, finely minced
Kosher salt to taste

Steaks:

4 12-ounce strip steaks
Salt and ground black pepper to taste
4 tablespoons olive oil

Spinach:

2 tablespoons olive oil
2 tablespoons unsalted butter
6 cloves thinly sliced garlic
1 shallot, thinly sliced
4 pounds spinach, stems removed, leaves well rinsed
Salt and ground black pepper to taste

To Make the Olive Oil Tomatoes:

- Bring a 2-quart saucepan of water to a boil. With a paring knife, cut an X in the bottom of each tomato. Drop tomatoes into boiling water and cook 10 to 15 seconds. Remove tomatoes and cool in ice water.
- When cooled, slip the skins off the tomatoes. (If the skin does not peel off easily, place the tomatoes back in the boiling water for 5 seconds, cool, and try again.) Cut each peeled tomato in quarters. With a paring knife, cut out and discard the center part of the tomatoes (the part with the seeds). You should have 16 tomato "petals" now.
- Preheat oven to 200 degrees F. Place tomato petals in a small oven-proof dish. Add olive oil, garlic and basil. Cover with foil and bake until tomatoes are tender but not mushy, about 6 hours. Set aside at room temperature until ready to serve.

To Make the Mashed Potatoes:

- Place potatoes in a saucepan and cover with cold water. Add sea salt and bring to a boil. Adjust heat and simmer until tender.
- While potatoes cook, in a small saucepan heat cream and 4 tablespoons of the butter until butter is melted. Keep warm.
- Heat 2 more tablespoons butter in a small skillet over medium heat. Add minced garlic and cook until garlic is softened. Set aside.
- Drain potatoes. Return them to the pot and place over medium heat. Cook for a few minutes, tossing, to remove any excess water.
- Pass potatoes through a food mill or ricer. Stir in half the butter-cream mixture and half the garlic. Add more butter-cream mixture as needed to make the potatoes light and fluffy. Taste and add salt and more garlic as needed. Keep warm.

To Make the Steaks:

- Preheat oven to 400 degrees F. Heat a large, heavy skillet over high heat. Season steaks with salt and pepper. Add 4 tablespoons of olive oil to the skillet. Sear steaks until nicely browned, about 3 minutes per side. Transfer skillet to the oven and cook until they reach the desired doneness, about 10 minutes for medium-rare.

To Make the Spinach:

- Heat a large skillet over medium heat. Add the olive oil and butter. Add the sliced garlic and shallot and cook for 2 minutes. Add the spinach and cook until wilted. Season with salt and pepper and keep warm.

Finish and Serve:

- Have ready four heated dinner plates. Divide spinach and potatoes between plates. Place a steak on each plate and top steaks with tomatoes. Serve.

Tournedos of Beef with Asparagus and Crabmeat

Chef Ed Leonard, CMC

Serves 4

Blender Hollandaise:

1 1/2 cups (3 sticks) unsalted butter

4 large egg yolks

2 teaspoons lemon juice

2 teaspoons water

4 drops hot sauce

Pinch cayenne

Beef and Asparagus:

16 medium asparagus spears, trimmed

8 pieces beef tenderloin, each about 1-inch thick

Kosher salt to taste

Ground black pepper to taste

1/4 cup olive oil

2 tablespoons unsalted butter

1/2 cup king crabmeat

Finish and Serve:

Chopped parsley or chives for garnish

To Make the Blender Hollandaise:

- Melt the butter in a small saucepan. Place yolks, lemon juice and water in a blender and blend until smooth. With the motor running, add the hot melted butter by droplets to the yolk mixture. Once you've incorporated 1/2 cup of the butter, begin pouring in a thin stream until all the butter is incorporated. Add the hot sauce and cayenne.
- Remove sauce from blender and season with salt and pepper. Keep in a warm place or in an insulated thermos until ready to serve.

To Make the Beef and Asparagus:

- Bring a medium saucepan of salted water to a boil. Add asparagus and cook until just tender, 3 to 4 minutes. Plunge into cold water to cool, drain and pat dry. Set aside.
- Preheat oven to 400 degrees F. Season beef with salt and pepper. Heat oil in a large, heavy skillet over high heat. Add beef and sear on both sides until nicely browned. Place in the oven and cook until beef reaches the desired doneness, about 8 minutes for medium rare.
- Meanwhile, melt 1 tablespoon of the butter in a small saucepan. Add crabmeat and cook until warmed through. Heat the remaining tablespoon butter in a small skillet and reheat asparagus. Season asparagus with salt and pepper.

Finish and Serve:

- Place two pieces of beef on each of four warmed dinner plates. Top beef with two asparagus spears. Divide the crabmeat between the plates, spoon warm hollandaise over beef and asparagus and garnish with chopped parsley.

Variety of Angus Beef

Chef Ed Leonard, CMC

Serves 4

Sirloin:

1 cup red wine

2 tablespoons crushed black peppercorns

2 tablespoons ChefNique Master Steak spice mix

1/2 cup extra-virgin olive oil

12-ounce certified Angus New York sirloin steak

Burger Chop:

8 ounces certified Angus ground beef

1 teaspoon minced shallot

1/2 teaspoon minced garlic

1/4 teaspoon ground cardamom

1 teaspoon chopped parsley

1 teaspoon ketchup

Salt and pepper to taste.

Filet:

10 ounces certified Angus beef tenderloin

8 tablespoons mushroom powder

2 tablespoons olive oil

Sauce:

2 tablespoons unsalted butter

1 cup diced oyster mushrooms

1/3 cup red wine

1/2 cup plus **2 tablespoons** beef broth

1 tablespoon arrowroot

2 tablespoons cold, diced unsalted butter

Salt and pepper to taste

To Make the Sirloin:

- Whisk together wine, peppercorns, spice mix and oil. Pour over steak and marinate overnight.
- Prepare a gas or charcoal grill or heat a grill pan. Remove steak from marinade and pat dry. Grill to desired doneness.
- Let steak rest 10 minutes, then cut into 12 slices.

To Make the Burger Chop:

- Mix all ingredients until well blended. Shape into four chop-shaped burgers.
- Grill or pan fry until cooked to medium.

To Make the Filet:

- Cut the tenderloin into four equal pieces. Coat each with mushroom powder. In a heavy skillet set over high heat, heat oil until very hot. Add fillet and sear on each side 1 to 2 minutes. Remove from pan and let rest 5 minutes.

To Make the Sauce:

- In a sauté pan, melt butter over medium-high heat. Add mushrooms and sauté until brown. Add wine and cook until liquid is reduced by half. Add 1/2 cup of the broth and bring to a simmer.
- Mix arrowroot with remaining 2 tablespoons broth and whisk into simmering broth. Simmer 2 to 3 minutes. Whisk in butter and season with salt and pepper.

Finish and Serve:

- Divide the potato salad and vegetables between four plates, placing them in the center. Place a piece of fillet, a burger and some sliced sirloin around plate. Drizzle with sauce and serve.

CHEF'S TIP:

- Chef Ed Leonard serves this dish with warm potato salad (see recipe on page 232) and pan roasted vegetables (see recipe on page 226).

Tart Cherry Glazed Pork Tenderloin Salad

Chef James Decker
Serves 4

Relish:
1/4 cup diced dried cherries
1/4 cup finely diced fennel
1/4 cup diced Granny Smith apple
1/4 cup peeled and finely diced celery
2 tablespoons toasted pine nuts
1/4 teaspoon finely diced jalapeño
1 tablespoon olive oil
1 tablespoon balsamic vinegar
Salt and pepper to taste

Pork:
4 thin slices prosciutto
1 teaspoon chopped thyme leaves
1 teaspoon chopped sage leaves
4 5-ounce pieces pork tenderloin
Salt and pepper to taste
2 tablespoons vegetable oil
1/4 cup tart cherry juice

Salad:
2 tablespoons red wine vinegar
1 tablespoon olive oil
1 tablespoon Dijon mustard
2 cups mesclun salad mix, rinsed and dried
2 cups arugula, rinsed and dried
1/4 cup coarsely chopped fennel fronds
Salt and pepper to taste

BEVERAGE RECOMMENDATION
Clos Pegase Sauvignon Blanc

To Make the Relish:
- Combine all the relish ingredients in a small bowl and toss well. Let flavors marry while assembling the other ingredients.

To Make the Pork:
- Preheat oven to 350 degrees F. Lay the prosciutto slices out and sprinkle them with the thyme and sage.Wrap a prosciutto slice around each piece of pork and season with salt and pepper. Heat the oil in a large sauté pan over medium-high heat and sear the outside of the pork, browning the prosciutto.
- Remove from the pan and brush each with some of the cherry juice. Place on a sheet pan and bake until pork reaches an internal temperature of 150 degrees, 10 to 12 minutes. Remove from the oven and brush again with cherry juice. Let rest for 5 minutes.

To Make the Salad:
- In a medium bowl, whisk together the vinegar, oil and mustard. Add the mesclun, arugula and fennel fronds and toss to coat evenly with the dressing. Season with salt and pepper to taste.

Finish and Serve:
- Place a quarter of the salad on half of each of four plates. Slice the ends off each pork piece to make a flat surface on which they can stand, then halve each piece on the bias. Place the pork standing on end on the plates. Surround with the relish and serve.

CHEF'S TIP:
- Tart cherry juice can be found in the refrigerated juice sections of some grocery stores.

Double-Cut Honey-Rosemary Glazed Pork Chops Stuffed with Crab

Chef Chad A. Durkin

Serves 2

Honey Glaze:

2 cups honey

4 cloves garlic, thinly sliced

3 sprigs rosemary

Salt and pepper to taste

Stuffing:

3 potatoes, roughly diced

4 cups half-and-half, or as needed

1/2 cup bread cubes

1 egg, beaten with a few teaspoons of water

7 sprigs chives, chopped

Salt and pepper to taste

2 cups lump crabmeat

1 cup Italian breadcrumbs

Pork Chops:

2 10-ounce double-cut pork chops

Salt and pepper to taste

Finish and Serve:

2 sprigs rosemary

To Make the Honey Glaze:

- Whisk together honey and just enough water so that it pours easily. Whisk in garlic and chopped leaves from rosemary sprigs. Season with salt and pepper and set aside.

To Make the Stuffing:

- Place the potatoes in a pot and pour in just enough half-and-half to cover. Bring to a simmer and cook until potatoes are tender.
- Combine bread cubes and egg. Stir in chives and season with salt and pepper.
- When potatoes are tender, drain them, reserving the cream. Rice or mash the potatoes and place in a large bowl. Thin with half-and-half as needed. Stir in crabmeat and breadcrumbs.

To Make the Pork Chops:

- Cut a pocket in the side of each pork chop for stuffing. Season chops with salt and pepper and stuff them until filling is just bursting out.
- Brush chops with honey glaze. Preheat a charcoal or gas grill and grill chops, brushing with glaze, until cooked through.

Finish and Serve:

- Place chops on plates and drizzle with honey glaze. Garnish each with a small sprig of rosemary and serve.

BEVERAGE RECOMMENDATION

With this you can serve white wine because of the heaviness of the meal, but personally your favorite ice cold beer would do just perfect.

CHEF'S TIP:

- These pork chops are excellent grilled, but you can also sear them on the stove top and then finish them in a hot oven. Chef Durkin serves them with baked apples, cabbage and glazed carrots.

Roasted Lamb over Potato and Turnip Gratin with Apple-Wood Bacon Green Beans

Chef Joachim Buchner, CMC

Serves 4

Lamb:

1 rack of lamb, chine bone removed and chops Frenched by your butcher

Salt and pepper to taste

3 tablespoons vegetable oil

2 tablespoons Dijon mustard

2 tablespoons ChefNique Best Lamb Seasoning

Turnip Gratin:

6 tablespoons butter

1 cup paper-thin slices of peeled turnip

1/2 cup paper-thin slices onion

1 cup paper-thin slices potato

Salt and pepper to taste

1/2 teaspoon fresh thyme leaves

3/4 cup heavy cream

1 clove garlic, mashed

Green Beans:

8 ounces green beans, ends trimmed

1 tablespoon vegetable oil

2 tablespoons diced apple-wood smoked bacon

1/2 small red onion, sliced

1 pinch chopped oregano

Salt and pepper to taste

To Make the Lamb:

- Preheat oven to 350 degrees F. Cut the rack in half so you have two pieces, each with four chops. Season lamb with salt and pepper. In a heavy roasting pan, heat the oil over high heat and sear lamb on all sides. Remove lamb from pan and set on a roasting rack.
- Brush lamb with mustard and sprinkle with ChefNique Best Lamb Seasoning. Roast lamb until it reaches desired doneness, about 15 minutes for medium-rare. Remove from oven and let rest for 10 minutes before carving. Cut lamb into four pieces of two chops each.

To Make the Gratin:

- Heat oven to 350 degrees F. In a heavy sauté pan, melt 4 tablespoons of the butter over medium heat. Add turnips and onion and sauté until soft. Add potato and continue to cook, stirring gently. Season with salt, pepper and fresh thyme. Fold in the heavy cream.
- Grease a baking dish with the remaining 2 tablespoons butter and spread with the mashed garlic. Fill baking dish with potato mixture and bake for 30 minutes.

To Make the Green Beans:

- Bring 6 quarts of salted water to a boil and cook green beans until tender.
- Meanwhile, in a sauté pan, heat oil over medium heat and sauté the bacon until almost crispy. Add red onion and continue to cook until bacon is crispy and onion is soft.
- Remove green beans from the boiling water. Drain very well and add to the onions. Add oregano and season with salt and pepper.

Finish and Serve:

- Divide beans between four dinner plates. Top beans with lamb and put gratin on the side.

CHEF'S TIP:

- Lamb is a great choice any time of the year, and this is a fabulously flavorful preparation. In the summer, you can carve the rack into individual chops and grill them quickly on your patio charcoal or gas grill.

BEVERAGE RECOMMENDATION

Patz and Hall "Hyde Vineyard," Carneros 1999 Pinot Noir

Grilled Maple and Balsamic Glazed Pork Chops with Sweet Potato Hash

Chef Joachim Buchner, CMC
Serves 4

Maple and Balsamic Glaze:

3 tablespoons maple syrup
3 tablespoons balsamic vinegar
2 tablespoons orange juice
1 teaspoon minced garlic

Pork Chops:

4 12-ounce bone-in pork rack chops
Salt and pepper to taste

Sweet Potato Hash:

3 tablespoons unsalted butter
1/2 cup diced sweet onion
1 cup diced sweet potato
1 cup diced Yukon gold potato
2 cups vegetable stock
Salt and pepper to taste
1 teaspoon chopped marjoram
1 teaspoon finely sliced scallion

BEVERAGE RECOMMENDATION

Domaine Bader-Mimeur, Chassagne Montrachet, 1999

To Make the Maple and Balsamic Glaze:

- In a small saucepan, combine syrup, vinegar, orange juice and garlic. Bring to a boil and simmer over low heat until mixture is reduced by half, about 15 minutes. Remove from heat and let cool.

To Make the Pork Chops:

- Preheat a gas or charcoal grill to medium. Season pork chops with salt and pepper and grill for 5 minutes on each side. Brush with some of the maple-balsamic mixture and continue to grill until medium. Keep warm.

To Make the Sweet Potato Hash:

- In a sauté pan, melt butter and sauté onion until tender. Add potatoes and half of the vegetable stock. Simmer until potatoes are tender, adding more vegetable stock as needed. Season with salt and pepper. Stir in marjoram and scallion.

Finish and Serve:

- Serve pork chops with potatoes and maple balsamic glaze.

CHEF'S TIP:

- This juicy cut of pork glazed with maple syrup and served with sweet potato hash is a nice combination for fall or winter. It goes well with green beans or stewed onions.

Hot Smoked Herb-Crusted Atlantic Salmon with Caviar Crème Fraîche

Chef Russell Scott, CMC

Serves 4

Herb Crust:

1/2 cup fresh breadcrumbs
2 tablespoons fresh chopped parsley
2 tablespoons grated Parmesan cheese
2 tablespoons olive oil
Salt and pepper to taste

Salmon:

1 cup kosher salt
1 cup granulated sugar
1 tablespoon ground cumin
2 teaspoons red pepper flakes
1 tablespoon curry powder
2 teaspoons black pepper
1 tablespoon dried dill
4 6-ounce salmon medallions

Caviar Crème Fraîche:

1 cup crème fraîche, at room temperature
1 tablespoon American sturgeon roe
1 tablespoon salmon roe
1 tablespoon chopped fresh dill
Salt and pepper to taste

Potatoes and Haricots Verts:

1/2 cup haricot verts
Stock as needed
Unsalted butter as needed
1/2 a small tomato, peeled, seeded and cut into thin strips
12 fingerling potatoes
Olive oil as needed
Garlic as needed
Thyme as needed
Salt and pepper to taste

Finish and Serve:

Braised Fennel (See page 229)

To Make the Herb Crust:

- Combine all ingredients.

To Make the Salmon:

- In a bowl, combine the kosher salt, sugar, cumin, pepper flakes, curry powder, black pepper and dill. Place salmon medallions in another bowl and cover with the salt mixture. Allow to set for 20 minutes.
- Under cold running water, rinse salt mixture off salmon and blot dry. Preheat oven to 325 degrees F.
- Hot smoke the salmon for 3 to 4 minutes only (see instructions below for smoking on the stove top). Top the salmon with a small amount of the Herb Crust and finish cooking in the oven at 350 degree F. for approximately 8 minutes.

To Make Caviar Crème Fraîche:

- Place crème in a bowl and stir until smooth. Gently stir in sturgeon roe, salmon roe and dill. Season to taste with salt and pepper.

To Make the Haricots Verts and Potatoes:

- Blanch the haricot verts. Plunge in ice water to cool, pat dry and refrigerate until needed. Heat the haricots in a sauté pan with stock, butter and tomato.
- Cook potatoes in salted water until tender. Slice in half. Lightly brown the potatoes in a small amount of olive oil. Finish the potatoes in the oven with a small amount of garlic and thyme. Adjust seasoning.

Finish and Serve:

- Blot of all excess moisture from the braised fennel and plate one piece in the center of each plate. Place the potatoes around the fennel. Spoon caviar crème fraîche around the fennel and potatoes. Drain any excess liquid from the haricot verts and tomatoes and place around the fennel on top of the sauce. Place the salmon on top of the fennel and serve.

CHEF'S TIP: To Hot Smoke on the Stove Top

- Organize the following items: One 4-inch hotel pan lined with foil; one 2-inch perforated hotel pan sprayed with vegetable spray; one handful of fine wood chips; one 2-inch full-size hotel pan. Have good ventilation.
- To begin, place the item to be smoked on an oiled perforated inset. Place the wood chips into the center of the deep hotel pan on the foil. Place the deep hotel on the stove the wood chips directly over the burner. Cover the pan loosely with foil and turn on the flame. Once smoke starts to appear place the pan with the item to be smoked into the deep pan; it must be at least 2 inches above the wood chips in the pan below to avoid excess heat. Leave for the amount of time required (3 to 4 minutes only for salmon medallions).
- Remove food from the smoker and cover the smoker again with foil until it cools down. Pour water over chips to make sure they are not still smoldering and discard.

Florida Rock Shrimp Cakes with Heart of Palm Salad, Creole Mustard and Sweet Pepper Sauce

Chef Russell Scott, CMC

Serves 4

Hearts of Palm Salad:

1/2 pound canned hearts of palm, sliced into 1/4-inch pieces on the bias
1 chayote squash, peeled and julienned
16 sprigs frisée lettuce
1 red bell pepper, finely diced
1 yellow bell pepper, finely diced
1 green bell pepper, finely diced
1 bunch scallions, sliced thinly on the bias
Mustard-Herb Vinaigrette (see page 230)
Salt and black pepper to taste

Shrimp Cakes:

2 teaspoons unsalted butter
1 stalk celery, finely chopped
1 pound fresh rock shrimp, cleaned, deveined and roughly chopped
1 bunch scallions, finely sliced
1/2 cup crushed saltine crackers
1 tablespoon hot sauce
2 tablespoons mayonnaise
1 tablespoon chives, finely chopped
3 large eggs, well beaten
1 1/2 cups panko (Japanese) breadcrumbs
Salt and pepper to taste
1 cup all-purpose flour
Vegetable oil and melted butter for frying the cakes.

Fried Plantain:

1 green plantain
Peanut oil for frying

To Make the Hearts of Palm Salad:

- Toss hearts of palm, chayote, frisée, peppers and scallions together with enough dressing to coat well. Season with salt and pepper.

To Make the Shrimp Cakes:

- Melt the butter and cook the celery over medium-low heat until softened. Remove from the heat and transfer to a clean bowl. Cool.
- When cooled, add the shrimp, scallions, saltines, hot sauce, mayonnaise and chives. Stir in one of the eggs and half a cup of the panko. Season with salt and pepper. Shape the cakes into 2-inch patties.
- Place the remaining 2 eggs and 1 cup panko separately in deep, shallow bowls. Place the flour on a plate. Dredge cakes in flour, dip into beaten egg, then coat in panko.
- Fry the cakes in a skillet with enough vegetable oil and butter to come half way up the cakes. Cook until golden brown, drain and keep warm.

To Make the Fried Plantain:

- Slice the green plantain on the bias into 1/16-inch-thick pieces.
- Deep fry the plantain slices in 350 degree F. peanut oil until golden brown. Remove from oil, blot dry and season with salt. Keep warm until service.

Finish and Serve:

- Drizzle Cilantro and Sweet Pepper Sauce over the surface of each of 4 plates. Place a quarter of the Heart of Palm Salad in the center of each plate. Place a shrimp cake on top of each mound of salad, garnish with fried plantain and serve.

CHEF'S TIP:

- Chef Scott serves this dish with cilantro and sweet pepper sauce (see page 233).

Crunchy Fried Haddock with Pickled Watermelon and Creamy Coleslaw

Chef Dan Scannell, CMC

Serves 4

Pickled Watermelon Rind:

1 cup rice-wine vinegar
1/4 cup water
1/2 cup sugar
1 bay leaf
4 juniper berries
1 star-anise pod
1/2 vanilla bean, split
4 pieces peeled watermelon rind, each approximately 1-by-3 inches with 1/2 inch of red flesh left intact on each

Creamy Coleslaw:

1 cup mayonnaise
1/3 cup apple-cider vinegar
1/2 cup sugar
2 teaspoons kosher salt
1/2 teaspoon freshly ground black pepper
2 cups thinly shredded cabbage
2 tablespoons shredded carrots

Fried Haddock:

1 quart vegetable oil
2 cups all-purpose flour
Salt
4 boneless, skinless haddock fillets (about 6 ounces each)
3 large eggs, lightly beaten
2 cups panko (Japanese) bread crumbs
2 teaspoons kosher salt

Finish and Serve:

Tartar sauce
Malt vinegar

To Make the Pickled Watermelon Rind:

- Combine vinegar, water, sugar, bay leaf, juniper and star anise in a stainless-steel 1-quart saucepan. Using the tip of a paring knife, scrape out the seeds from the vanilla bean and add them to the pot. Toss in the pod as well. Bring the mixture to a boil and remove from heat. Add the watermelon rind, cover, and allow to steep for 20 minutes. Store in the refrigerator until ready to use.

To Make the Creamy Coleslaw:

- In a large bowl, whisk together mayonnaise, vinegar, sugar, salt and pepper. Stir in cabbage and carrots. Cover and refrigerate at least 2 hours before serving.

To Make the Fried Haddock:

- Heat the oil in a 2-quart stockpot until it reaches 350 degrees F. (Make sure that the pot is filled no more than half way for safety.)
- Season flour with salt. Dredge fillets in the flour, then dip into the beaten eggs. Coat fillets with breadcrumbs and gently shake off any excess breading.
- Gently place the breaded fillets into the hot oil and cook until golden brown. Using a slotted spoon, remove fillets and drain on a large plate covered with paper napkins or paper towels.

Finish and Serve:

- Serve the Fried Haddock immediately after cooking with the watermelon, coleslaw tartar sauce and malt vinegar on the side.

CHEF'S TIP:

- Chef Scannell likes to serve this dish with fried or roasted potatoes.

Poached Lobster with Ricotta Gnocchi and Sage

Chef Dan Scannell, CMC

Serves 4

Ricotta Gnocchi:

16 ounces Ricotta cheese, drained
1 large egg
2 teaspoons truffle oil
1 tablespoon extra-virgin olive oil
2 teaspoons salt
1 3/4 cups flour, or as needed

Emulsified Butter:

2 pounds cold, unsalted butter, cut into 1-inch cubes

Lobster in Sage-Butter Sauce:

16 ounces cooked, shelled Maine lobster meat
6 morel mushrooms (medium size)
2 cups emulsified butter (see above)
2 teaspoons truffle oil
Fleur de sel sea salt or kosher salt to taste
1/2 teaspoon ground black pepper
10 fresh sage leaves
2 teaspoons fresh lemon juice

Finish and Serve:

1/4 cup finely grated Parmigiano-Reggiano cheese
2 teaspoons Lobster Dust (optional; see below)

To Make the Ricotta Gnocchi:

- Place ricotta in a large stainless-steel bowl. Make a well in the center of the cheese and add the egg, oils and salt. Using a fork, very slowly work the flour into the wet ingredients until the flour has been incorporated. Dough should be soft but not sticky; amount of flour needed may vary. Place the dough in a floured cloth and wrap with plastic wrap. Refrigerate until ready to use.
- Dust a clean work surface lightly with flour. Using your hands, roll pieces of dough out to logs approximately 1/2 inch in diameter and 12 inches long. Cut the logs into 1-inch lengths. Form gnocchi by pinching the pieces to flatten them lightly, then roll them one by one over the surface of your palm with the index finger of your other hand. (Remember that if the gnocchi dough is too moist just dust them with a little flour.)
- When ready to cook, bring 1 gallon of well-salted water to a rolling boil. Gently place gnocchi into the water and cook them until they begin to float. Do not over cook.

To Make the Emulsified Butter:

- In a stainless-steel 2-quart saucepan, bring a half cup of water to a boil. Measure out 2 tablespoons of the water, discard the rest, and return the 2 tablespoons to the pot. Reduce the heat and whisk in the butter little by little until all has been incorporated. Set aside 2 cups for the lobster; leftover butter can be saved for another use.

To Make the Lobster in Sage-Butter Sauce:

- Slice lobster meat and mushrooms thinly on the bias and add to the emulsified butter. Heat gently until lobster and mushrooms are just warmed through. Gently stir in truffle oil, salt, pepper, sage leaves and lemon juice.

Finish and Serve:

- Gently add cooked gnocchi to the lobster and sage-butter sauce. Sprinkle with Parmesan and lobster dust and serve hot in a warm bowl.

Lobster Dust

Serves 4 as a garnish

Lobster Dust:

2 tablespoons lobster roe
1/2 cup water

To Make the Lobster Dust:

- Remove lobster roe from live Maine lobsters and remove and discard as much of the membrane between the egg sacks as possible. Place roe and water in a small saucepan and gently poach, uncovered, until all of the water has evaporated. Continue to dehydrate the roe until it is very dry.
- Place dried roe into a spice grinder and grind until powdery. You can use the lobster dust to season butters, sauces or sprinkle on top of dishes as a garnish.

New England Lobster Roll

Chef Dan Scannell, CMC

Serves 4

Lobster Rolls:

16 ounces cooked Maine lobster meat

3 tablespoons diced, blanched celery

1 tablespoon minced onions

3/4 cup mayonnaise

2 teaspoons lemon juice

2 teaspoons Old Bay Seasoning

1 teaspoon celery salt

1 teaspoon ground black pepper

2 teaspoons dry mustard powder

1 tablespoon minced red bell pepper

1 tablespoon chopped Italian parsley

Polenta Fries:

4 1/2 cups water

2 teaspoons kosher salt, plus more for sprinkling on the fries

4 tablespoons unsalted butter

1 cup yellow cornmeal

1/2 cup grated Parmigiano-Reggiano cheese, plus more for sprinkling on the fries

2 cups flour

2 cups vegetable oil

Finish and Serve:

4 New England rolls or slices white bread

3 tablespoons melted unsalted butter

4 leaves lettuce

4 slices tomato

4 pickle planks sprinkled with celery salt

To Make the Lobster Rolls:

- Cut lobster meat into chunks. Set aside in a large mixing bowl.
- In another bowl, mix together blanched celery, onions, mayonnaise, lemon juice, Old Bay, celery salt, pepper and mustard. Stir in bell pepper and parsley. Fold in the lobster meat and refrigerator for at least 2 hours and up to 24 hours.

To Make the Polenta Fries:

- In a 2-quart stainless-steel saucepan, bring water and salt to a rolling boil. Add 2 tablespoons of the butter. Whisking constantly, very slowly whisk the cornmeal into the water.
- Once all the cornmeal has been incorporated, lower the heat to low and switch to a wooden spoon. Continue to cook, stirring, for 10 minutes. Remove from heat and stir in the remaining 2 tablespoons butter and the cheese.
- Line a baking sheet with parchment paper. Spread the polenta evenly over the parchment. Cover with plastic wrap and refrigerate for 2 hours.
- Using a sharp knife, cut the polenta into strips the size of French fries and gently flour the polenta. Heat oil to 350 degrees F. Working in batches, fry polenta until golden and crisp. Drain the fries, sprinkle with a little salt and grated parmesan cheese and serve hot. They are a wonderful garnish for all types of grilled or roast-ed meats.

Finish and Serve:

- Brush the rolls with butter and grill on both side until golden brown. Fill the rolls with lobster salad and garnish with polenta fries, lettuce, tomato and pickle.

Potato-Crusted Grouper with Chive Butter Sauce

Chef Richard Rosendale, CC
Serves 4

Sauce:
1 small minced shallot
3 sprigs parsley
4 black peppercorns
1 bay leaf
2 tablespoons white wine vinegar
1/2 cup white wine
2 tablespoons heavy cream
1 cup unsalted butter, diced
Juice from 1/2 lemon
1 bunch fresh chives, sliced
Salt and white pepper to taste

Grouper:
1 large Idaho potato
4 5- to 6-ounce grouper fillets, or any firm white fish
Salt and white pepper to taste
1 large egg yolk, lightly beaten
1/4 cup clarified butter
1 pinch cream of tartar
1/2 cup oil for frying

To Make the Sauce:

- Place the shallot, parsley, peppercorns, and bay leaf in a small heavy bottom saucepan. Pour in the vinegar and the wine. Simmer until the liquid is reduced by three-fourths. Next, add the heavy cream and reduce this by half.
- Remove from the heat and slowly whisk in the butter little by little. Strain the sauce and stir in lemon juice and chives. Season with salt and pepper.

To Make the Grouper:

- Julienne the potato on a mandolin and place in cold water to keep them from browning. Run cold water over the potatoes until the water is clear and not starchy looking.
- Season the fillets with salt and white pepper on both sides. Brush the top of the fillets with the egg yolk. Squeeze the potatoes dry and toss with the melted clarified butter and cream of tartar until potatoes are completely coated. Divide the potatoes equally between the four fillets. Lightly press the potatoes to cover the surface evenly.
- Heat the oil in a large sauté pan over medium-high heat. Carefully lay in the fish, potato-side down. Be careful not to brown the potatoes too fast. Let them fry gently. When the potatoes are fully cooked and browned, flip the fish and cook for an additional 1 minute. Remove the fish from the pan and serve with the butter sauce.

CHEF'S TIP:

- The fish and potatoes can be crusted 2 hours in advance — the potatoes will not discolor.
- Chef Rosendale serves this dish with fresh steamed asparagus.

Prosciutto-Wrapped Scallops with Truffle-Scented Lobster Ragout, Sweet Corn Ravioli, Fennel and Creamy Roasted Corn Sauce

Chef Craig Peterson

Serves 4

Scallops:

4 thin strips prosciutto
4 dry-pack sea scallops
Freshly cracked pepper and kosher salt to taste
2 tablespoons clarified butter

Sweet Corn Ravioli:

1 egg, lightly beaten
2 tablespoons water
1/8 teaspoon squid ink
8 ounces flour
1/4 teaspoon salt
1 teaspoon unsalted butter
4 ounces roasted corn kernels
1 tablespoon diced onion
1 teaspoon chopped roasted garlic
1/4 cup heavy cream
1 teaspoon finely chopped chives
1/4 teaspoon chopped thyme
Salt and pepper to taste

Creamy Roasted Corn and Fennel Sauce:

6 tablespoons unsalted butter
2 ounces fresh corn
1 ounce fennel, coarsely chopped
1 ounce diced onion
1 teaspoon chopped roasted garlic
2 sprigs thyme
1 bay leaf
1 cup shellfish stock or clam juice
3/4 cup heavy cream
Salt and pepper to taste

To Make the Scallops:

- Wrap a piece of prosciutto around the side of each of the scallops and secure in place with a toothpick. Season scallops with fresh cracked pepper and kosher salt.
- In a moderately hot sauté pan, sauté the scallops in the clarified butter until they reach the desired doneness. Keep warm.

To Make the Sweet Corn Ravioli:

- In a small bowl, whisk together egg, water and squid ink. Stir this mixture into the flour and salt. Knead for 5-10 minutes. Cover dough with a kitchen towel and rest on the counter 30 minutes.
- Using a pasta machine, roll out dough to desired thickness.
- In a small skillet over medium heat, melt the butter and cook the corn, onion and garlic until tender. Add the cream and cook on low heat for 3 to 5 minutes. Stir in chives and thyme. Season to taste with salt and pepper.
- Pick the straightest edge of the sheet (trim if necessary) and put heaping teaspoon of filling about an inch and a half apart and an inch and a half from the margin of the sheet. Carefully fold the pasta over the filling and cut the strip of pasta and filling free from the sheet with a serrated pasta wheel. Tamp down the pasta around the balls of filling with your fingers, pressing hard to make sure the pasta adheres so the ravioli won't come apart while cooking, and cut the individual ravioli free. Set the finished ravioli to dry on a lightly floured cloth and repeat the process, continuing until the stuffing is used up.

To Make the Creamy Roasted Corn and Fennel Sauce:

- Melt 2 tablespoons of the butter in a medium sauté pan over medium heat. Add corn, fennel, onion and garlic and cook until vegetables are softened. Add thyme, bay leaf, stock and cream. Cook over low heat for 20 minutes.
- Remove and discard the bay leaf. Transfer to a blender, purée and strain through a fine-mesh sieve.
- Place the skillet back over medium-high heat and slowly whisk in the remaining 4 tablespoons butter. Season to taste with salt and pepper. Keep warm.

Finish and Serve:

- In the center of the plates, spoon a good amount of the lobster ragout. On top of the ragout, place the ravioli and braised fennel.
- To finish, top off the ravioli with the prosciutto wrapped scallop and spoon sauce around the ragout

---

CHEF'S TIP:

- Chef Peterson serves this with truffle-scented lobster ragout (see recipe page 231) and braised fennel (see recipe page 236).

Grilled Shrimp, Bacon and Fennel Risotto

Chef Ed Leonard, CMC
Serves 4

Shrimp:
2 tablespoons honey
Juice from 2 limes
1 tablespoon fresh thyme leaves
1 tablespoon extra-virgin olive oil
18 large shrimp, peeled and deveined

Risotto:
1/4 cup unsalted butter
2 tablespoons olive oil
1/4 cup diced bacon
1/4 cup diced shallots
1/4 cup diced fennel
1 cup Canaroli rice
1/4 cup Merlot wine
3 cups shrimp or chicken broth
2 teaspoons chopped parsley
1 teaspoon chopped sage
1/4 cup grated Parmesan cheese
4 tablespoons diced cold unsalted butter
1/4 cup heavy cream, heated
Sea salt to taste
1/4 cup cooked petite green peas or frozen, defrosted peas

To Make the Shrimp:

- Whisk together the honey, lime juice, thyme and olive oil. Toss with the shrimp and let sit for 20 minutes.
- Remove shrimp from marinade. Cut six of the shrimp into small dice and reserve. Grill remaining 12 shrimp for 2 to 3 minutes on each side just after risotto is finished.

To Make the Risotto:

- In heavy bottom, stainless-steel pan set over medium heat, cook butter, oil and bacon until bacon is lightly browned. Add shallots and fennel and cook 2 to 3 minutes. Add rice and stir quickly to coat rice.
- Add wine, lower heat, and cook until all the wine is absorbed. Add half the broth and cook, stirring constantly, until the broth is almost completed absorbed by the rice.
- Add remaining broth and cook, stirring constantly, until almost all broth is absorbed. The rice should be slightly firm and creamy, with a nice feel on the mouth. (Risotto shouldn't be crunchy or starchy.)
- Remove from the heat and fold in reserved diced shrimp (the heat of the rice will cook the shrimp completely). Stir in parsley, sage, cheese, cold butter, and cream. Season to taste with salt. Fold peas into the risotto.

Finish and Serve:

- Divide risotto between four bowls. Top each with three grilled shrimp and serve.

CHEF'S TIP:

- Risotto is not the complicated dish restaurants make it seem. The key is to cook the rice in two stages and let it absorb the broth slowly while you stir. It's worth the effort.
- A parmesan cookie is a nice garnish for risotto. To make, just take an 8-inch skillet and wipe with some oil and place on low to medium heat. Place a 2- or 3-inch cookie cutter in the pan, sprinkle grated parmesan cheese inside the cookie cutter, remove cutter and repeat; you should be able to get three or four to a pan. Cook cheese until lightly brown and turn the cookie over using a spatula. Cook on the other side for an additional 1-2 minutes, remove and let rest on the counter.

Grilled Red Snapper and Shrimp With a Hot Salad of Fennel, Corn, Zucchini and Roasted Tomatoes

Chef Ed Leonard, CMC
Serves 4

Snapper and Shrimp:
4 red snapper fillets, 5 to 6 ounces each
2 tablespoons olive oil
1 teaspoon chopped fresh thyme
2 tablespoons lemon juice
Kosher salt to taste
8 extra-large shrimp, peeled and deviened
2 tablespoons honey
1 tablespoon lime juice
1 tablespoon soy sauce

Dressing:
6 tablespoons extra-virgin olive oil
2 tablespoons cherry balsamic vinegar
Juice of 2 limes
1 teaspoon chopped mint
Salt and freshly ground pepper to taste

Salad:
1 pint grape tomatoes
3 tablespoons olive oil
Kosher salt to taste
3 tablespoons butter
1 zucchini, diced
1 bulb fennel, very thinly sliced
1/2 cup roasted corn kernels

To Make the Snapper and Shrimp:

- Marinate fillets in oil, thyme, lemon juice and salt to taste. Marinate shrimp in honey, lime juice and soy sauce. Set aside to marinate at least 1 hour.

To Make the Dressing:

- Whisk together oil, vinegar, lime juice and mint. Season to taste with salt and pepper and set aside.

To Make the Salad:

- Preheat oven to 375 degrees F. Toss tomatoes with 2 tablespoons of the oil and salt place in a small pan. Roast for 3 to 5 minutes and set aside.
- In a skillet, heat the remaining oil and butter over medium-high heat. Sauté snapper 3 to 4 minutes on each side. Remove from pan and keep warm. Sauté shrimp 1 to 2 minutes on each side. Remove shrimp from pan and keep warm.
- While pan is still hot, add zucchini and sauté on high heat until lightly browned. Add fennel and corn and cook 2 minutes. Add tomatoes and half the dressing. Remove pan from heat and toss.

Finish and Serve:

- Divide salad equally among four dinner plates. Top with snapper fillets and shrimp. Drizzle remaining dressing over the fish and plates and serve.

Just-Cooked Salmon with Warm Lobster and Celeriac Salad and Mango Sorbet

Chef Ed Leonard, CMC

Serves 4

Salmon:

2 1/2 cups extra-virgin olive oil
2 cups grape seed oil
4 sprigs thyme
1 bay leaf
1 vanilla bean, slit
1 cinnamon stick
4 basil leaves
4 5-ounce pieces skinless salmon fillet
Sea salt as needed
Freshly ground pepper as needed

Mango Dressing:

3/4 cup grape seed oil
1/4 cup balsamic vinegar
1/3 cup mango purée or nectar
1 teaspoon chopped mint

Salad:

1/4 cup grape seed oil
2 tablespoons unsalted butter
1 minced shallot
8 shiitake mushrooms, stems discarded, tops sliced
1 cup peeled and sliced matchstick-size pieces of celeriac
8 ounces cooked lobster meat
1/2 cup diced peeled pears
2 tablespoons champagne vinegar
2 teaspoons creamed horseradish
2 tablespoons heavy cream
4 scoops mango sorbet

To Make the Salmon:

- In a stainless-steel heavy saucepan or a portable fryer, heat oils to 140 degrees F. Add thyme, bay leaf, vanilla bean, cinnamon stick and basil. Keep at this temperature for 30 minutes. Reduce temperature to 110 degrees F.
- Sprinkle salt and pepper on both sides of salmon. Place salmon fillets in oil and cook at 110 degrees F. until flesh is a bright pink-orange color, 25 to 40 minutes. Remove fillets and place on paper towels.

To Make the Dressing:

- Combine all ingredients in a blender and blend until smooth. Set aside.

To Make the Salad:

- In a sauté pan, heat oil and butter over medium heat. Add shallots and mushrooms and sauté 2 to 3 minutes. Add all other items except the sorbet and cook over high heat for 1 to 2 minutes.

Finish and Serve:

- Place equal amounts of salad in the center of each of four plates. Top each with a salmon fillet and then a small scoop of mango sorbet. Drizzle plate with mango dressing and serve.

Baked Ruby Trout with Wild Mushroom-Ramp Sauté and Heirloom Tomato Picallily

Chef Scott Fetty
Serves 4

Tomato Picallily:
1/2 cup sugar
1/4 cup sherry vinegar
1 teaspoon minced garlic
1/4 cup yellow onion, diced small
1/8 cup golden raisins
2 cups diced assorted heirloom tomatoes (use a variety of tomato types and colors)
2 tablespoons minced chile pepper (jalapeño or other mild, hot pepper is suggested)
Kosher salt and pepper to taste

Trout:
4 ruby trout fillets, skinned with pin bones removed (have your fishmonger do this for you)
2 teaspoons minced chives
1 teaspoon minced lemon zest
1/2 teaspoon minced shallot
1/4 teaspoon grape seed oil
Kosher salt and pepper to taste

Mushrooms and Ramps:
3 slices slab bacon, diced small
2 cups assorted wild mushrooms, tough stems removed (morels are recommended, but other types will work also)
1 cup ramps, washed and split in half length-wise
1/2 teaspoon unsalted butter
1 teaspoon sherry vinegar
Kosher salt and pepper to taste

To Make the Tomato Picallily:

- In a non-reactive pan, combine sugar and vinegar and cook over low heat until the mixture is the consistency of honey. Add the garlic, onion and raisins to the pot and cook until the vegetables have softened. Fold in the tomatoes and chile pepper and remove from the heat. Allow the mixture to cool in the pot for 1/2 hour. Season with salt and pepper and refrigerate (overnight would be best).

To Make the Trout:

- Cut the trout fillets in half. Combine chives, zest, shallot and oil. Pour over fillets and marinate 20 minutes. Transfer to a baking sheet and set aside.

To Make the Mushrooms and Ramps:

- Cook the bacon in a sauté pan over medium heat until crisp. With a slotted spoon, remove the bacon and set aside. Add the mushrooms and ramps to the pan and sauté in the fat until mushrooms are softened. Add the sherry vinegar and the butter to the pan and remove from the heat. Season with salt and pepper to taste. Keep warm.

Finish and Serve:

- Preheat oven to 350 degrees F. Sprinkle fish with salt and pepper and bake until it it has changed from bright orange to light pink, about 6 minutes. Remove from the oven.
- To plate, place a warm potato and apple hash patty on the upper middle of each of four plates. In front of each hash patty, spoon a quarter of the mushroom and ramps. Place two pieces of the trout on top of the mushrooms and the hash. Top each fish fillet with a dollop of the picallily and serve.

CHEF'S TIP:

- Chef Fetty serves this with warm potato and apple hash (see recipe page 236).
- This entrée features seasonal ingredients from Chef Fetty's home state of West Virginia. Picallily is a local condiment that is something like chowchow. Other types of trout, like brook, golden or rainbow trout, can be substitute for the ruby trout.

Minestra del Mare

Chef Chad A. Durkin
Serves 4-6

Minestra del Mare:

Olive oil as needed
1 onion, chopped
5 cloves garlic
1 can tomato paste
1 cup white wine (optional)
4 medium cans stewed whole tomatoes
4 fresh plum tomatoes, chopped
1/2 to 1 cup sugar
1/2 bunch fresh parsley, chopped
1/2 bunch basil, chopped
5 to 6 crabs, depending on size
2 pounds mussels
1 pound large shrimp, peeled and deviened
1 pound sea scallops
1/2 pound calamari or squid, cut into rings and tentacles
2 pounds linguine
Salt and pepper to taste
Crushed red pepper to taste

Finish and Serve:

Italian bread
Grated Parmesan cheese

BEVERAGE RECOMMENDATION

A nice rich Chianti.

To Make the Minestra del Mare:

- Cover the bottom of a large pot with oil place over medium heat. When hot, add onion. Add garlic. Let cook until lightly browned. Stir in tomato paste and cook for a minute or two.
- Add wine. Crush the tomatoes between your fingers and add them and the juice from the cans to the pot. Fill three of the cans with water and add that to the pot as well.
- Add plum tomatoes and 1/2 cup of the sugar. Simmer, skimming off any foam that forms on the surface of the sauce. Add parsley and basil and let the sauce simmer until slightly reduced. Taste the sauce and add more sugar if necessary.
- Add crabs first, then, waiting a minute or two between additions, add mussels, shrimp, scallops and finally squid. Let cook until all seafood is done.
- Meanwhile, fill a large pot 3/4 full of salted water to a boil. Cook the pasta until al dente. Strain and run cool water over pasta.
- Season sauce with salt, pepper and red pepper flakes to taste. Add more sugar if the sauce isn't sweet enough.
- Transfer the crabs to a separate serving bowl. Pour some of the sauce in the bottom of a very large pasta bowl. Add pasta and toss with the remaining sauce. (If there's too much sauce you can serve some in a gravy boat on the side.) Let cool 10 to 15 minutes so sauce thickens slightly.

Finish and Serve:

- Serve with warm Italian bread and grated Parmesan.

CHEF'S TIP:

- This Italian pasta dish translates as "soup of the sea." It's traditionally served family style around Easter and Christmas.

Grilled Salmon Mignon with Yellow Pepper Sauce and Potato Fried Shrimp

Chef James Decker

Serves 4

Yellow Pepper Sauce:

2 tablespoons olive oil
4 yellow bell peppers, stem and seeds removed, cut into large pieces
1/4 cup finely diced yellow onion
1 clove garlic, sliced
1 tablespoon finely sliced basil leaves
1 cup chicken stock
Salt and pepper to taste
1 sweet potato, peeled
1 large golden beet, peeled
1 large carrot, peeled
1 zucchini
1 large red-skin potato, scrubbed

Savory Salt:

2 tablespoons kosher salt
2 tablespoons summer savory

Salmon:

4 8-ounce salmon fillets
Vegetable oil as needed

Potato Fried Shrimp:

1 large Idaho potato, peeled
4 large shrimp, peeled and deveined (leave the tail section of the shell on)
4 cups vegetable oil for frying

BEVERAGE RECOMMENDATION

Grand Archer Syrah or Chalk Hill Chardonnay

To Make the Yellow Pepper Sauce:

- Place the olive oil in a medium stockpot set over low heat. Add the yellow peppers and cook until softened. Add the onion, garlic and basil and cook a few more minutes. Add the chicken stock and simmer until reduced by half. Once reduced, purée in a blender and strain through a fine-mesh strainer. Season with salt and pepper.
- Using a small Parisienne spoon or small melon baller, make tiny balls of the sweet potato, beet, carrot, zucchini and red-skin potato. Blanch each separately in boiling salted water until tender. (Each vegetable will take a different amount of time, so cook them separately.) Transfer vegetables to a bowl of ice water to cool. Set the vegetables aside.

To Make the Savory Salt:

- Place the kosher salt and summer savory in a spice or coffee grinder and grind until the salt starts to take on a green color. Set aside for seasoning the salmon after it cooks.

To Make the Salmon:

- Heat a gas or charcoal grill to high. Slice each salmon fillet in half lengthwise and roll one fillet around the other to make a large, round, flat fillet, then secure each with a long bamboo skewer so it holds its shape. Brush the salmon with a small amount of the vegetable oil and sear on a hot grill to achieve nice grill marks. Move the salmon to a cooler part of the grill until cooked through, or finish in the oven. Keep warm.

To Make the Potato Fried Shrimp:

- Place the Idaho potato on a spiral vegetable cutter. Using the smallest blade, cut spiral potatoes to wrap around the shrimp. Pat the shrimp dry, and using a length of potato 12 inches long and a few strands wide, start at the tail of the shrimp and wrap the potato around the shrimp until you reach the large end. Heat the vegetable oil in a medium, heavy bottom saucepan to 350 degrees F. Fry the shrimp until golden brown and drain on paper towels. Keep warm.

Finish and Serve:

- Reheat the pepper sauce and cover the bottom of four dinner plates with a layer of it. Remove the skewers from the salmon and place a medallion in the middle of each plate. Reheat the vegetable balls in a sauté pan with a little simmering water. Once hot, drain and spread the vegetables, like confetti, around the salmon. Sprinkle the savory salt on the salmon as needed. Place the fried shrimp, standing up, on top of the salmon and serve.

CHEF'S TIP:

- A spiral vegetable cutter can be purchased at equipment specialty stores like William Sonoma, or sometimes at Asian markets.

Gremolata-Crusted Sea Bass with Saffron Risotto and Roasted Tomato Croquette

Chef James Decker
Serves 4

Roasted Tomato Croquette:
4 Roma tomatoes, peeled, cut in half lengthwise and seeded
2 tablespoons olive oil
1/2 teaspoon finely chopped basil
1/2 teaspoon finely chopped rosemary
Salt and pepper to taste
1/4 cup all-purpose flour
2 large eggs, lightly beaten
1 cup fine breadcrumbs

Sea Bass:
2 tablespoons finely chopped parsley
2 tablespoons finely grated lemon zest
2 tablespoons finely chopped garlic
4 6-ounce sea bass fillets, patted dry

Saffron Risotto:
5 cups chicken stock
6 saffron threads
6 tablespoons unsalted butter
1/4 cup finely diced onion
1 1/2 cups Arborio rice
1 cup grated Parmesan cheese

To Finish and Serve:
4 cups vegetable oil for frying

BEVERAGE RECOMMENDATION
Cakebread Chardonnay

To Make the Roasted Tomato Croquette:

- Preheat oven to 200 degrees F. Place tomatoes on a baking sheet and sprinkle with olive oil, basil, rosemary and salt and pepper. Roast for 1 1/2 hours.
- Remove tomatoes from the oven and pat them dry with paper towels. Place two halves on a sheet of plastic wrap and roll into a log by twisting the plastic from both ends in opposite directions. Place in the freezer. Repeat with remaining tomatoes. Freeze until firm.
- Place flour, eggs and bread crumbs in separate wide, shallow bowls. Once tomatoes are firm, unwrap and dredge in flour. Dip in the egg wash and shake off any excess egg. Roll in the breadcrumbs until fully coated. Repeat the flour-egg-breadcrumb process with each tomato log again so that they are double coated. Place on a sheet pan covered with parchment paper or waxed paper and chill until needed.

To Make the Sea Bass:

- Preheat oven to 350 degrees F. Combine the parsley, lemon zest and garlic. Spread the mixture evenly on top of the sea bass fillets. Place on a sheet pan and bake until cooked through, 12 to 15 minutes. Remove from the oven and keep warm.

To Make the Saffron Risotto:

- While the fish is baking, in a medium saucepan, bring the stock and saffron to a boil and let steep for 5 minutes. In a separate pan, melt the butter over medium heat. Add the onion and cook, stirring, until soft. Add the rice and stir until the grains are well coated, about 1 minute. Add the stock in three additions, stirring constantly and waiting until the liquid is absorbed between each addition.
- Once all the stock is added, fold in the cheese and season with salt and pepper. Keep warm.

Finish and Serve:

- Heat the vegetable oil in a large, deep pan to 350 degrees F. Fry the tomato logs until golden brown.
- Place a quarter of the risotto in the center of each of four plates. Place a sea bass fillet in the center of the rice. Cut the tomato croquettes in half on the bias, place on top of the fish and serve.

CHEF'S TIP:

- Chef Decker serves this dish over steamed asparagus.

Coriander-Dusted Black Bass over Sautéed Frisée with Onion-Bacon Sauce

Chef Scott Campbell

Serves 6

Frisée:

2 tablespoons bacon fat

2 heads frisée, well rinsed and dried

2 cloves garlic, sliced

1/2 cup water

Salt to taste

Pepper to taste

Onion-Bacon Butter Sauce:

1 pound thick-cut bacon

2 tablespoons olive oil

1 medium onion, thinly sliced

Salt to taste

White pepper to taste

1/4 cup aged sherry vinegar

1 cup chicken stock

1/2 cup unsalted butter, cut into chunks

1 teaspoon Tabasco

Black Bass:

1 cup flour

1 teaspoon ground coriander

Sea salt to taste

Pepper to taste

6 6-ounce black bass fillets, skin on

1/4 cup blended oil

To Make the Frisée:

- Place two large sauté pans on over medium-high heat. Divide the bacon fat between the pans. Add half the frisée to each pan along with half the garlic. Sauté until lightly browned. Transfer the frisée to one pan. Add water and cook until evaporated. Season with salt and pepper to taste. Keep warm.

To Make the Onion-Bacon Butter Sauce:

- Cut three slices of the bacon in half and cook until crisp. Set aside for garnish.
- Cut remaining bacon into 1-inch pieces and cook until crisp. Reserve bacon fat and bacon pieces separately.
- In a skillet, heat oil and sauté onions over medium-high heat until golden brown. Season with salt and pepper. Add sherry and cook, stirring, until it is evaporated. Set aside.
- In a small sauce pan, bring chicken stock to a boil and whisk in butter. When butter is incorporated add the bacon mixture, onions and Tabasco. Blend together with a hand-held blender and season to taste with salt and pepper. Keep warm.

To Make the Black Bass:

- Preheat oven to 350 degrees F. In a small bowl, combine flour, coriander, salt and pepper. Dredge fillets in mixture and shake off excess flour.
- Heat a large cast-iron skillet over medium-high heat. Add oil. Place three of the fillets in the pan skin-side down. Cook, turning once, until lightly browned, about 2 minutes per side. Repeat with the remaining fillets. Transfer the fish to the oven and roast until done, 2 to 3 minutes

Finish and Serve:

- Divide frisée between six plates. Top with a bass fillet and drizzle with sauce. Garnish with reserved bacon and serve.

Scott Campbell helps lead the youth team to gold-medal victory in hot food.

Olive Oil Poached Halibut with Oven-Dried Tomato and Roasted Eggplant

Chef Joachim Buchner, CMC

Serves 4

Oven-Dried Tomatoes:

8 plum tomatoes, quartered
2 tablespoons olive oil
Salt and pepper to taste
4 sprigs fresh thyme

Red Wine Reduction:

1 bottle red wine

Vegetables:

4 slices eggplant, each 1/2 inch thick, approximately 3 inches in diameter
Salt and pepper to taste
5 tablespoons olive oil
1 shallot, diced
4 baby artichokes, trimmed, cooked and halved
1 1/2 cups oven-dried tomatoes
1/2 cup kalamata olives, pitted and halved

Halibut:

2 cups olive oil
4 4-ounce pieces Alaskan halibut

Finish and Serve:

1 tablespoon chopped parsley
1 tablespoon sliced basil leaves
1 tablespoon finely sliced chives

BEVERAGE RECOMMENDATION

Grove Mill, Marlborough 01
Sauvignon Blanc

To Make the Oven-Dried Tomatoes:

- Preheat oven to 250 degrees F. Lay tomatoes on a wire rack set over a sheet pan. Drizzle with olive oil. Season with salt, pepper and the thyme leaves. Place in oven and dry for 2 to 3 hours, until slightly firm.

To Make the Red Wine Reduction:

- Place the wine in a medium stainless-steel saucepan and bring just to a boil. Adjust the heat and simmer until reduced to about 1 cup, watching closely and lowering the heat further as the wine reduces to prevent scorching. Transfer the reduced wine to a small saucepan and continue simmering very gently until you have a thick, syrupy liquid; sweeter wines will become syrupy more quickly. Measure out 1/4 cup of the reduced wine and set aside.

To Make the Vegetables:

- Sprinkle eggplant with salt and pepper and let stand for 1 hour. Rinse off salt and drain eggplant.
- Heat a large sauté pan over medium heat. Add 3 tablespoons of the oil and sauté eggplant until very tender, about 10 minutes. Keep warm.
- In another sauté pan, heat 2 tablespoons of the remaining oil and sauté the shallot and artichokes until shallot is are soft. Add oven-roasted tomatoes and olives. Keep warm.

To Make the Halibut:

- In a heavy saucepan, warm 2 cups of olive oil over very low heat until it reaches 150 degrees F. Season halibut with salt and pepper and submerge it in the warm olive oil. Poach fish for 5 minutes. Remove from oil and let drain thoroughly.

Finish and Serve:

- Spoon the cooked eggplant in the center of each of four dinner plates. Place a piece of fish on top of each and spoon tomato and artichoke around and on top of the fish. Sprinkle parsley, basil and chives over the tomato and artichoke. Drizzle the reduced red wine around the fish and serve.

CHEF'S TIP:

- Quality ingredients are an absolute necessity to achieve the light but bold flavor of this dish. Use only high-quality olive oil and top-of-the-line olives.

Wild Mushroom and Goat Cheese Strudel

Chef Russell Scott, CMC
Serves 4

Strudels:

2 tablespoons olive oil, or as needed
4 pounds wild mushrooms, quartered
2 tablespoons chopped shallots
1 tablespoon chopped garlic
1/2 cup dry sherry
4 ounces soft goat cheese
1/2 bunch chives, chopped
1 tablespoon fresh thyme leaves
1 egg
Salt and pepper to taste
10 sheets phyllo dough
3/4 cup clarified butter or olive oil
Olive oil

Lentils:

2 tablespoons olive oil
1 cup cooked lentils
2 cups roasted red bell pepper
Salt and pepper to taste

To Make the Strudels:

- Heat oil in large skillet. Working in batches, sauté mushrooms until golden brown. Transfer to a large bowl.
- Add shallots and garlic to the skillet mushrooms cooked in. Sauté until soft. Add sherry and cook until reduced and syrupy. Combine with mushrooms and cool to room temperature.
- When cool, stir in goat cheese, chives, thyme and egg. Mix well and season to taste with salt and pepper.
- Lay a sheet of phyllo out and brush it with clarified butter. Top with another phyllo sheet, brush with butter, and repeat until you have used 5 sheets total. Using a knife, halve the sheets lengthwise. Place about a quarter of the mushroom mixture on top of each half. Tuck the sides over the filling and then roll up as if you were rolling up a burrito. Repeat with remaining phyllo and stuffing until you have 4 strudels.
- Brush outside of rolls with clarified butter and roast carefully on a parchment paper-lined baking sheet, rotating the strudels as needed to encourage even browning.

To Make the Lentils:

- In a small sauté pan, heat the olive oil and cook the lentils and peppers until heated through and season to taste with salt and pepper.

Finish and Serve:

- Evenly distribute the lentils and creamed spinach between 4 plates. Cut each strudel on the bias in half and place on top of the lentils and spinach, serve.

CHEF'S TIP:

- Chef Scott serves this with creamed spinach (see recipe page 230).
- To roast bell peppers, rub them with oil, broil or grill until charred, cool and peel, remove stems and seeds.

Raspberry Martinis

Chef Roy Pell

Serves 8

Shortbread Cookies:

1/2 cup softened unsalted butter

5 tablespoons sugar, plus more for sprinkling on the cookies

Zest of 1 orange

1/8 vanilla bean

1/4 cup all-purpose flour

Lady Finger Sponge:

6 tablespoons cornstarch

6 tablespoons bread flour

1 cup egg whites

10 tablespoons sugar

1/2 cup egg yolks, lightly beaten

Raspberry Mousse:

3/4 teaspoon powdered gelatin

2 tablespoons cold water

1 cup raspberry purée

6 tablespoons sugar

2 cups heavy cream

Raspberry Sauce:

4 teaspoons cornstarch

1 cup raspberry purée (see Chef's Tip)

2 tablespoons sugar

Finish and Serve:

2 cups raspberries

Mint sprigs for garnish

To Make the Shortbread Cookies:

- Preheat oven to 350 degrees F. In the bowl of a mixer, cream the butter and sugar together until fluffy. Beat in zest. Scrap seeds from vanilla bean and beat them in. Stir in flour.
- Form dough into an 8-inch circle and place on a non-stick baking pan. Bake until just golden brown around the edges, about 15 minutes. Remove from oven, sprinkle with sugar and allow to cool. Cut into eight wedges.

To Make the Lady Finger Sponge:

- Sift cornstarch and flour together and set aside. Whip the egg whites until foamy. Slowly whip in the sugar, whipping until soft peaks form. Fold the whipped whites into the egg yolks, then fold in the cornstarch and flour mixture.
- Preheat oven to 390 degrees F. Pour into a greased 10-inch round cake pan. Bake at until a toothpick inserted into the center of the cake comes out clean, about 10 minutes.
- Cool briefly in the pan, then turn the sponge cake out onto a wire rack to cool completely.

To Make the Raspberry Mousse:

- In a small cup, combine gelatin and water and allow to soften.
- In a small saucepan, heat half of the purée until it just begins to bubble. Remove from heat and stir in the gelatin.
- Mix well and strain onto the rest of the purée. Allow to cool to room temperature.
- Whip cream and sugar until it forms soft peaks. Fold in purée. Refrigerate until ready to serve.

To Make the Raspberry Sauce:

- Place the cornstarch in a small saucepan. Very slowly stir the purée into the cornstarch, forming a smooth paste. Bring to a simmer over medium heat and stir in the sugar. Simmer for 1 minute.
- Allow to cool and adjust thickness by adding water if necessary.

Finish and Serve:

- Have ready eight martini glasses. Split the lady finger sponge into 1/2 inch thick slices, then cut into circles that will fit into your martini glasses. Set aside.
- Place three raspberries in the bottom of each glass and cover with raspberry sauce. Cover with mousse, filling half way up the glasses. Add a sponge circle to each glass. Fill glass until 7/8 full of mousse. Refrigerate until set, about 1 hour.
- Once set, cover the top with raspberry sauce and decorate with raspberries and a mint sprig. Serve each with a shortbread cookie on the side.

CHEF'S TIP: Raspberry Purée

- The easiest way to make raspberry purée is to start with frozen, sweetened raspberries. Thaw the berries and put them in a food processor. Process until smooth. Stain the purée to remove seeds and use as directed.

Warm Chocolate Tarts

Chef Roy Pell
Serves 8

Chocolate Tart Shells:
14 tablespoons softened unsalted butter
1/4 cup sugar
1/2 teaspoon vanilla extract
1/2 large egg
1 1/4 cups all-purpose flour
1 tablespoon cocoa powder

Chocolate Tart Filling:
2 cups heavy cream
1 3/4 cups chopped semisweet chocolate
2 eggs

Chocolate Sauce:
1 cup water
10 tablespoons sugar
1/4 cup corn syrup
1/4 cup cocoa powder
1 cup chopped semisweet chocolate

Finish and Serve:
Fresh fruit for garnish

To Make the Chocolate Tart Shells:

- In a large bowl, cream together the butter, sugar and vanilla extract. Beat in the egg.
- Sift the cocoa powder and flour together and add to the butter mixture. Stir until a dough is formed. Refrigerate until chilled.
- Preheat oven to 350 degrees F. Roll dough out to a thickness of 1/4 inch and cut into circles large enough to line 8 individual 4-inch tart pans. Ease the dough circles into the pans and trim the edges. Line the shells with parchment paper and weight with pie weights or dry beans. Bake until the dough appears dry and just cooked through.
- Allow to cool and remove paper and weights. Release shells from tart pans and set aside.

To Make the Chocolate Tart Filling:

- In a small saucepan, heat the cream just until bubbles form on the edge of the pan. Place the chocolate in a large bowl and stir in the hot cream, stirring until melted and smooth. Allow to cool slightly, then stir in the eggs. Mix well.

To Make the Chocolate Sauce:

- Combine water, sugar and corn syrup in a small saucepan and bring to a boil. Stir in cocoa powder to form a paste.
- Place chocolate in a medium bowl and pour hot cocoa and sugar mixture over it. Stir until all melted. Strain and keep at room temperature until needed.

Finish and Serve:

- Preheat oven to 325 degrees F. Pour the chocolate filling into prepared tart shells and bake 5 minutes. Allow to cool until partially set but still warm. Serve on plates decorated with chocolate sauce and fruit.

In its first-ever participation in pastry at the "Culinary Olympics," Team USA's pastry team places second in the world. (l. to r.) Team coach Gilles Renusson, captain Darrin Aoyama and Roy Pell.

Warm Chocolate Decadence in a Minted Raspberry Essence with Crispy Tuile and Fresh Strawberry Ice Cream

Chef Patricia Nash

Serves 8

Chocolate Decadence:

8 ounces dark couverture chocolate, chopped

1 cup unsalted butter

1/2 cup sugar

4 large eggs

Minted Raspberry Essence:

2 pints raspberries

1/4 cup sugar

1/2 teaspoon fresh lemon juice

2 tablespoons Chambord

4 tablespoons water

Leaves from 2 sprigs fresh mint, thinly sliced

Tuiles:

1/4 cup all-purpose flour

1/4 cup sugar

1 tablespoon egg whites

2 tablespoons melted unsalted butter

Strawberry Ice Cream:

3/4 cup heavy cream

1/4 cup milk

1/4 cup sugar

1/2 vanilla bean

3 egg yolks

1/2 cup strawberries, finely chopped or puréed

To Make the Chocolate Decadence:

- Preheat oven to 310 degrees F. Melt dark chocolate and butter in the top of a double boiler set over simmering water. Stir in sugar. In a large bowl, whisk eggs together. Slowly whisk in chocolate mixture.
- Place greased 3-inch metal rings on a parchment-lined sheet pan. Fill the rings with custard. Bake until custard is set, about 12 minutes. Set aside.

To Make the Minted Raspberry Essence:

- Combine raspberries, sugar, lemon juice, Chambord and water in a bowl. Cover with plastic wrap. Place over simmer water in the top of a double boiler and heat for about 45 minutes.
- Strain the raspberry mixture. Discard the solids. Taste the liquid and stir in more sugar if it is not sweet enough. Cool.
- Just before serving, stir in mint.

To Make the Tuiles:

- Combine flour and sugar. Whisk in egg whites until there are no lumps. Stir in butter, stirring until incorporated. Refrigerate until thickened and no longer runny.
- Preheat oven to 350 degrees F. Line a sheet pan with a Silpat baking liner. Form tuiles on Silpat by either using a stencil or simply spreading the batter into thin circles about 3 inches in diameter. Bake until cookies loose their shine, about 2 minutes. Remove from oven and cool.
- Once cool, return the cookies to the oven and bake a second time until lightly browned, about another 2 minutes. While still hot, remove the cookies from the sheet pan with a spatula and drape them over a small ladle or upturned glass to form small bowls.

To Make the Strawberry Ice Cream:

- Combine heavy cream, milk, sugar and vanilla bean in a small, heavy saucepan. Bring just to a boil. In a bowl, whisk yolks. Slowly whisk in hot cream mixture. Return to the pan and cook, stirring, briefly over medium heat. Pour into a clean bowl and chill well.
- Stir in strawberries. Freeze according to the instructions for your ice cream maker.

Finish and Serve:

- Warm chocolate decadence in the oven or microwave. Place each in the center of a bowl. Pour in raspberry essence. Top decadence with tuile and ice cream and serve.

Chocolate Butter Mousse and Vanilla Bean Mousse Terrine with Chocolate Peanut Butter Ice Cream

Chef Patricia Nash

Serves 8

Chocolate Butter Mousse:

12 ounces couverture milk chocolate (Callebaut), chopped
6 ounces softened unsalted butter
1 ounce cocoa powder
6 ounces sugar
Pinch salt
1/4 cup egg yolks
4 gelatin sheets, gold grade
4 cups heavy cream
1/4 cup Godiva chocolate liquor

Vanilla Bean Mousse:

1 1/4 cups egg yolks
1 1/4 cups powdered sugar
Seeds from 2 vanilla beans
4 gelatin sheets, gold grade
3 cups heavy cream
1/4 cup vanilla extract

Chocolate Peanut Butter Ice Cream:

2 ounces couverture dark chocolate, melted
4 tablespoons peanut butter
3/4 cup heavy cream
1/4 cup milk
1/4 cup sugar
1/2 vanilla bean
3 egg yolks

Cherries:

1 cup pitted fresh cherries, halved
1/4 cup sugar
1 vanilla bean, seeded

To Make the Chocolate Butter Mousse:

- In the top of a double boiler over simmering water, melt chocolate. Set aside.
- Meanwhile, in a mixer fitted with a paddle attachment, combine butter, cocoa powder, sugar and salt and beat until light. Beat in yolks.
- Soften gelatin leaves in cold water for 1 to 2 minutes. Whip cream until it forms soft peaks. Set aside.
- Strain water from gelatin. Combine the gelatin and Godiva liquor together and heat over simmering water until gelatin is melted.
- When gelatin is dissolved and chocolate is melted, add both to the butter mixture and stir to combine. Fold in the cream. Pour into a mold or loaf pan or terrine. Freeze.

To Make the Vanilla Bean Mousse:

- In a mixer, whip yolks, sugar and vanilla bean seeds until light and about triple in volume.
- Meanwhile, soften gelatin leaves in cold water. Whip cream until it holds soft peaks. Set aside.
- Strain off water from gelatin, add vanilla extract and heat over simmering water until gelatin is melted. Beat gelatin and vanilla mixture into yolks. Fold in whipped cream. Pour mixture over the chocolate butter mousse in the mold. Freeze.

To Make the Chocolate Peanut Butter Ice Cream:

- Combine the melted chocolate and 2 tablespoons of the peanut butter. Pour onto a small sheet pan lined with parchment paper. (This will become 'chips' for the ice cream.)
- Combine the heavy cream, milk, sugar and vanilla bean in a saucepan and bring to slow boil. In medium bowl, whisk the yolks until smooth. Slowly whisk in the hot cream. Cook slightly.
- Discard the vanilla bean and stir the remaining 2 tablespoons peanut butter into the cream mixture. Refrigerate until well chilled.
- Freeze the chilled cream mixture according to the directions for your ice cream maker. Chop the frozen chocolate and peanut butter mixture into small pieces and add them to the ice cream mixture during the last few minutes of freezing. Transfer the ice cream to a container and freeze.

To Make the Cherries:

- Combine the cherries, sugar and vanilla bean in a bowl and toss.

Finish and Serve:

- Unmold the terrine by inverting it onto a platter; if it doesn't release, place the bottom of the terrine briefly on a damp, heated towel and try again.
- Slice the terrine and serve with the ice cream and cherries.

CHEF'S TIP:

- Any type of mold can be used for the mousses; if you don't have round or rectangular custom terrine molds, a large loaf pan will suffice. Chef Nash serves this dessert with raspberry sauce.

Bread-and-Butter Pudding

Chef Roy Pell
Serves 8

Vanilla Sauce:

1 1/2 cups milk
1 1/2 cups cream
1/2 vanilla bean
4 tablespoons sugar
1/2 cup egg yolks

Pudding:

2 cups milk
1 1/2 teaspoons vanilla extract
1/2 cup sugar, plus more for sprinkling on the pudding
4 large eggs
16 slices white bread
1/2 cup softened unsalted butter
1/2 cup raisins

To Make the Vanilla Sauce:

- In a medium, heavy saucepan, combine milk and cream. Slit vanilla bean down the middle and use the tip of a knife to scrape out the seeds. Add seeds and bean to the saucepan. Place over medium-high heat and heat until bubbles just begin to form around the edges of the pan.
- In a large bowl, whisk together sugar and egg yolks. Whisking constantly and pouring in a very thin stream, whisk the hot milk and cream into the yolks. Discard vanilla bean.
- Return the mixture to the saucepan. Place over medium heat and, using a wooden spoon, stir the mixture constantly. Cook until the mixture thickens just enough to coat the back of the spoon.
- Immediately remove from the heat and strain into a clean bowl. Place the bowl over a larger bowl filled with ice and cool, stirring occasionally. Cover with plastic wrap and refrigerate until needed.

To Make the Pudding:

- Preheat oven to 350 degrees F. In a small saucepan, combine milk and vanilla and heat until bubbles just form around the edges of the pan. Remove from heat. Whisk together sugar and eggs. Very slowly whisk in hot milk. Strain and set aside.
- Spread bread slices with butter and cut to fit inside an 8-inch-square baking dish. Alternate layers of bread and raisins, ending with a layer of bread, butter-side up.
- Pour in the milk mixture and push the bread down into the liquid to help absorption. Sprinkle the top with sugar and bake until all the liquid has set, approximately 30 minutes.

Finish and Serve:

- Serve warm with vanilla sauce.

CHEF'S TIP:

- This dessert can be made in a single baking dish or in individual serving dishes. Just decrease the baking time slightly if you bake them individually.

Frozen Grand Marnier Soufflé

Chef Roy Pell
Serves 8

Soufflé:

2 1/4 cups heavy cream
Zest from 1 orange
7 tablespoons Grand Marnier
3/4 cup sugar
1/4 cup water
3/4 cup egg yolks

Finish and Serve:

Powdered sugar for garnish
Fresh fruit for garnish

To Make the Souffle:

- Have ready eight 6-ounce soufflé dishes or ramekins. Cut strips of paper 1 inch wider than the depth of your soufflé dishes or ramekins and long enough to wrap around them twice. Secure each to the outside of your dishes with a rubber band, making "collars" that are 1 inch higher than the dishes.
- In a large bowl, combine cream, zest and Grand Marnier. Whip until the mixture holds soft peaks. Set aside.
- In a small saucepan, combine sugar and water and cook until you have even and consistent bubbles coming to the surface (110 C./230 F.).
- Whip the egg yolks to a foam. Continue whipping while you slowly pour the hot sugar mixture into the bowl (to avoid spattering the hot liquid, do not pour it directly on the beaters). Continue beating until the mixture is no longer warm to the touch.
- Fold the cream into the yolk mixture. Fill your dishes and place in the freezer for at least 3 hours.

Finish and Serve:

- When frozen, remove from freezer, remove paper collars and dust soufflés with powdered sugar. Place each on a plate decorated with fresh fruits of your choice and serve.

Gratin of Citrus Fruit with Grapefruit Sorbet

Chef Roy Pell
Serves 8

Grapefruit Sorbet:
1 3/4 cups water
1 1/4 cups sugar
4 tablespoons glucose
1 1/4 cups grapefruit juice
1 cup orange juice

Tulipes:
3 tablespoons all-purpose flour
1/4 cup powdered sugar
1/4 cup egg whites
2 1/2 tablespoons unsalted butter, melted and cooled

Champagne Sabayon:
6 large egg yolks
1/2 cup sugar
1 cup champagne

Finish and Serve:
4 grapefruits, peeled and cut into segments
6 oranges, peeled and cut into segments
8 sprigs mint, for garnish

To Make the Grapefruit Sorbet:

- In a small saucepan, heat the water, sugar and glucose, stirring, just until the sugar melts. Remove from heat and stir in grapefruit and orange juices. Allow to cool.
- Freeze according to the directions for your ice cream maker. Transfer to a container and freeze until ready to serve.

To Make the Tulipes:

- Mix together flour and powdered sugar. Beat in egg whites, beating until smooth. Beat in cooled melted butter. Refrigerate overnight.
- Preheat oven to 350 degrees F. Using the back of a spoon, spread batter thinly onto a non-stick baking sheet in 3-inch circles; make only four circles per batch. Bake until golden brown, 3 to 4 minutes.
- Remove from oven and, while still hot, use a spatula to transfer each cookie onto the bottom of an upended glass. The sides of the cookie should drape over the glass, forming an inverted "tulip" or basket shape.
- Let cool, then remove from the glasses. Repeat until you have used all the batter. Store the tulips in an airtight container until ready to use.

To Make the Champagne Sabayon:

- Add water to the bottom of a double boiler and bring to a simmer. In the top of the double boiler, whisk together yolks, sugar and champagne. Place over simmering water and whisk until foamy and thick. (The mixture should hold its shape if you drag the whisk through the center.) Serve immediately.

Finish and Serve:

- Arrange fruit segments in a circle on each of eight dessert plates, alternating between grapefruit and orange. Warm the plates in the oven if desired.
- Cover the citrus segments with sabayon and brown with a blow torch or by placing them briefly under the broiler. Place a tulipe in the center of the segments and place a scoop of sorbet in the tulipe. Garnish with a mint sprig and serve immediately.

Crème Brulée with Honeyed Raspberries

Chef Patricia Nash
Serves 8

Crème Brulée:

3 cups heavy cream
3/4 cup sugar, plus more for sprinkling over the crème brulées
Seeds from 1 vanilla bean
1 1/4 cups egg yolks

Finish and Serve:

2 pints raspberries
3 tablespoons honey

To Make the Crème Brulée:

- Preheat oven to 310 degrees F. In a saucepan, combine cream, sugar and vanilla bean seeds and bring just to a boil. Whisk yolks together in a bowl. Slowly whisk the hot cream into the yolks. Transfer to crème brulée dishes. Set dishes in a roasting pan, pour in water to come half way up the sides of the dishes and bake until custard is set. Refrigerate until ready to serve.

Finish and Serve:

- Sprinkle the tops of the crème brulées with sugar. Brown the sugar under a broiler or with a blowtorch until crispy. Top with raspberries, drizzle with honey and serve.

CHEF'S TIP:

- If you don't have special crème brulée dishes, you can bake these in ramekins, oven-proof bowls or oven-proof coffee cups. If you have extra custard mix leftover, refrigerate it and use it later — it makes a rich base for bread pudding.

Summer Sherbet Cocktail

Chef Patricia Nash
Serves 8

Watermelon Sherbet:
1 cup puréed watermelon
1 tablespoon Rose's sorbet base
4 ounces thawed frozen yogurt mix
1 tablespoon Madori liqueur
1 tablespoon grenadine
1/4 cup sugar
1 tablespoon lemon juice

Cantaloupe Sherbet:
1 cup cantaloupe purée
1 tablespoon Rose's sorbet base
4 ounces thawed frozen yogurt mix
1 tablespoon Madori liqueur
1/4 cup sugar
2 tablespoons fresh pineapple juice
1 tablespoon lemon juice

Honeydew Sherbet:
1 cup honeydew purée
1 tablespoon Rose's sorbet base
4 ounces thawed frozen yogurt mix
1 tablespoon Madori liqueur
2/3 cup sugar
1/4 cup pineapple juice, fresh
1 tablespoon lemon juice

Finish and Serve:
Sprigs of mint
Chocolate decorations

To Make the Watermelon Sherbet:

- Combine all ingredients and run them through a juice machine. Freeze according to the directions for your ice cream machine. Transfer to a small container and freeze.

To Make the Cantaloupe Sherbet:

- Combine all ingredients and run them through a juice machine. Freeze according to the directions for your ice cream machine. Transfer to a small container and freeze.

To Make the Honeydew Sherbet:

- Combine all ingredients and run them through a juice machine. Freeze according to the directions for your ice cream machine. Transfer to a small container and freeze.

Finish and Serve:

- Place one scoop of each of the three sorbets in martini glasses. Garnish with sprigs of mint or a chocolate decorations and serve.

CHEF'S TIP:

- The amount of sugar added to each sherbet recipe should be adjusted according to the ripeness of the melon. Chef Nash runs these mixtures through a juice machine prior to freezing to produce perfect creaminess in the final product.

Chocolate Caramel Cashew Crunch-Ups

Chef Heather Hurlbert
Serves 4

Tuiles:
2 large eggs
1/2 cup powdered sugar
1/2 teaspoon vanilla extract
1 pinch salt
1/2 cup plus **2 tablespoons** all-purpose flour
1/4 cup chopped cashews

Cereal Crunch:
1/2 cup chopped bittersweet chocolate, melted
1/3 cup Grape Nuts cereal
1/3 cup chopped cashews

Caramel Cream Filling:
1 cup sugar
1/4 cup water
1/2 cup plus **2 tablespoons** heavy cream
1 cup whipped cream

Pineapple-Caramel Sauce:
1/4 cup sugar
3 tablespoons water
1/4 cup heavy cream
1/4 cup pineapple purée
1/2 vanilla bean
1/2 cup finely diced pineapple

Pineapple Fan:
1/3 cup water
1/2 cup sugar
4 pieces very thinly sliced pineapple

Finish and Serve:
Shaved chocolate

To Make the Tuiles:

- Preheat oven to 325 degrees F. Whisk together eggs, sugar, vanilla and salt. Stir in flour. Fold in nuts.
- Spoon 2-tablespoon portions of the batter onto a parchment-lined baking sheet. Bake until golden brown, 8 to 10 minutes. Allow to cool slightly. While still warm, press cookies around a tube or narrow bottle about 1 1/2 inches in diameter, forming a tube. Allow to cool until firm. Gently slip the cookie off and store in an airtight container until ready to serve.

To Make the Cereal Crunch:

- Gently stir together melted chocolate, cereal and nuts. Spread the mixture out onto a baking sheet lined with parchment paper and refrigerate. When set, break into small pieces. Keep refrigerated in an air tight container until ready to serve.

To Make the Caramel Cream Filling:

- Combine sugar and water in a small, heavy saucepan. Place over medium heat and cook until the mixture turns a deep amber color. Remove from heat and very carefully stir in the cream (the mixture will sputter). Return to heat and cook, stirring constantly, until the mixture is smooth.
- Refrigerate until cool to touch. Fold in whipped cream. Refrigerate until ready to use.

To Make the Pineapple-Caramel Sauce:

- Place sugar and water in a small saucepan over medium-low heat. Cook until amber in color. Remove from the heat and very carefully stir in the cream (the mixture will sputter). Return to the heat and add pineapple purée and vanilla bean. Bring to a boil and stir until smooth. Refrigerate. When chilled, stir in the diced pineapple.

To Make the Pineapple Fan:

- Heat water and sugar until sugar is completely dissolved (simple syrup). Cool.
- Dip the pineapple slices into the simple syrup (make sure the simple syrup is cool) and lay carefully onto a Silpat.
- Place into a 150 degree F. oven for an 1 1/2 hours, flip the pineapple slices and continue to cook for an additional 1 1/2 hours.

Finish and Serve:

- Fold cereal crunch pieces into caramel cream filling. Transfer to a pastry bag fitted with a large plain tube and pipe the mixture into tuile cylinders. Place on plates. Garnish plates with pineapple-caramel sauce, shaved chocolate and pineapple fan and serve.

Banana Cake, Spiced Banana Compote, Roasted Banana Ice Cream and Banana-Lime Essence

Chef Darrin Aoyama, CEPC
Serves 8

Cake:
1/2 cup unsalted butter
1 cup sugar
2 large eggs
2 tablespoons milk
1 teaspoon vanilla extract
2 cups all-purpose flour
1 teaspoon baking soda
1 1/2 teaspoons baking powder
1 teaspoon ground cinnamon
1/2 teaspoon salt
3 large, ripe bananas, peeled

Compote:
1/4 cup unsalted butter
1/2 cup brown sugar
1/4 cup orange juice
1/4 cup dark rum
4 large, ripe bananas, peeled and cut into 1/4-inch dice
1/2 teaspoon cinnamon
Juice from 1/2 lemon

Ice Cream:
3 large, ripe bananas, peeled
1/4 cup unsalted butter, diced
1/2 cup brown sugar
1/2 cup granulated sugar
2 large eggs
1 large egg yolk
1 1/4 cups milk
1 1/2 cups heavy cream
1 tablespoon corn syrup
1 vanilla bean, split and seeds scraped out

Banana-Lime Essence:
1 cup granulated sugar
1 cup banana liqueur
3 large, ripe bananas, peeled and cut into 1-inch slices
Juice of 2 limes

Finish and Serve:
Powdered sugar
Chocolate curls (optional)
Fresh fruit

To Make the Cake:

- Preheat oven to 350 degrees F. and butter a 9-inch cake pan or eight individual molds. Cream together the butter and sugar. Whisk together the eggs, milk and vanilla. Sift together the flour, baking soda, baking powder, cinnamon and salt. Working in three additions, add the wet and dry ingredients alternately to the creamed butter and sugar.
- Smash the bananas until they are fairly smooth but you still have some chunks. Add bananas to the batter and mix. Scrape batter into prepared pan or pans and bake until a toothpick inserted into the center of the cake comes out clean, about 30 minutes for the 9-inch pan or 20 minutes for individual pans. Let the cake cool for 10 minutes, then remove from pan or pans and cool completely on a rack.

To Make the Compote:

- Melt the butter in a sauté pan over medium heat and add the brown sugar. Cook, stirring, until mixture is smooth. Remove from the heat and stir in the orange juice and rum. Return to the heat and bring to a simmer. Add the bananas, lemon juice and cinnamon. Cook until the banana are tender. Set aside.

To Make the Ice Cream:

- Preheat oven to 350 degrees F. Place the bananas in a parchment-lined casserole dish. Dot with the butter and sprinkle the brown sugar over the bananas. Bake until the bananas are soft enough to be mashed easily, 20 to 30 minutes. Remove from the oven and mash bananas with a fork. Set aside to cool.
- In a large bowl, beat granulated sugar, eggs and yolk together until pale yellow and fluffy. In a saucepan, combine the milk, cream, corn syrup and scraped vanilla bean and bring just to a simmer. Very slowly whisk the hot liquid into the egg mixture.
- Return the mixture to the saucepan and place over medium-low heat. Cook, stirring constantly, until the mixture thickens enough to just coat the back of a spoon. Immediately remove from the heat and strain into a clean bowl. Discard vanilla bean pod. Place the bowl over an ice bath or refrigerate until mixture is well chilled.
- When chilled, pour into an ice cream maker and process according to the manufacturer's directions. Fold in the cooled roasted bananas, transfer the ice cream to a container and freeze.

To Make the Banana-Lime Essence:

- In a saucepan, combine the sugar and liqueur and bring to a simmer. Add the bananas and let simmer until the bananas expand and soften but don't fall apart, about 10 minutes. Strain the mixture and discard the solids. Chill the liquid. Stir in lime juice to taste.

Finish and Serve:

- Cut cake into eight pieces if you have one large cake. Dust pieces or individual cakes with powdered sugar and place each in a shallow bowls or soup plates. Place a mound of the compote on the side of the cakes and place a scoop of the ice cream on top of the compote. Pour some of the essence around the cakes, garnish with chocolate curls and fresh fruit and serve.

Ginger Pudding

Chef Heather Hurlbert
Serves 4

Pudding:
1 1/2 tablespoons grated ginger
3/4 cup milk
1 cup plus **2 tablespoons** heavy cream
1/2 vanilla bean
1/3 cup plus **2 tablespoons** sugar
2 leaves gelatin
1 tablespoon water

Mango-Passion Fruit Jelly:
1 sheet gelatin
1 1/2 teaspoons water
1/3 cup plus **2 tablespoons** passion fruit purée
1/3 cup plus **2 tablespoons** mango purée

Chocolate Fudge Cookies:
2 tablespoons unsalted butter
1/8 teaspoon sugar
1/4 teaspoon vanilla extract
1/4 cup chopped semisweet chocolate, melted
1 tablespoon cocoa powder
1/4 cup all-purpose flour
Pinch salt
Pinch baking soda
1/4 cup chopped semisweet chocolate
1/4 cup chopped macadamia nuts

Coconut Sable Cookies:
4 tablespoons unsalted butter
Pinch salt
2 tablespoons powdered sugar
1 large egg yolk
1/2 cup all-purpose flour
1 tablespoon almond flour
2 tablespoons unsweetened, desiccated coconut
1/2 teaspoon coconut extract

Chocolate Twirl:
Acetate
1 pound bittersweet chocolate, melted and tempered

Finish and Serve:
Berries for garnish

To Make the Pudding:
- In a small saucepan, combine ginger, milk, heavy cream, vanilla bean and sugar. Bring to simmer, remove from heat, cover and let infuse 1 hour. Strain and discard the solids.
- In a bowl, combine water and gelatin and let sit until gelatin leaf has completely absorbed water. Add gelatin to warm cream mixture and stir until completely dissolved. Pour the mixture into four parfait glasses and refrigerate until set.

To Make the Mango-Passion Fruit Jelly:
- In a bowl, combine gelatin and water and let sit until gelatin has absorbed water. Place bowl over simmering water and stir until gelatin has melted. Stir gelatin into mango and passion fruit purées. Pour the mixture on top of the pudding in the parfait glasses and refrigerate until set.

To Make the Chocolate Fudge Cookies:
- In a large bowl, cream together butter and sugar. Stir in vanilla and melted chocolate. Sift flour, cocoa powder, salt and baking soda together. Stir into butter and sugar mixture. Fold in chopped chocolate and macadamia nuts.
- Preheat oven to 350 degrees F. Spoon or scoop quarter-sized portions of dough onto parchment-lined baking sheet. Bake until you smell the aroma of chocolate and the surface of the cookies lose their shine and become dull, about 12 minutes. Cool on pan.

To Make the Coconut Sable Cookies:
- Preheat oven to 350 degrees F. In a large bowl, cream together butter, salt and powdered sugar. Beat in yolk. Sift together all-purpose flour and almond flour and stir into butter-sugar mixture. Stir in coconut and extract.
- Spoon or scoop quarter-sized portions of dough onto parchment-lined baking sheet. Bake until browned, about 12 minutes. Cool on pan.

To Make the Chocolate Twirl:
- Cut strips of patterned acetate (1 inch by 4 inches).
- Apply a thin layer of chocolate on acetate and let sit for 1 minute, then form into twirls (use a terrine mold to shape). Let set completely.
- Peel acetate from chocolate.

Finish and Serve:
- Garnish puddings with fresh berries, chocolate twirls, fruit jellies and cookies and serve.

Autumn Poached Pear and Spice Soufflé with Cinnamon Crème Anglaise

Chef Darrin Aoyama, CEPC

Serves 8

Cinnamon Crème Anglaise:

2 cups milk

1/2 vanilla bean, split and seeds scraped out

1/2 cup sugar

4 large egg yolks

1/2 teaspoon cinnamon

Pears:

8 Seckel pears

1 cup white wine

4 cups sugar

1 vanilla bean, split and seeds scraped out

1 cinnamon stick

Juice of 1 lemon

3 cups water

Soufflé:

2 cups milk

3/4 cup all-purpose flour

1 cup plus 1 tablespoon sugar

2 large eggs

6 large eggs, separated

1 teaspoon cinnamon

1/4 teaspoon ground nutmeg

1/4 teaspoon ground cloves

1/2 cup sugar

To Make the Cinnamon Crème Anglaise:

- In a small saucepan, combine the milk and vanilla bean pod and seeds. Heat just until bubbles form around the edges of the pan. Set aside.
- In a large bowl, whisk together the sugar, yolks and cinnamon. Very slowly whisk in the hot milk. Return the mixture to the saucepan and cook over medium heat, stirring constantly, until it thickens just enough to coat the back of the spoon.
- Strain immediately into a clean bowl and chill over an ice bath. Cover and refrigerate until ready to serve.

To Make the Pears:

- Peel and core the pears and place in large bowl of water to which some lemon juice has been added. Set aside.
- In a large saucepan, combine wine, sugar, pod and seeds of the vanilla bean, cinnamon stick, lemon juice and water. Bring to a simmer. Add pears and poach until pears are tender, 10 to 15 minutes. Drain and set aside to cool. (Discard the liquid or save for another use.)

To Make the Soufflé:

- Preheat the oven to 375 degrees F. and butter and sugar eight soufflé ramekins. Place the milk in a small saucepan and heat just until bubbles form around the edges of the pan. In a medium bowl, combine flour, 1/2 cup plus 1 tablespoon of the sugar and the 2 whole eggs. Very slowly whisk in the hot milk. Return the mixture to the pan and cook over low heat, stirring constantly. As the mixture cooks it will become lumpy, then smooth out to a thick paste. Remove from the heat and transfer to a mixing bowl.
- Whisk in the 6 egg yolks one at a time, whisking until you have a smooth batter. Stir in cinnamon, nutmeg and cloves.
- Whip the six egg whites with the remaining 1/2 cup of sugar until you have soft peaks. Add half of the whites to the bowl with the batter and fold gently. When almost fully incorporated fold in the rest of the whites.
- Fill a ramekin 1/2 to 3/4 full with batter. Push a pear into the middle of each ramekin until it hits the bottom, making sure the batter comes to just below the edge of the ramekin (you may need to adjust how much batter you put in initially depending on the size of your pears). There should not be any batter on the edges of the ramekin---if there is, gently wipe the edges clean with your finger.
- Bake the soufflés until puffed and golden brown, about 30 minutes.

Finish and Serve:

- Serve immediately when they come out of the oven with the crème anglaise on the side.

CHEF'S TIP:

- The cinnamon crème anglaise for this soufflé can be made the day before and stored in the refrigerator.

Marinated Berries with Sabayon

Chef Darrin Aoyama, CEPC

Serves 8

Berries:

1 pint raspberries
1 pint blueberries
1 pint blackberries
1 pint strawberries, hulled and quartered
1/4 cup sugar
1/4 cup freshly squeezed orange juice
1/4 cup orange liqueur
Juice of 1 lemon

Sabayon:

4 whole large eggs
8 large egg yolks
1/4 cup sugar
1/4 cup orange juice
1/2 cup orange liqueur

Tuile Cookie Crisp:

1/2 cup melted butter
1/2 cup powdered sugar
1/2 cup egg whites
1/2 cup bread flour

Finish and Serve:

Powdered sugar for dusting
Cookie twist

To Make the Berries:

- In a large bowl, toss together the raspberries, blueberries, blackberries and strawberries. Whisk together the sugar, orange juice, liqueur and lemon juice and pour over the berries. Cover with plastic wrap and refrigerate for 1 hour.
- Drain the berries, discarding the juice or saving it for another use. Place the berries in either a shallow oven-proof ceramic platter or on 8 individual oven-proof plates.

To Make the Sabayon:

- Fill a large pot or the bottom of a double boiler with an inch or two of water. Bring to a low simmer. In the top of a double boiler or in a bowl that fits over your pot, combine the eggs, yolks, sugar, orange juice and liqueur.
- Reduce the heat of the water so that it is no longer simmering. Place bowl over the pot and begin whipping the egg mixture. Continue to whip the mixture over the heat until it is light and fluffy. When the entire mixture is fluffy, with no liquid part on the bottom of the bowl, the sabayon is done. Be careful not to over heat or over cook the mixture or the eggs will scramble.

To Make the Tuile Cookie Crisp:

- Combine all of the ingredients and mix well. Refrigerate the batter for 4 hours.
- Preheat over to 325 degrees F. Spread the batter thinly on a Silpat in desired shape or use a stencil pattern and bake until golden brown (approximately 5 to 6 minutes). When the cookies come out of the oven and are still warm, they can be bent or formed into desired shape. Let cool and store in an airtight container until needed.

Finish and Serve:

- Preheat the broiler. Pour the sabayon over the berries. Place the platter or plates under the broiler until sabayon is golden brown on top; rotate plates or platter so sabayon does not burn.
- Dust top of sabayon with powdered sugar, garnish with a cookie crisp and serve immediately.

CHEF'S TIP:

- A Silpat is a nonstick silicone mat that can be found in most specialty cooking stores.

Summer Peach and Apricot Soup with Raspberry Sorbet and Almond Cake

Chef Darrin Aoyama, CEPC

Serves 8

Soup:

8 peaches

8 apricots

1 cup peach nectar

1/4 cup sugar

1/4 cup peach liqueur

Lemon juice as needed

Sorbet:

2 cups water

1 cup sugar

1 cup raspberry purée (see Chef's Tip)

Juice of 1 lemon

Almond Cake:

1 cup almond paste

1/2 cup unsalted butter, at room temperature

1/2 cup sugar

3 large eggs

2 tablespoons Grand Marnier

1/4 cup cake flour

1/2 teaspoon baking powder

Finish and Serve:

Fresh fruit for garnish

To Make the Soup:

- Peel the peaches by bringing a large pot of water to a boil. Using a paring knife, mark the bottom of each peach with an "X." Place the peaches into the boiling water for 30 to 45 seconds and immediately transfer to a bowl of ice water. Slip the skins off and discard.
- Cut the peaches and apricots into quarters and discard the pits. Combine the fruit, nectar and sugar in a saucepan and place over medium heat. Cook, stirring occasionally, until fruit is tender, 15 to 20 minutes.
- Purée the fruit mixture in a blender and stir in the liqueur. Chill.
- Once chilled, taste and stir in lemon juice or more sugar as needed.

To Make the Sorbet:

- Combine the water and sugar and bring to a simmer. Cool. Stir in the purée and lemon juice. Taste and adjust with sugar or lemon juice if necessary. Chill well.
- Process in an ice cream maker according manufacturer's directions. Place in a small container and freeze.

To Make the Almond Cake:

- Preheat oven to 350 degrees F. and grease a muffin pan. In a mixer fitted with a paddle, cream the almond paste, butter and sugar. Beat in eggs, one at a time, beating well after each addition. Beat in Grand Marnier.
- Sift together the flour and baking powder. Stir into batter until smooth. Fill eight of the muffin cups about half full with batter and bake until a toothpick inserted into the center of a cake comes out clean, 15 to 20 minutes.

Finish and Serve:

- Let the cakes cool for 5 minutes, then pop them out of the pan onto a wire rack and cool completely.
- To assemble, place an almond cake in the middle of each of eight shallow serving bowl. Pour some soup around the cakes. Place a scoop of sorbet on top of each cake, garnish with seasonal fresh fruit and serve.

CHEF'S TIP: Raspberry Purée

- To make raspberry purée, pulse fresh raspberries in a blender until smooth. Strain through a sieve to remove the seeds.

Passion Fruit Curd Tarts

Chef Darrin Aoyama, CEPC
Serves 8

Sugar Dough:
2 cups all-purpose flour
3 tablespoons sugar
1/2 teaspoon salt
1 cup cold unsalted butter, diced
2 large egg yolks
1/4 cup cold water

Curd:
7 large egg yolks
1 cup sugar
1/2 cup passion fruit juice
12 tablespoons unsalted butter, cut into 1/4-inch cubes

Whipped Cream:
2 cups heavy cream
1/4 cup sugar
1 teaspoon vanilla extract

Finish and Serve:
Sugared currants
White chocolate twirls (optional)

To Make the Sugar Dough:

- Combine the flour, sugar and salt in a food processor fitted with the dough attachment (if a dough attachment is unavailable the standard blade will work). Pulse to combine. Add the cold butter and pulse until the butter is the size of peas. Add the yolks and pulse again. With the motor running, slowly add the water and process until you have a dough that pulls away from the sides of the bowl.
- Remove the dough from the processor and form it into a disk. Wrap in plastic and refrigerator for 30 to 35 minutes.
- Preheat oven to 350 degrees F. Roll the dough out to thickness of 1/8 inch. Cut circles 5 inches in diameter and use them to line eight 3-inch tart shells. Trim the edges of the dough and refrigerate the tart shells briefly. (There will be leftover dough and scraps; this can be reformed and baked as sugar cookies.)
- Line each tart pan with parchment paper and fill with pie weights or dried beans. Bake until the edges of the shells are lightly browned. Remove weights and parchment and continue to bake until the shells are browned and fully baked. Set aside to cool.

To Make the Curd:

- Combine the yolks, sugar and passion fruit juice in a heat-proof bowl or in the top of a double boiler. Cook, stirring, over simmering water until the mixture thickens to the consistency of pudding.
- Remove from the heat and stir in the butter; stir the curd gently so as not to incorporate air, mixing until the butter has melted and is completely incorporated. Immediately pour into the prepared tart shells and chill until set, about 4 hours.

To Make the Whipped Cream:

- Whip the cream, sugar and vanilla extract until stiff peaks form.

Finish and Serve:

- Top chilled tarts with whipped cream, sugared currants, white chocolate twirls and serve.

CHEF'S TIP:

- Passion fruit juice can be found in gourmet or health food stores, or you can extract juice from fresh passion fruits.

Simply the Best Lobster Mashed Potatoes

Chef Ed Leonard, CMC
Serves 4

Lobster Mashed Potatoes:

1 1/2 pounds Yukon gold potatoes, scrubbed but not peeled
Cold spring water
Kosher salt
1/2 cup heavy cream
1/2 cup milk
16 tablespoons (2 sticks) high-quality unsalted butter, diced
Sea salt to taste
1 teaspoon fresh thyme leaves
8 ounces cooked, diced lobster meat

To Make the Lobster Mashed Potatoes:

- Place potatoes in a large stainless-steel pan. Cover with cold spring water by 2 inches. Add 1 tablespoon of kosher salt for every 4 cups of water you add.
- Bring to a boil, reduce heat and simmer until potatoes are tender. Drain potatoes immediately and place on a clean kitchen towel.
- In a saucepan, combine cream and milk and bring to a boil. Set aside.
- When cool enough to handle, peel potatoes and cut into pieces. Pass the potatoes through a ricer twice and then transfer to a heavy bottomed stainless-steel saucepan.
- Place pan on low heat and beat with a wooden spoon for 3 to 5 minutes. A little at a time, stir in 12 tablespoons of the butter, beating well until butter is incorporated and potatoes are fluffy. Slowly stir in the cream and milk. Season with salt and set aside.
- In a small skillet combine the remaining 4 tablespoons butter, thyme and lobster meat. Heat just until butter is melted and lobster is well coated. Fold lobster meat into the potatoes. Add more cream if potatoes are too thick. Reheat if necessary and serve.

CHEF'S TIP:

- Though delicious on their own, these mashed potatoes are unforgettable when served with either grilled shrimp, seared fish or sea scallops. They can be either a part of a main plate or a first course.

Pan Roasted Vegetables

Chef Ed Leonard, CMC
Serves 4

Vegetables:

12 baby turnips, peeled
1 cup carrot, peeled and sliced on the bias
1/2 cup diced rutabaga
Chicken broth as needed
2 tablespoons unsalted butter
2 teaspoons sugar
1 tablespoon chopped parsley
1 tablespoon chopped sage
1 tablespoon extra-virgin olive oil
Salt to taste

To Make the Vegetables:

- Blanch turnips, carrot and rutabaga until tender in chicken broth. Drain well.
- Melt butter in a skillet and sauté vegetables and sugar for 3 to 4 minutes. Toss with parsley, sage and oil. Season to taste with salt and serve.

CHEF'S TIP:

- Chef Leonard suggests serving this with variety of angus beef (see recipe page 150)

Glazed Carrots

Chef Kevin Zink, CCC
Serves 4

Carrots:

8 baby carrots, peeled and tops removed
2 cups water
1/4 cup sugar
1/4 cup unsalted butter, cut into chunks
2 teaspoons finely chopped parsley
Salt and pepper to taste

To Make the Carrots:

- In a 2-quart saucepan, combine carrots, water and sugar. Bring to a simmer and cook until carrots are tender. Remove carrots from pan and continue simmering syrup until very thick and reduced. Remove from heat and whisk in butter and parsley. Return carrots to the pan, toss, season with salt and pepper and serve.

CHEF'S TIP:

- Chef Zink serves these carrots with pecan roast bison hanger steak with red wine reduction and peruvian mashed potatoes (see page 128). Double the quantities here for more generous servings.

Sautéed Spinach

Chef Kevin Zink, CCC
Serves 4

Spinach:

1 tablespoon soybean oil
1 tablespoon finely diced fennel
2 teaspoons unsalted butter
3 cups baby spinach
1 tablespoon finely diced shallot
1 teaspoon chopped garlic
1 tablespoon toasted pine nuts

To Make the Spinach:

- Heat a sauté pan over high heat. Add oil and heat just to the point where the oil begins to smoke. Add fennel and butter. When butter starts to brown, add spinach. Stir and then immediately add shallot and garlic. Toss quickly, remove from heat and add pine nuts. Season to taste with salt and pepper and serve hot.

CHEF'S TIP:

- Double the quantities for more generous servings.

Braised Greens

Chef Scott Fetty
Serves 4

Greens:

1/2 cup yellow onion, diced small
1 clove garlic, minced
2 slices slab bacon, diced small
16 ounces assorted braising greens (collard, turnip, beet, kale, or mustard greens), well rinsed and stems removed
1/2 cup chicken stock or water
Kosher salt and pepper to taste
Red wine vinegar as needed

To Make the Greens:

- Combine the onion, garlic and slab bacon in a medium skillet. Place over medium-low heat and cook until the onions become translucent and the bacon has rendered fat. Add the greens to the pot and wilt over medium heat. Add the stock, bring to a simmer, cover, and cook until the greens are tender, 20 to 25 minutes. Season with salt, pepper and red wine vinegar.

CHEF'S TIP:

- Chef Fetty serves these tender, flavorful greens with his smoked quail stuffed with country ham, leeks and quince (see page 120).

Fried Cornbread

Chef Russell Scott, CMC
Makes about 30 fritters

Cornbread:
1/2 cup yellow cornmeal
1/2 cup all-purpose flour
1 teaspoon salt
1 teaspoon baking powder
1 tablespoon unsalted melted butter
1 large egg, lightly beaten
6 tablespoons milk
1 jalapeño, seeded and minced
2 teaspoons onion powder
1/4 teaspoon garlic powder
1 teaspoon ground cumin
1/4 teaspoon cayenne
2 cups oil for deep frying

To Make the Cornbread:

- Mix the cornmeal, flour, salt, and baking powder. Add the melted butter and egg and milk and mix well. Stir in jalapeño, onion powder, garlic powder, cumin and cayenne. You should have a thick batter.
- In a deep pot, heat oil to 375 degrees F. Drop batter by rounded tablespoons into fat and fry until puffed, crispy, golden brown and cooked completely through. Drain on paper towels. Serve hot.

CHEF'S TIP:

- Chef Scott serves this cornbread with wedge of boston lettuce with heirloom tomato salad and cucumber-buttermilk dressing (see page 60).

Braised Fennel

Chef Russell Scott, CMC
Serves 4

Fennel:
2 bulbs fennel
2 tablespoons olive oil
1 shallot, cut into 1/4-inch-thick slices
1 bay leaf
1/4 bunch parsley
1/4 bunch thyme
1 cup white wine
2 cups chicken stock
1 cup water
Salt and pepper to taste

To Make the Fennel:

- Preheat oven to 300 degrees F. Wash and trim fennel bulbs and remove any bruised or damaged outer layers. Trim the root bottom and trim off the stems at the top of the bulb.
- Slice the each fennel bulb into four 1-inch-thick slices across the grain. Remove any excess core, being careful to kept the slices intact. (You may stick a tooth pick through the slices to hold them together.) Set aside.
- Spread oil on the bottom of a large roasting pan. Place over medium heat and cook shallots just until tender. Spread the shallots evenly around the pan, then add the herbs evenly around the pan and place the fennel slices on top. Add enough wine, stock and water to come half way up the sides of the fennel pieces.
- Season to taste with salt and pepper. Cover the roasting pan with oiled parchment and then foil. Bake until fennel is tender. Remove fennel from cooking liquid and serve.

CHEF'S TIP:

- Chef Scott serves this fennel with hot smoked herb-crusted atlantic salmon with caviar crème fraîche (see page 160).

Creamed Spinach

Chef Russell Scott, CMC
Serves 4

Spinach:
2 tablespoons olive oil
1 1/2 cups finely sliced onions
1 teaspoon minced garlic
2 pounds spinach leaves, well rinsed, stems and tough leaves removed and discarded
1 1/2 cups heavy cream, simmered gently until reduced by half
1/4 cup grated Parmesan
Grated nutmeg to taste
Salt and pepper to taste

To Make the Spinach:

- Heat the oil in a large sauté pan. Add the onions and sauté until they begin to turn translucent, 1 to 2 minutes. Add the garlic and sauté until it begins to release its aroma.
- Add the spinach, filling the pan and adding more as the spinach cooks down. Cook until spinach is completely wilted and tender. Add the cream and cheese. Season to taste with nutmeg, salt and pepper.

CHEF'S TIP:

- Chef Scott serves this spinach with wild mushroom and goat cheese strudel (see page 192).

Mustard-Herb Vinaigrette

Chef Russell Scott, CMC
Serves 4

Mustard-Herb Vinaigrette:
1/4 cup cider vinegar
1 1/2 teaspoons Creole mustard
1/2 teaspoon sugar
1/4 clove minced garlic
3/4 cup olive oil
Salt and black pepper to taste
1/2 teaspoon Tabasco sauce
1/4 teaspoon chopped thyme
1 1/2 teaspoons chopped parsley
1 1/2 teaspoons chopped cilantro

For the Mustard-Herb Vinaigrette:

- In a small bowl, combine vinegar, mustard, sugar and garlic. Mix well. Whisk in the olive oil, season with salt and black pepper and Tabasco. Stir in thyme, parsley and cilantro. Chill.

CHEF'S TIP:

- Chef Scott serves this dish with florida rock shrimp cakes (see page 162).

Mac and Cheese

Chef Russell Scott, CMC
Serves 4

Mac and Cheese:
3 tablespoons clarified butter
1/2 cup finely diced onion
3 tablespoons all-purpose flour
1 bay leaf
1 whole clove
2 cups whole milk, hot
Pinch cayenne
1/4 teaspoon mustard powder
1/4 teaspoon Worcestershire sauce
2 cups macaroni, cooked and cooled
1/4 cup cooked crisp bacon, finely diced
1/4 cup caramelized onions
1/2 cup chopped cooked spinach, excess moisture squeezed out
1 pound cheddar cheese, shredded
1/2 cup grated parmesan cheese
Salt and freshly ground white pepper to taste
3 tablespoons fresh breadcrumbs
1/4 teaspoon paprika

To Make the Mac and Cheese:

- In a large pot, heat clarified butter and cook onion until soft. Add the flour, bay leaf and clove. Cook over low heat for about 2 minutes. Whisk in the hot milk and bring up to a simmer. Add the cayenne, mustard and Worcestershire sauce. Cook, stirring frequently, until thick and no longer starchy tasting.
- Place cooked macaroni in a large stainless bowl. Remove and discard bay leaf and clove from sauce and pour sauce over macaroni. Fold in bacon, caramelized onions, spinach, cheddar cheese and a half of the parmesan cheese. Season to taste with salt and white pepper.
- Preheat oven to 375 degrees F. and divide macaroni and cheese evenly between large buttered ramekins. Mix together the breadcrumbs, paprika and the remaining 1/4 cup cheese. Sprinkle over the ramekins. Bake until golden brown on top.

CHEF'S TIP:

- Chef Scott serves this with yankee-style pork pot roast (see page 130)
- When adding a dairy product to a hot dish, heat the dairy product first to avoid disaster.

Lobster Ragout

Chef Craig Peterson
Serves 4

Lobster Ragout:
2 tablespoons unsalted butter
1 tablespoon sliced leek
1 teaspoon chopped roasted garlic
1 teaspoon chopped roasted shallot
2 ounces fresh lobster meat, coarsely chopped
2 tablespoons lobster stock
1 ounce goat cheese
2 tablespoons peeled, seeded, finely diced tomato
1 teaspoon finely sliced basil leaves
1 teaspoon truffle oil
Freshly cracked pepper and kosher salt to taste

To Make the Lobster Ragout:

- Melt the butter in a medium sauté pan over medium heat. Add the leek, garlic and shallot and cook until softened. Add lobster meat and stock. Cook 1 minute. Remove from heat and stir in cheese, tomato, basil and truffle oil. Season with freshly cracked pepper and kosher salt. Keep warm.

CHEF'S TIP:

- Chef Peterson serves this with prosciutto-wrapped scallops with truffle-scented lobster ragout, sweet corn ravioli, caramelized fennel and creamy roasted corn sauce (see recipe page 172).

Warm Potato Salad

Chef Ed Leonard, CMC
Serves 4

Warm Potato Salad:

3 medium Yukon Gold potatoes, peeled and diced
1 shallot, diced
1/4 cup finely diced celery
1/4 cup finely diced peeled, seeded tomato
1 thinly sliced garlic clove
1/3 cup chicken broth
1 teaspoon chopped parsley
2 tablespoons red wine vinegar
6 tablespoons extra-virgin olive oil
1 tablespoon unsalted butter
Kosher salt and freshly ground pepper to taste

To Make the Potato Salad:

- Cook potatoes in salted water until tender. Drain well and keep warm.
- In a saucepan, combine shallot, celery, tomato, garlic and chicken broth and simmer for 4 minutes. Drain, reserving broth and vegetables separately.
- Toss vegetables, potatoes with 4 tablespoons of broth together with the parsley, vinegar oil and butter. Season to taste with salt and pepper. Serve warm.

CHEF'S TIP:

- Chef Leonard suggests serving this with variety of angus beef (see recipe page 150).

Skillet Cornbread

Chef Scott Fetty
Serves 4

Cornbread:

1/2 cup yellow cornmeal
1 cup all-purpose flour
1 teaspoon baking powder
1/2 teaspoon salt
1/2 cup sugar
6 tablespoons vegetable oil
3 large eggs
1/4 teaspoon vanilla extract
10 tablespoons milk

To Make the Cornbread:

- Preheat a small cast-iron skillet in a 350 degree F. oven. Combine the cornmeal, flour, baking powder, salt and sugar in a bowl. In a separate bowl, whisk together the oil, eggs, vanilla and milk. Add the wet ingredients to the dry, mixing very briefly. (Over-mixing will create a tough bread.)
- Scrape the batter into the hot skillet and bake until golden brown on top and a toothpick inserted into the center comes out clean, about 25 minutes. Allow the bread to cool and cut into wedges.

CHEF'S TIP:

- This cornbread is an old family recipe that has been handed down to Chef Scott Fetty. He serves it with smoked quail stuffed with country ham, leeks and quince (see page 120).

Cilantro and Sweet Pepper Sauce

Chef Russell Scott, CMC
Serves 4

Cilantro and Sweet Pepper Sauce:

2 tablespoons unsalted butter
2 yellow bell peppers, coarsely chopped
2 shallots, coarsely chopped
3 tablespoons onion, minced
2 cloves garlic, sliced
1 1/2 cups vegetable stock
1 sachet (see Chef's Tip)
1 cup heavy cream
2 teaspoons chili powder
1 tablespoon hot sauce
Salt and pepper to taste
1/2 cup chopped cilantro leaves

To Make the Cilantro and Sweet Pepper Sauce:

- Melt the butter over medium heat and cook the peppers, shallots and onion until tender. Do not allow them to brown. Stir in garlic. Add the vegetable stock, sachet and cream. Simmer for about 30 minutes. Add chili powder and hot sauce. Remove and discard the sachet. Transfer to a blender and blend until smooth.
- Strain through a sieve. Season to taste with salt and pepper. Add more stock if the sauce is too thick. Stir in cilantro leaves and serve at room temperature.

CHEF'S TIP:

- Chef Scott serves this dish with Florida rock shrimp cakes (see page 162).
- Chef Scott makes his sachets by tying 2 chopped parsley stems, 1 bay leaf, 1/4 teaspoon cracked black peppercorns, and a 1/4 teaspoon dried thyme loosely in a piece of cheesecloth.

Sun-Dried Fruit Relish

Chef Craig Peterson
Serves 4

Sun-Dried Fruit Relish:

1/4 cup white wine
6 tablespoons sugar
2 sun-dried apricots, thinly sliced
1 tablespoon sun-dried cranberries
1 tablespoon sun-dried cherries
1 tablespoon chopped walnuts
1 teaspoon chopped chives
Cracked pepper to taste

To Make the Sun-Dried Fruit Relish:

- In a small saucepan, combine wine and sugar. Heat until sugar is dissolved. Combine apricots, cranberries, cherries and walnuts in a small bowl. Pour in hot wine, cover and marinate overnight.
- Before serving, stir in chives and cracked pepper to taste.

CHEF'S TIP:

- Chef Peterson serves this with honey-maple breast of duckling with rosemary polenta, caramelized pearl onions, port wine poached pear, sun-dried fruit relish and natural duck jus (see recipe page 116).

Stuffed Zucchini

Chef Ed Leonard, CMC
Serves 4 or 8

Zucchini:
4 long zucchini
3 tablespoons olive oil
1 small onion, diced
8 ounces ground fresh Italian sausage meat
3 cloves garlic, thinly sliced
1/4 cup diced tomatoes
1/4 cup red wine
2 slices white bread, crusts removed
1/2 cup heavy cream
1/2 cup Italian breadcrumbs
1/2 cup freshly grated Parmigiano-Reggiano cheese
1 large egg
2 tablespoons extra-virgin olive oil
1 teaspoon chopped basil leaves
1 teaspoon chopped oregano leaves
salt and pepper to taste
4 tablespoons diced unsalted butter
3/4 cup chicken broth

To Make the Zucchini:

- Rinse the zucchini well and trim off the ends. Split each in half lengthwise. With a teaspoon, scoop out the flesh, leaving 8 "shells."
- Set shells aside. Finely dice the flesh. In a sauté pan set over medium heat, heat oil and add diced onion. Add sausage meat and garlic and cook 3 to 4 minutes. Add zucchini flesh, tomatoes and wine and cook 5 to 7 minutes on low heat.
- Dice bread slices and toss with heavy cream in a small bowl. In a large bowl, combine cooked sausage and vegetable mixture, soaked bread, bread crumbs, cheese, egg, oil, basil and oregano mix well. Season to taste with salt and pepper if needed.
- Preheat oven to 350 degrees. Fill the zucchini shells with the stuffing mixture and place shells in a casserole or stainless steel pan. Dot with butter. Pour broth into pan. Bake for 20 to 25 minutes.

Braised Swiss Chard

Chef Russell Scott, CMC
Serves 4

Swiss Chard:
1 pound Swiss chard, well rinsed
2 tablespoons unsalted butter
2 strips smoked bacon, cooked and crumbled
4 ounces diced onion
1 clove minced garlic
1 cup chicken stock
Salt and pepper to taste

To Make the Swiss Chard:

- Separate the leaves and stems of the Swiss chard. Mince the stems and roughly chop the leaves and set aside separately
- Heat the butter in a large skillet. Add the cooked bacon, onion and garlic and cook until the onion is lightly brown. Add the chard stems and sauté for 5 minutes, then add the leaves. Add stock if the mixture becomes too dry and cook, uncovered, until tender and almost dry. Season to taste with salt and pepper and serve.

CHEF'S TIP:

- Chef Scott serves this dish with buttermilk fried chicken (see page 110).

Warm Potato and Apple Hash

Chef Scott Fetty
Serves 4

Potato and Apple Hash:

Grape seed oil as needed
2 Russet potatoes, diced and cooked until tender
1 Gala apple, peeled and cored, diced small
1 teaspoon minced shallot
1/2 teaspoon minced garlic
1 teaspoon minced flat-leaf parsley
Kosher salt and pepper to taste
Cornstarch for dusting

To Make the Potato and Apple Hash:

- Heat a sauté pan and add oil. When hot, add cooked potato, apple, shallot and garlic and sauté until apple is soft. Stir in parsley, season with the salt and pepper and remove from the heat. Cool to room temperature.
- Once the mixture has cooled, form the hash into patties about 2 1/2 inches in diameter and 3/4 inch thick. Lightly dust the patties with the cornstarch. Heat grape seed oil in a non-stick pan and fry patties until browned on both sides and crispy. Keep warm.

CHEF'S TIP:

- Chef Fetty serves this with baked ruby trout with wild mushroom-ramp sauté and heirloom tomato picallily (see recipe page 180).

Braised Fennel

Chef Craig Peterson
Serves 4

Braised Fennel:

2 tablespoons unsalted butter
4 wedges of fennel
1 cup shellfish stock or clam juice
1 bouquet garni (thyme, garlic, leek, bay leaf, parsley stems tied in cheesecloth)

To Make the Braised Fennel:

- In a medium skillet, melt butter over medium-low heat. Add fennel and cook, turning, until slightly softened. Add stock and bouquet garni, cover and cook simmer gently for 20 minutes.

CHEF'S TIP:

- Chef Peterson serves this with prosciutto-wrapped scallops with truffle-scented lobster ragout, sweet corn ravioli, fennel and creamy roasted corn sauce (see recipe page 172).

Chef Certification: A Lifetime of Advancement and Opportunity

The career path of the chef in the 21st century incorporates a lifetime of learning, sharing, progressive skill development and professional networking into a busy lifestyle. For every type of person who enters the foodservice/hospitality industry, there are just as many different types of jobs, positions and segments within the industry in which they can work.

Quality foodservice at any level can only be accomplished by professionals who strive for perfection. Anyone can cook, but not everyone has the expertise or passion of a trained culinarian who can transform the simplest ingredients into the most exquisite foods. Unless a cook or chef sets goals to deliberately prepare and serve the best foods possible, only mediocrity can be guaranteed. Quality foodservice is never accomplished by accident.

Setting the Bar for Professional Development

ACF's certification program for professional cooks and chefs was devised in the early-1970s as a validation process to measure competencies at various stages of professional development. The modern professional cook and chef must study and train in all facets of quality foodservice to maximize career potential. Cooking and baking are still the foundations upon which all professional chef careers are based, but sanitation and food safety, nutrition, food costs, supervision and management are now added to the expected repertoire of skills.

Indeed, 32 years after its launch, ACF's certification program has been continuously tested, revised and improved to meet the ever-growing demands of the evolving industry.

ACF's certification program is based on a natural progression of a cook's and chef's career from cook to master chef and provides an ideal career ladder to guide culinarians along the way. Each level is based on a specific amount of experience and knowledge, and offers both short- and long-term goals to which the culinarian can aspire.

In all cases, ACF certification is based on the same foundation of knowledge, progressive skill development and demonstration of proficiencies.

Who Benefits from Certification?

All who offer their culinary knowledge and skill in the marketplace, employ them or are served by them are beneficiaries of ACF's certification program.

Certification helps employers verify that applicants have the knowledge and skills required for the positions they are applying for. In today's business environment, workers move from job to job using a cluster of transferable, knowledge-based skills. Certification provides professional cooks and chefs with concrete credentials that differentiate their applications from dozens, if not hundreds, of others.

Demand for proper supervision and delivery of safe and healthful foods is also increasing. While not all quality-minded chefs are certified, certified cooks and chefs have publicly made a commitment to providing the best, safest food possible. Certification itself is a voluntary, yet deliberate, process that can only improve chances for personal success and, therefore, the success of employers and customers.

The public is demanding the safe preparation of their food, and operators are forced to pay attention. Without certification, consumers can only hope for the best. An ACF-certified chef provides that assurance.

For more information on ACF chef certification, call (800) 624-9458, e-mail certify@acfchefs.net, or visit www.acfchefs.org.

ACF operates the only comprehensive certification program for chefs in the United States. Currently, more than 4,000 culinarians are certified by ACF, with more than 20,000 certifications awarded since 1973.

ACF awards many levels of certification:

CC/CPC: Certified Culinarian/ Certified Pastry Culinarian

CCA: Certified Culinary Administrator

CCC: Certified Chef de Cuisine

CCE: Certified Culinary Educator

CEC/CEPC: Certified Executive Chef/Certified Executive Pastry Chef

CSC: Certified Sous Chef

CMC/CMPC: Certified Master Chef/Certified Master Pastry Chef

CSCE: Certified Secondary Culinary Educator

CWPC: Certified Working Pastry Chef

PCC: Personal Certified Chef

PCEC: Personal Certified Executive Chef

Certification is awarded for five years and must be renewed by providing documentation of required continuing education including nutrition, sanitation and supervisory management.

Acidulated Water: Water with lemon juice or other acid added, intended to keep raw fruit or vegetables from discoloring.

Adobo Sauce: Seasoning paste used in Mexican cuisine made with ground chiles, herbs and vinegar.

Albumin: Clarifying protein found in egg whites, leeks, blood, and connective tissue.

- Soluble in cold liquid.
- It congeals when heated and traps impurities.

Al Dente: Cooked to the point of tenderness but with some texture remaining.

A la Minute: At the last minute, just before service.

Au Jus: Served with unthickened pan juices, often with the addition of stock or other flavorings.

Bain-Marie: A hot water bath used to insure gentle cooking. Water is placed in a pan and other foods, in separate containers, are set into the water; the whole is then usually placed in the oven. Also, a double boiler insert for slow cooking over simmering water. Also, a steam table in which smaller pans and their contents are kept hot.

Barfing: Wrapping meats with thin slices of fat or fatty meats, like bacon, before cooking.

Bechamel: Basic white sauce.

Beurre Manié: A 60/40 mix of whole butter and flour used as a liaison.

Bird Chiles: Slender, straight, chiles, bitingly hot and resembling the arbol.

Blanch: To immerse food briefly in boiling water, either to help loosen the skin or to precook briefly to set color and flavor.

Boil: To cook liquid rapidly so that bubbles constantly rise and break on the surface. To cook food in boiling liquid.

Bouquet Garni: Little bundles of herbs and spices, usually wrapped in cheesecloth.

- Classic combination – parsley, peppercorns, thyme, and bay leaves.

Braise: To cook a seared product in a tightly covered pan with varying amounts of a flavorful liquid for a lengthy period of time.

- Best for tough cuts of meat.
- Usually completed in the oven.
- Braised vegetables are usually not seared.

Bread: To coat with bread or cracker crumbs before cooking, usually after first dipping food into beaten egg or other liquid so crumbs will adhere.

Brine: A salt solution. Also the act of soaking a product in a salt solution.

Brown: To cook in a small amount of fat until browned on all sides, giving food an appetizing color and flavor and, in meats, sealing in natural juices.

Brunoise: To dice vegetable minutely, or the resulting diced vegetable mixture.

Capon: Castrated and fattened rooster.

Carryover Cooking: The cooking that takes place after a product is removed from the oven.

- Remove roasts from the oven at least 5 degrees below the desired temperature.

Chard: A member of the beet family that produces large leaves and thick stalks.

Chèvre: Goat's milk cheese.

Chiffonade: To finely cut greens to produce thin strips.

Chinois: A metal, conical strainer with fine-mesh. Sometimes known as a "China cap."

Concasser: To chop roughly – often used to describe a rough chop of blanched, peeled, and seeded tomatoes.

Confit: Meats cooked and preserved in fat. Fruits preserved in sugar or liquor.

Consommé: Clarified stock that has been fortified with lean ground meat and additional mirepoix and bouquet garni.

Coral: The roe of lobster or other crustaceans.

Court-Bouillon: A poaching liquid that contains water, an acid (wine, citrus, vinegar), aromatics and other flavorings.

- Acids help flavor and coagulate the proteins of the products being poached.

Cube: To cut into small cubes (about 1/2 inch). In meats, to tenderize by pounding with a special tool that imprints a checkered pattern on the surface, breaking tough fibers to increase tenderness.

Darne: A thick slice of a large raw fish.

Dash: A very small amount, less than 1/8 teaspoon.

Deglaze: To dissolve and pick up the flavorful bits left on the bottom of a pan after cooking.

- Acids like wine work best because they help extract flavor.
- Stock, water or other liquids can also be used.

Demi-glace: "Half glaze" — a brown sauce reduction.

Depouillage: To skim the impurities off the top of a stock, soup or sauce.

Dice: To cut into very small pieces. (about 1/8 to 1/4 inch)

Dredge: To coat or cover food lightly but completely with flour, sugar, or other fine substance.

Emulsion: A mixture of one liquid with another with which it cannot normally combine smoothly.

Farce: Stuffing or forcemeat.

Fat: Generic term for butter, margarine, lard or vegetable shortening; also the rendered drippings of meat or fowl.

Fat Cap: Layer of fat that surrounds muscle tissue.

Fines Herbes: A fine mixture of fresh herbs used to season meats, fish and sauces.

Foie Gras: Fattened goose or duck liver.

Fry: To cook in hot fat — pan-frying in a skillet (very little fat) or deep-frying in a heavy pan (food immersed in fat).

Fumet: White stock with other flavorings added, simmered and reduced by 50%.

Galanga: A root that is a relative of ginger, used in Thai cuisine — sometimes spelled galangal.

Glacé: Brown stock reduced by 85% to 90%.

Grease: To rub fat or oil on a cooking surface or utensil to prevent food from sticking.

Grill: To cook on a rack over direct heat - gas, electricity, or charcoal; to broil on a grill.

Haricot Vert: Thin French green beans.

Herbs: Leaves of plants used either fresh or dry.

- When substituting dry for fresh, use 1/3 the amount.

Hydrogenation: A process in which extra hydrogen atoms are pumped into unsaturated fat.

Ice Bath: A container of ice water used to stop the cooking process or cool foods or liquids quickly.

Jus: The natural juice of a meat, vegetable or fruit.

Jus Lie: Pan juices thickened with a slurry.

Julienne: Matchstick pieces of vegetables, fruits or cooked meats.

Kale: Curly-leafed vegetable from the cabbage family.

Kohlrabi: Root vegetable that resembles a turnip but has a more delicate flavor.

Larding: Threading strips of fat into a piece of meat before cooking.

- Larding needle – hollow needle

Liaison: Thickening or binding agent used in the preparation of a soup or sauce.

Liaison Finale: Finishing or enriching agent added to soups or sauces at the end of the cooking process.

Madeira: Fortified wine, either sweet or dry, from the Portuguese island of Madeira.

Maillard Reaction: When natural sugars and proteins react to heat by carameliz-ing-browning and forming a crust.

Mandoline: A slicer with adjustable blades.

Marinade: A flavorful liquid used to tenderize and flavor products.

- Usually includes an acid, oil, herbs and spices

Mince: To cut or chop into very fine particles.

Mirepoix: Rough cut flavorful vegetables–traditionally carrots, onions, celery and sometimes leeks.

Monder: To blanch, peel and seed tomatoes.

Monter au Beurre: To swirl small chunks of cold, whole butter into a sauce at the end of the cooking process.

Nage: A light sauce created from a court bouillon.

Napper: To lightly coat with a sauce or to cook a sauce until it coats the back of a spoon.

Pan-Fry: To cook in a moderate amount of fat; sauté.

Pan Gravy: Pan drippings thickened with flour.

Parboil: To boil until partially cooked; remainder of cooking is done by another method.

Poach: To gently simmer in liquid.

Purée: To sieve or whirl food into a smooth, thick mixture.

Quenelle: A dumpling made of meat, poultry or fish. It also refers to the basic quenelle shape — An oval formed by using 2 spoons that have been moistened in water.

Ragout: A rich stew.

Reduction: The result of boiling down liquids in order to concentrate flavors.

Remouillage: Second, weaker extraction made from the remnants of a stock.

- Half the water, half the cook time
- Used to start another stock

Render: To liquefy the fat from a meat product over low heat.

- Product should be diced or scored.

Resting: Letting a roast rest for 5 to 15 minutes after cooking.

- Equalizes internal pressure so juices can be re-absorbed
- Allows for carryover cooking

Roast: Oven-cook foods in an uncovered pan to produce a well-browned product with a moist interior.

- Dry cooking method
- Best for tender cuts of meat

Rondeau: Heavy pan with straight sides that are less than the width of the base. It is commonly used for braising.

Roux: A cooked combination of fat and flour used to thicken sauces and soups.

Sabayon: A mixture of egg yolks and an acid whisked over hot water just until the yolks start to thicken.

Sambal: A chile paste, often with garlic, salt, sugar and other spices, used in Asian cuisine.

Sauté: To cook quickly over high heat in a minimal amount of oil.

Sauternes: A fruity, sweet white wine from the Bordeaux region.

Scald: To heat milk just below the boiling point (tiny bubbles appear around the edge of the pan when it has reached the proper temperature).

Sear: To brown meat quickly either in a hot pan with very little oil or in a hot oven.

Shock: To stop the cooking process by plunging a food in ice water.

Simmer: To cook in liquid over low heat just below the boiling point (bubbles form slowly and burst before reaching the surface).

Singer: To dust with flour after sautéing or roasting – flour mixes with the fat to create a quick roux.

Skim: To remove fat or scum from the surface of a liquid with a spoon or ladel.

Slurry: 50/50 mixture of cold liquid and refined starch – most often arrowroot or cornstarch.

Smoke Point: The temperature at which oils begin to smoke, burn and/or break down.

Spices: Buds, fruits, flowers, bark, berries, seeds and roots of plants and trees, used as seasonings.

Star Anise: the brown, fragrant pod of a Chinese evergreen used as a spice.

Steam: To cook in water vapors, on a rack or in a steam basket, in a covered pan above boiling water.

Steep: To infuse in liquid.

Stew: To cook a product barely covered in a flavorful liquid until the product is tender.

- Good for tough, small cuts of meat.
- Usually completed on top of the stove.
- Stewed vegetables are usually not seared.

Stir: Using a spoon or a whisk in a broad, circular motion, to mix ingredients without beating or to prevent them from sticking.

Sweat: To cook slowly over medium/low heat without browning.

- Good for flavor extraction.
- Moisture development encouraged.

Tamarind Concentrate: A sour-flavored paste made from the the pod of a tropical tree.

Texture: The structural quality of a food— roughness, smoothness, graininess, or creaminess.

Truss: Tie products prior to cooking.

- Helps maintain a products shape.
- Ensures even cooking.

Tuile: A thin, crisp, curved wafer.

Turmeric: The root of a musky-smelling tropical plant, used as a spice — usually used in powdered form.

Whip: To beat rapidly with a wire whisk, or electric mixer, incorporating air to lighten a mixture and increase its volume.

Whisk: To beat with a wire whisk until blended and smooth.

Whitewash: 50/50 mixture of cold liquid and flour.

Zest: Outer colored peel of citrus fruits. Also, the act of removing this outer peel.

CHILI

DESSERT

FIRST PLATES—SEAFOOD

FIRST PLATES—VEGETARIAN

SALAD

SAUCES

SECOND PLATE—MEAT

SECOND PLATE—POULTRY

SECOND PLATE—SEAFOOD

SECOND PLATE—VEGETARIAN

SIDES

SOUPS

STEW

2004 American Culinary Federation Sponsors

Specials thanks to our sponsors for their continued support.

PLATINUM

SILVER

BRONZE